'Comprehensive in its scope and attuned to the impacts of lifespan, culture and evidence-based perspectives, this book will be a valuable resource in the diagnosis and management of depression, perhaps the most pressing mental health condition of our times.'

—**Zindel Segal, PhD,** *Distinguished Professor of Psychology in Mood Disorder, University of Toronto Scarborough*

Depression

Depression, now recognized as a significant source of disability across the globe, is something many of us will be familiar with. This book explores the way people have discussed depression and examines how scientific understanding has led to ways to better appreciate and treat the condition.

Through evaluations of contemporary research and literature, this book examines how depression has been depicted throughout history and presents an up-to-date account of how a diagnosis is made. Offering a narrative steeped in cognitive neuropsychology and emotion regulation, chapters explore the different theories behind current explanations of why depression develops and how this understanding drives the different ways to treat and manage the condition. It presents a holistic approach that considers depression in the context of physical health and how it impacts across the lifespan.

This book is an essential read for practising and trainee clinical psychologists, but its accessible and readable style will appeal to a broader audience of those looking to further understand depression.

Gary Christopher, PhD, is a gerontologist working in the Centre for Innovative Ageing at Swansea University. His research focuses on memory and emotion regulation within the context of older adult mental health. He is particularly interested in dementia as an existential threat and ways to mitigate the impact.

Depression

Current Perspectives in Research and Treatment

Gary Christopher

Routledge
Taylor & Francis Group

LONDON AND NEW YORK

Designed cover image: © Getty Images

First published 2023
by Routledge
4 Park Square, Milton Park, Abingdon, Oxon OX14 4RN

and by Routledge
605 Third Avenue, New York, NY 10158

Routledge is an imprint of the Taylor & Francis Group, an informa business

British Library Cataloguing-in-Publication Data
A catalogue record for this book is available from the British Library

Library of Congress Cataloging-in-Publication Data
Names: Christopher, Gary (Lecturer in psychology), author.
Title: Depression : current perspectives in research and treatment / Gary Christopher.
Description: New York, NY : Routledge, 2023. | Includes bibliographical references and index.
Identifiers: LCCN 2022045800 (print) | LCCN 2022045801 (ebook) | ISBN 9781138904132 (hardback) | ISBN 9781138904149 (paperback) | ISBN 9781315688879 (ebook)
Subjects: LCSH: Depression, Mental. | Depression, Mental—Treatment.
Classification: LCC RC537 .C495 2023 (print) | LCC RC537 (ebook) | DDC 616.85/27—dc23/eng/20221214
LC record available at https://lccn.loc.gov/2022045800
LC ebook record available at https://lccn.loc.gov/2022045801

ISBN: 9781138904132 (hbk)
ISBN: 9781138904149 (pbk)
ISBN: 9781315688879 (ebk)

DOI: 10.4324/9781315688879

Typeset in Times New Roman
by Apex CoVantage, LLC

Contents

Acknowledgements

I have so many people to thank for their guidance and support throughout my career that I will not be able to capture them all here. My work as an academic has always been grounded in the experiences of those whose lives have been touched by depression in so many ways. I have gained so much personally and professionally from working with them. It is impossible to put it into words. I continue to work with some fantastic people whose dedication to making the world a better place for people with mental health conditions is genuinely astounding. This book was beset with many a setback, but Marie has always been there to motivate me. I dedicate this book to my mother, who sadly passed away in September 2020, days before her 80th birthday.

Chapter 1

What is depression?

Defining depression

Even though there is a surfeit of books in the market now providing instruction on how to be happy—which is a good thing, on the whole—it is essential to know that we cannot expect to always feel positive. That is just not achievable. It is not realistic. Some days we wake ready to take on the challenge of another day; other days, we would instead prefer to stay wrapped up in our beds. This is usual. We have all experienced times in our lives when we feel down. Such feelings often accompany times of significant change. We spend most of our lives either in school or at work, and each of us knows the challenges that these bring. Even though we may feel downhearted at times, most of us are adept at bouncing back. These feelings do not last long. They may last for a few days, maybe a couple of weeks, but then we begin to feel our equilibrium restored and can cope with life as usual. In depression, this does not happen. Instead, such feelings continue for months, sometimes years, and take over a person's life.

Distinguishing between clinical depression and non-clinical mood states remains problematic. The most appropriate way to view depression, as it is with many mental health conditions, is to envisage a continuum of increasing severity (1). However, the severity of symptoms is not the only characteristic to mark out those who meet the diagnostic criteria for depression. In addition, the duration and persistence of these symptoms and the level of functional impairment the individual experiences help clinicians decide upon an accurate diagnosis.

The Fifth Edition of the *Diagnostic and Statistical Manual of Mental Disorders*, or DSM-5 (2), lists several symptoms. A person diagnosed with depression will exhibit five or six. Symptoms include experiences lowered mood most of the time; persistent irritability; a loss of interest in life (anhedonia); loss of self-confidence; feelings of hopelessness; suicidal thoughts; difficulty making decisions; feeling tired and/or agitated; weight loss or weight gain; poor sleep; withdrawing from social situations.

For the majority, there is little impact of positive life events on the emotional state of someone with depression. This may not always be the case, with some showing a degree of change throughout the day, referred to as diurnal variation (3).

DOI:10.4324/9781315688879-1

For many, depression creeps upon them. The realization that one is experiencing depression may not occur until someone close to us makes the connection and tentatively broaches the topic. Physical symptoms are often the first sign that something is wrong. People talk about general lethargy, fatigue, headaches, pain sensations in the body, and disturbed sleep. Other behavioural symptoms include increased irritability, tearfulness, reduced libido, and social withdrawal (4).

Sleep is affected by depression. We know that sleep problems occur due to depression, and we are also aware that poor sleep can exacerbate the condition. Sleep can be involved in many ways, although insomnia—an inability to sleep—is prevalent and may, in fact, be a risk factor for depression. A person's appetite will also vary, with people either not eating enough or, conversely, overeating, which often leads to marked changes in a person's weight.

There are many cognitive difficulties associated with depression. Although there is an entire chapter set aside to explore these in more detail (see Chapter 4), it is crucial at this stage to indicate some of the problems people with depression face in terms of their ability to think and respond in everyday situations. The main cognitive issues include a combination of poor attention and problems with memory (5). This makes it difficult for the person to concentrate and remember important things throughout the day. Underlying all this is a constant stream of negative thoughts that compete for the already limited attention of the person with depression. These negative intrusions bombard the individual with troublesome thoughts about who they are, their past, and their future. In combination, this leads to a predominantly slowed, ruminative style of thinking (6). Cognitive problems feed into the cycle of depression, emphasizing further the behavioural and psychological symptoms of the condition. For many who experience depression, there is the comorbid issue of increased anxiety to also contend with. As we shall see in Chapter 4, anxiety is also associated with a discrete set of cognitive challenges.

There are several causes of depression. For some, a specific event, or a series of related events, leads to these feelings. However, often there is no apparent cause. Events such as bereavement or divorce can lead to depression. Our physical health can also contribute here, especially if a person has been diagnosed with a severe illness, be it a life-threatening or long-term condition. Hormonal dysfunction can lead to marked effects on mood as well. We all experience these events. We respond in an idiosyncratic way, often feeling sad, withdrawing from those around us, retreating into ourselves.

In most cases, the veil lifts eventually. For those who experience depression, ways of behaving and responding become engrained. They become stuck in a particular mode of responding. As humans, we quickly adapt our behaviours, often for the better. In the case of depression, these changes are maladaptive. Once entrenched, they are challenging to change.

As with most conditions, whether depression develops is determined by biological, psychological, social, and environmental variables. Personality is a significant contributing factor to depression, making some more vulnerable than others. Excessive alcohol is often chosen as a way to help deal with life's stressors. If taken to an extreme, regular excessive drinking will contribute to and maintain the depression. Alcohol is, after all, a depressant. It also eats away at a person's physical health, consuming money and eroding friendships. One aspect which we have no control over is our genes. There is evidence to show that depression can run in families. We shall explore these and many other factors later in the book.

Historical perspective

Before further ado, we shall start looking at how depression has been conceptualized and treated in the past. It is always worth remembering that, when looking back in time at how a condition is portrayed, we must consider as of utmost importance the beliefs and norms of the period referred to. The way terms have been employed clearly change with time, although what those words describe remains essentially unchanged.

Before turning attention to the rise of the modern classification of mental health conditions, we shall turn the clock back to look at how enduring sadness was addressed in ancient Greek society. It never ceases to amaze me how contemporary definitions of a psychological phenomenon are better described in the texts of writers in ancient Greece. With depression in mind, Hippocrates saw such extreme sadness resulting from an excess of black bile, hence the term melancholia. At this time, the body was seen to be composed of four humours. Any imbalance thus led to specific medical disorders (7).

Paracelsus, in the sixteenth century, introduced the notion of chemical underpinnings of behaviour. This was developed a century later by Willis Dewhurst (8). What superseded this was a view that the cause was physical rather than chemical, and was the result, according to Pitcairn, of sluggish blood.

Two millennia from Hippocrates, the year 1621 saw the publication of a critical text that contributed significantly to our understanding of depression. I am, of course, referring here to Burton's *The Anatomy of Melancholy* (9). It is a fascinating account, one that I can heartily recommend to anyone who has an interest in depression, as well as those who desire to know more about how psychological understanding has developed over time. Even given the subject, it remains an engaging and thought-provoking read. It is also encyclopaedic in scope, bringing together all relevant thought on the matter at hand. It is famous for the sheer number and prestige of its devotees. I must confess that I have not read this monumental tome in its entirety, although I hope to do so one day. However, I would direct interested parties to the excellent abridged version published by Penguin entitled *Some Anatomies of Melancholy* (10).

In the chapter setting out the various forms of melancholy, the concept that the body comprises multiple humours is paramount. Although it is emphasized that there is almost infinite variety, the argument espoused here is that there are three forms. The first form that melancholy takes is caused by the brain and is described as head-melancholy; the second form is due to imbalance across the whole body; the third and final form originates in the bowels mainly and is called windy—unclear why—or hypochondriacal melancholy.

Before the advent of a formalized classification—nosology—of mental health conditions was first mooted, words we use today had vastly different meanings. Take mania as an example. At the turn of the nineteenth century, this referred not to heightened mood and activity by which we currently understand the term, but rather it described an intense madness. Melancholia was a term used to describe someone who exhibited milder madness, once again deviating from a term we still use today to describe lowered mood. Dementia likewise did not reflect neurodegeneration—a process unknown then—but was used to refer to a range of states of varying mental incapacity (11).

However, with the growth of psychiatry, there was an interest in attempting to group together various conditions regarding whether they were primarily problems with intelligence, emotion, or will. At the time, psychiatrists were referred to as alienists, from the French, *médecin aliéniste*. The appropriate word then to describe a mood disorder was lypemania—one example of the monomanias, a group of conditions characterized by repetitive thoughts or actions—although it was not long before this word was replaced by the term (mental) depression (12). In light of Kraepelin's nosology, depression and mania were intimately linked.

With the dawning of the twentieth century, depression and madness were entwined in the minds of clinicians. However, it was clear that this was not entirely accurate, leading to the introduction of the term neurotic or reactive depression to differentiate it from what is seen as being the more severe endogenous depression (13). As its name suggests, reactive depression is the response to a specific situation. This distinction was further validated in the clinician's eyes with the observation that those with the endogenous form appeared to be more responsive to medication when compared to those with reactive depression. Indeed, these terms found their way into the DSM (14). However, this was later dropped with DSM-III (15). It was not until the paradigm shift associated with the rise of cognitive psychology and its accompanying approaches to therapy that the purely biological view of depression was once more challenged.

Depression is an inherent aspect of the human character, independent of time and cultural boundaries. It is undeniable then that depression is an unmistakable, clinical entity that exists outside of professional doctrines or ideologies. Although it is clear that the profession of psychiatry has had an impact on how we view mental health disorders, and as a result, treat them, it would not be accurate to say that depression is in any way a construct created to preserve the *status quo* of physicians (8). The real change occurred in how differences in states of mind were explained. The ancient Greeks disposed of earlier accounts steeped in superstition (except for a version of melancholia associated with prophetic visions (16)) and instead referred to objective changes in the body, a precursor of modern evidence-based medicine.

Now that we have looked at how depression has been conceptualized over the years, it is vital to take the time to consider how depression feels from the perspective of someone diagnosed with the condition.

The experience of depression

This section aims to present a descriptive account of what it is like to actually experience depression. I have made extensive use here of first-hand accounts of depression and academic texts on mood disorders. One book I am particularly fond of and draw upon heavily in my work is *Symptoms in the Mind*, by Andrew Sims, specifically the updated version by Oyebode (17). The subtitle says it all, *An Introduction to Descriptive Psychopathology*. It is a wonderful work that talks about various conditions from an experiential point of view. I certainly urge anyone interested in going beyond mere lists of symptoms to read this book. It brings you closer to the reality of the situation and, in so doing, enables one to more fully understand the many challenges faced by thousands of individuals worldwide.

Mood changes are the fundamental characteristic of depression. Depression, after all, is a mood disorder. Before we continue, it is essential to distinguish between various nouns often used interchangeably in the literature but referring to rather specific states. Starting with emotion, this refers to an immediate response to a situation. Feeling refers to a nuanced response to a challenge, either positive or negative. Affect is a term used clinically to describe how emotions manifest, such as a look of fear. On the other hand, mood refers to a protracted state, a general temperament that colours people's views.

When assessing mood in a clinical setting, it is necessary to consider two fundamental things. To start with, a judgement has to be made as to whether the individual is experiencing anguish in any way. If they are, then is it in keeping with the situation at hand.

In depression, people talk, often with fear, of a loss of feeling. They do not experience emotion in response to anything they are exposed to. People are often at a loss at this. Because they do not understand why this is happening, for many, this emotional void brings with it a sense of guilt. It is a loss of feeling rather than an alteration in a person's beliefs. In depression, a common state is anhedonia, which is a specific form of this loss of feeling. This relates to an inability to react to events positively. This pervades all aspects of the person's behaviour, including facial expressions, speech, and overall bodily movement. Because enjoyment is no longer experienced, people make marked changes to what they do and how they behave purely due to this change in the experiential nature of their existence.

With depression, movement and action are slowed down. The same can be said for thought processes. This is referred to as psychomotor retardation. All aspects of thinking are affected. People find it difficult to concentrate, and decision making is fraught with difficulty. The all-encompassing nature of this experience means that the individual can no longer maintain the type of activities that once were taken for granted. Their ability to deal with the usual demands of life is diminished. This sense of failure often results in self-directed blame that eats away at self-esteem.

Although depression is generally characterized as a condition where all sign of movement is reduced to a bare minimum, and to a large extent, this is entirely accurate, there are times when the person experiences intense restlessness and agitation.

Linked to this are feelings of anxiety. It is common for someone with depression to also be diagnosed with anxiety.

Having described a loss of feeling in depression, one should be aware of the contrasting state where mood intensifies. In this case, overwhelming unhappiness. To differentiate the lowered mood one experiences with depression from common bouts of sadness, many have described the intense melancholia as akin to a physical sensation, specifically pain (18). The ever-descriptive James talked about "a sort of psychical neuralgia wholly unknown to normal life" (19). Just as a brief diversion, if you relish florid accounts of psychological phenomena, you need to look no further than William James. His descriptions of our inner states are almost baroque in their ornamentation but provide insightful glimpses into our being.

Depression is a much more complicated beast than common misconceptions would have us believe. It also sees the individual experiencing intense fear and anger, often manifesting as tetchiness and general unease.

We have already explored the lack of response to previously enjoyable experiences. However, not only is the inner response dialled down to such an extent that nothing sends out emotional ripples to signify pleasure, but external cues to how one is feeling are also absent. Clinicians in such cases describe a flattening of affect to reflect the lack of expression seen in such cases. There is an absence of expression in the face, gesture, and voice. Minimal eye contact is made during social exchanges (20).

Depression can also manifest as myriad bodily sensations. An apparent predominance of which can lead to confusion when initial diagnosis is being considered. This somatization is often associated with a sense akin to a build-up of pressure on the skull in those with depression; "a feeling of misery, like a black cloud pressing on my head" (21). Other parts of the body are involved in similar stages of upset, including the stomach, eyes, and legs. People described experiencing an overwhelming sense of exhaustion that clouds the eyes and make the legs heavy. Such symptoms were deemed vital feelings by Wernicke (21). We shall examine this later in more detail in Chapter 2.

Thoughts of suicide are prevalent here. Feelings of hopelessness abound. The person with depression feels thwarted at every turn. There is nowhere left to go. Death appears to offer the only reasonable means of escape. Rather worryingly, it is often the case that a person is at higher risk of suicide following treatment, such as electroconvulsive therapy (ECT), because they feel more energized. Yet, their mood is still dark and guilt-ridden. In cases of completed suicides, those who were with the person before the act recall someone who appeared more at peace than previously.

A subsequent section concerns bereavement, so it is pertinent to talk here about feelings of loss that accompany depression. Loss of any kind is a stressor. We generally think about the loss of a person that one is close to; however, loss can be equally about losing a job, a home, a part of one's body, and so on (22). The depression surrounding loss is exacerbated in those who attach guilt or self-blame to the events.

Loss is often initially experienced as a sense of detachment, a state of intense shock. Many deny that it has happened. Grief is often close on the heels of denial. This sudden realization of what has actually happened catalyses extreme anxiety and, often, panic. Depression develops as the person begins to accept that the loss has indeed occurred. It is now time to turn to the topic of bereavement.

Bereavement

The experiencing of grief is very personal. We all grieve in different ways. There is no single, correct way to grieve. There is no agreed time limit for grief. Having said that, many factors can influence the grieving process.

To a great extent, one's own personality shapes how grief will manifest. Previous experiences of grieving for some loss will influence how one will grieve on subsequent occasions. The culture in which we were brought up and live will largely determine what that grief will look like. The cause of the distress will bring with it its own influence on how a person responds to the situation.

The experiencing of grief is a highly physical thing. It is not just a cluster of psychological warning signs. A person reacting to loss will likely experience a range of symptoms such as heart palpitations, tension in various parts of the body, hallucinations, and sleep disturbances. One of the most marked symptoms is excessive crying.

For some, grief can bring some rather unexpected emotions to the fore. Aside from the profound sense of sadness, some might also feel an element of resentment, annoyance, and possibly antagonism to the recently departed person. People who have lost someone dear will often express that they feel abandoned by the person who has died.

There is a debate about whether someone experiencing bereavement should be treated for their symptoms or whether it is a natural process that needs to be worked through. Hypnotics may be prescribed to help with sleeplessness. Often, people need to resolve their grief by talking to friends and family or seeking solace from their religious beliefs. Bereavement counselling is an option many find beneficial.

However, there are some cases where the situation is more complicated, such as when a person loses someone they were heavily dependent on. This is an adjustment disorder—now called stress response syndrome—and refers to a protracted stress response.

It is important to remember that not everyone who loses someone close to them will develop depression. However, death in these circumstances is a common trigger for such depression. In other words, depression and grief can coincide (23). Grief is a process whereby someone adapts to the loss of a person who was an integral part of their life. People oscillate between intense sadness and moments of joy as they remember the times they shared. People often describe waves of grief that encompass them. In the case of depression, despair and negativity are unceasing.

So far in this chapter, we have defined what we mean by depression, looked at how depression has been depicted in the past, and examined what depression is like for the individual experiencing it. We shall now turn our attention to how depression is seen in modern society.

Current views of depression

Throughout the history of psychology and psychiatry, an internal struggle has continuously been waged between those who seek to medicalize depression (and other mental health conditions) and those who wish to focus only on the individual and their unique needs. There are pros and cons for each viewpoint, and it is certainly not within the scope of this book to address any of these. However, it is a fascinating area of debate. To label or not to label, that is the question that has plagued clinicians and academics alike, and no doubt shall continue to do so for all time. One might argue that the two are not mutually exclusive. The medical approach offers the benefits promised by drug therapy, for example. However, this does not mean the clinician is not interested in exploring the uniqueness of the individual, although time and other constraints are significant barriers to this.

In a recent account (24), the ethos of the medical approach is criticized, arguing that the premise that depression is a biological problem that requires a biological fix is erroneous. The basis of the argument here is that it is wrong to approach the situation to reboot individual functioning to an agreed normative state. Leader (24) talks here about the idea of mental hygiene. In other words, the removal of the problem rather than encouraging elucidation.

In Leader's (24) account, an argument is made to exclude the word "depression" to refer to the types of experiences people describe. It is too vague to be of any value. Instead, we should return to previous notions of "mourning" and "melancholy," as these better capture the range and severity of the symptoms people experience.

We talked about bereavement and mourning previously. A shared understanding of the word *mourning* refers to a response to loss, more specifically, to recover from the event. The question here is whether the true aim of mourning is to move on from a loss. Might it not be the case that we do not actually get over a loss, but instead somehow incorporate that loss into our lives (24). The person is still with us in that sense, providing us with a sense of comfort. They live on in our hearts and minds.

The word *melancholy* is often seen as being consigned to the pages of the early poets and philosophers. As such, it does not really have a place in our modern world. It brings to mind works such as Durer's engraving, *Melancholia*, from 1514. Some argue that this is not actually the case. The argument is that melancholy better fits the emotional turmoil people experience. The word *depression* is too anodyne a term for anguish encountered (24). It is undoubtedly the case that "depression" as a word has been adopted into everyday parlance to refer to everything from slightly lowered mood to severe, disabling states. Generally, however, it is the former that people refer to when using the word. Because of this, the impact of the word *depression* is lost. The sheer existential weight of the condition experienced by many is neither captured nor understood by this term any longer.

As we have shown, terminology may have changed, but the underlying condition remains the same. However, over-familiarity with diagnostic labels can bring ignorance of the true nature of the situation. This has certainly happened with the word *depression*. The way it is used in everyday conversation fails to reflect the menace of the condition. Throughout the history of psychiatry and psychology, there has been a debate raging about using diagnostic labels. One might argue that having received a diagnosis allows individuals to access the much-needed treatment to help them back onto the road of recovery. The assumption here is that the diagnosis is an accurate one. On the other hand, others argue that diagnostic labels are dehumanizing and only reduce the individual to a cluster of symptoms. Many more arguments aim to set out the pros and cons of adopting a diagnostic system for mental health conditions, but this is not the place to explore this further.

Summary

Having explored the concept of depression from ancient times to the modern-day, the overriding message is that depression is a severe and potentially debilitating condition. It is not a single entity. There are many forms, and with each manifestation, there are unique triggers and events that either presage or cause an episode of depression. Cultural norms also play a significant role in how depression pans out, which will be explored further in Chapter 2. The final section of this chapter set out some of the main issues associated with public understanding of the condition. The main message from all this is that we should endeavour to see beyond the label and its associated list of symptoms. We need to know the person as an individual, not a diagnosis. Easier said than done. People focus on the diagnosis and symptoms mainly with the sole intention of helping the person. However, unless carefully monitored, this can slide irretrievably into making assumptions and holding expectations that are not steeped in fact but are fuelled by serial misinterpretation. The individual is lost in all future transactions.

References

1   Lewinsohn PM, Solomon A, Seeley JR, Zeiss A. Clinical implications of "subthreshold" depressive symptoms. J Abnorm Psychol. 2000;109(2):345.
2   American Psychiatric Association. Diagnostic and statistical manual of mental disorders: DSM-5. 5th ed. Washington, DC: American Psychiatric Association; 2013.
3   Andrews G, Jenkins R. Management of mental disorders. Sydney: World Health Organization Collaborating Centre for Mental Health and Substance Abuse; 1999.
4   Anderson I, Pilling S, Barnes A, Bayliss L, Bird V. The NICE guideline on the treatment and management of depression in adults. National Collaborating Centre for Mental Health, National Institute for Health and Clinical Excellence. London: The British Psychological Society & The Royal College of Psychiatrists; 2010.
5   Christopher G, MacDonald J. The impact of clinical depression on working memory. Cogn Neuropsychiatry. 2005;10(5):379–399.

6 Cassano P, Fava M. Depression and public health: An overview. J Psychosom Res. 2002;53(4):849–857.

7 Wakefield JC. Definition of depression. In: Ingram RE, editor. The international encyclopedia of depression. New York; London: Springer Publishing Company; 2009.

8 Dewhurst W. Melancholia and depression: From Hippocratic times to modern times. J Psychiatry Neurosci. 1992;17(2):81.

9 Burton R. The anatomy of melancholy. London: Everyman's Library; 1961.

10 Burton R. Some anatomies of melancholy. London: Penguin Books; 2008.

11 Berrios GE. History of depression. In: Ingram RE, editor. The international encyclopedia of depression. New York; London: Springer Publishing Company; 2009.

12 Berrios GE. The history of mental symptoms: Descriptive psychopathology since the nineteenth century. Cambridge: Cambridge University Press; 1996.

13 Gaddy MA. Endogenous and reactive depression. In: Ingram RE, editor. The international encyclopedia of depression. New York; London: Springer Publishing Company; 2009.

14 American Psychiatric Association. Diagnostic and statistical manual of mental disorders. 2nd ed. Washington: American Psychiatric Association; 1968.

15 American Psychiatric Association. Diagnostic and statistical manual of mental disorders. 3rd ed. Washington, DC: American Psychiatric Association; 1980(1983).

16 Jackson SW. Melancholia and depression: From Hippocratic times to modern times. New Haven: Yale University Press; 1986.

17 Oyebode F, Sims ACPSitm. Sims' symptoms in the mind: An introduction to descriptive psychopathology. 4th ed. Edinburgh: W. B. Saunders; 2008.

18 Styron W. Darkness visible: A memoir of madness. London: Vintage Books; 2004.

19 James W. The varieties of religious experience: A study in human nature. London: Penguin Books; 1985.

20 Andreasen NC. Affective flattening and the criteria for schizophrenia. Am J Psychiatry. 1979;136(7):944–947.

21 Wernicke C. Grundriss der Psychiatrie in klinischen Vorlesungen. Leipzig, Germany: Thieme; 1906.

22 Parkes CM. The psychological reaction to loss of a limb: The first year after amputation. In: Modern perspectives in the psychiatric aspects of surgery. New York: Springer; 1976, pp. 515–532.

23 Pies R. How the DSM-5 got grief, Bereavement Right 2018. Available from: https://psychcentral.com/blog/how-the-dsm-5-got-grief-bereavement-right/.

24 Leader D. The new black: Mourning, melancholia and depression. London: Penguin; 2008.

Chapter 2

Diagnosis and assessment

Epidemiology

Depression is one of the most common mental health conditions globally, with over 300 million people being affected worldwide (1). According to the World Health Organization (WHO), depression brings a substantial economic burden in terms of disability. It is also implicated in the premature death of those aged between 15 and 44, as seen in 800,000 completed suicides annually (2). In fact, the prediction is that depression will be the second biggest cause of disability across all age groups by 2020 (3). When looking at reports at the primary care level, prevalence is around 5–10 per cent (4). Worryingly, about a fifth of the population will require treatment for a mood disorder, with roughly a half of that figure meeting the criteria for major depressive episode (5). Rates of depression among women are twice as high as those occurring in men. Where a parent or sibling has experienced depression, the risk increases up to three times (6). For the vast majority, depression first occurs between 12 and 24, with another jump after 65.

The prevalence of depression appears to be higher among those unemployed, in lower social classes (below social class 4), with no formal education, and who live in urban areas, among other things (7).

Aetiology

Over the years, there have been various explanations for what causes depression. These will be explored in more detail in Chapter 3 when we look at the different models of depression. However, given the focus of this chapter, it would be remiss not to at least indicate various factors that are at play. Explanations include individual genetics, biochemical imbalances, structural changes in the brain, psychological mechanisms, and social aspects. The received wisdom is that, as with most conditions, it is not merely the case that any single one of these causes depression. Instead, it is a combination of many that lead to depression developing. The profile is likely to be different for each individual (8). There are also a host of risk factors that, in separate cases, increase the likelihood that someone will develop depression, some of which we will look at shortly.

DOI:10.4324/9781315688879-2

Genetics

Studies abound that try to find links between a person's genome and the development of a range of conditions. In the case of depression, one recent study indicates 15 genetic loci that appear to increase a person's risk of developing depression (9). Although an interesting study, it is essential to remember that data were obtained from those who self-reported experiencing depression.

The critical thing to consider about every study that indicates a genetic component to a condition is that the environment plays a fundamental role in all this. There are a few instances where this might not be the case. Still, on the whole, there needs to be some eliciting factor(s) that determines whether a specific gene or a combination of genes is expressed. The genetic profile contributes only a small amount to the overall risk of developing a particular condition in many cases.

Risk factors

As with most conditions, depression occurs as a result of a combination of many competing influences. These include stressors from the environment, psychological factors, biological events, and genetic predisposition. As we will see in Chapter 6, depression is also associated with several medical conditions, including heart disease and cancer. In many cases, depression exacerbates the symptoms related to these conditions. The significant risk factors for depression include a history of depression in the family, personality, major life-changing events, stress, and physical illness (10).

Looking at some of these in more detail, depression in families explains just under 40 per cent of cases (11). A child's early years can influence this. At increased vulnerability to depression are those who had a poor relationship with their parent(s) or some form of conflict (12).

Time and again, personality crops up as a critical determiner of a person's mental and physical well-being. Indeed, concerning depression, the personality trait of neuroticism has been identified as a significant risk factor, especially as it influences how someone responds to adverse life events (12). Relevant here are individual differences in what is perceived as being a sufficiently stressful life event. Clearly, this varies hugely across individuals (13).

Noteworthy also is the stress-vulnerability model (14). The premise here is that a person is host to myriad vulnerability factors either on interaction with their environment or in response to a specific physical stressor. This eventuates in a particular condition, in this case, depression.

It should be noted, however, that this is not always so. Sometimes, a person will develop depression in the absence of any apparent stressful trigger. Still, in other cases, a person may experience a stressor but not develop depression. We know that several emotional buffers can help reduce the likelihood that depression will occur following a stressful event, such as being in a confiding relationship (15).

Having looked at what might lead to depression, or at least increase the risk of developing the condition, we shall look at the process of screening before listing the various forms that depression can take. To assess and diagnose someone, they first have to present at a clinic or surgery. Although people are becoming more open to discussing their emotions with their family doctor, there is still a barrier in many cases. Such barriers can hamper accurate diagnosis should a person choose to discuss their condition. It also contributes to under-reporting and under-diagnosing of a severe mental health condition.

Course and prognosis

Although a person may experience depression for the first time at any stage in their life, generally, people experience their first episode in their mid-20s, with a large number developing depression in childhood and adolescence (12).

When looking at the symptoms that indicate the onset of depression—the prodromal phase—we can see a great deal of variation among individuals. For some, the beginning of full depressive symptoms occurs rapidly, often due to some serious life event. However, for many, the onset is subtler, with people experiencing various symptoms, such as anxiety, phobia, panic, and lowered mood. Still, in other cases, physical symptoms are to the fore. In these instances, it is usually the recourse of the clinician to examine for an underlying physical condition. However, at some stage later down the line, the behavioural and psychological symptoms of depression become increasingly noticeable.

In terms of the life course of depression, although it is the case that there appears to be a finite time for each episode—usually four to six months—in many cases, the remission phase is not entirely symptom-free. It is also the case that, although bouts of depression are generally followed by recovery, relapse occurs all too often. Around half of those who first experience depression will experience at least one more episode at some point later in their life (16). The likelihood of future relapse increases with each subsequent episode of depression, with the chance of relapse rising to 90 per cent in those who have experienced four bouts of depression (16). The likelihood of relapse is also higher for those who experienced depression in their childhood or where depression occurs for the first time later in life (17, 18).

Seasonal affective disorder—or recurring major depression with a seasonal pattern as it is now referred (19)—follows a particular course. Depression that recurs during winter is more common than depression that returns in the summer (20, 21). These regular relapses occur purely due to the time of the year and do not hinge around life events. In the majority of cases, individuals experience a reduction in their level of activity. Symptoms mirror those seen in atypical depression to a large extent (21). This seasonal form of depression is more common among younger adults (20).

In various sections of this book, I refer to treatment-resistant depression. Indeed, it is a term widely used in the literature and in practice. However, it is not without issues. It refers to individuals who fail to respond to a range of treatments, specifically antidepressants. It can be a term that is used in a derogatory way. As already mentioned, it is primarily associated with non-response to medication. It does not necessarily reflect psychological interventions (22), although this is not always the case. In such instances, it is essential to consider whether there are extrinsic factors, such as the person's home situation, that contribute to the lack of response to treatment (23).

Accurate detection

If we were lucky enough to have robust, accurate tools for detecting a universally agreed idea of depression in our arsenal, success would be hampered by peoples' disinclination to seek help. Studies have revealed a number of explanations people give for being loath to ask for help, including, among other things, the belief that it is something they should be able to deal with themselves, that the situation will improve at some stage anyway, as well as feelings of embarrassment and fear, and a dread of what might happen should they admit to how they really feel (24). There is a fear that antidepressants are addictive. In the case of older adults, there is also the assumption that what they are experiencing are just symptoms of growing old. Lurking in the background, as always, is the stigma levelled at depression, impacting at both individual and societal levels (25).

Even when a person does present their symptoms to their GP, because of the nature of the reporting, specifically a focus on bodily sensations and physical complaints, in many cases, the GP understandably does not suspect depression (26). This is particularly pertinent when considering older adults (27). Indeed, when we look at depression in those with physical health conditions (Chapter 6), the mere presence of comorbid physical complaints might act to mask the symptoms of depression, making accurate diagnosis incredibly difficult (28).

There are significant variations in how well individual GPs can accurately diagnose depression (29). When depression is diagnosed, the majority are treated within primary care. Only around a fifth are referred to a consultant psychiatrist. Those referred to specialist mental health services tend to comprise individuals who have not shown the expected improvement following a course of antidepressants and/or who manifest more severe symptomatology. It is also the case that a more substantial proportion of single women and those below 35 are referred to more specialist services (30).

It is not merely an issue of under-detection. There is the issue of people receiving a diagnosis of depression when they are, in fact, not experiencing depression at all. These are referred to as false positives (22).

There is some concern that GPs shy away from delving too deeply if depression is suspected as they are inhibited by severe time constraints. This has been described as therapeutic nihilism (31). The GP feels there is little they can do to help the individual with their depression. The concept of therapeutic nihilism has been around for millennia. It is characterized by the belief that many diseases are untreatable, with interventions being largely ineffective. Heraclitus suggested that doctors are "just as bad as the diseases they claimed to cure" (32). In many cases, such a response may partly be fuelled by frustration over a lack of availability of potential interventions.

Screening

Screening is an essential aspect of clinical work. It is defined as the methodical testing of an individual to recognize if they are at risk of developing a particular condition. It is also used to gauge whether the case warrants additional examination and/or treatment to help reduce the likelihood of it developing further (32). Screening, then, is about detecting those at particular risk and not about making a diagnosis at that stage. It is about trying to stop or delay the onset of a specific condition. Suppose an individual is suspected of experiencing depression. In that case, it is helpful to administer a screening tool to, on the one hand, clarify if further investigation is needed and, if so, just what needs to be investigated. Screening is also essential from a research perspective. Studies generally stipulate a range of inclusion and exclusion criteria. One might, for example, want to exclude all individuals who exceed the clinical cut-off for depression. In the majority of cases, such screening tools are self-report scales.

Screening is not without its malcontents. There are weighty ethical issues surrounding screening. One of the main problems is that most screening tools tend to be less than perfect in their ability to predict what might happen in the future. The issue here is that some will be deemed at risk when they are perfectly fine, instances referred to as false positives (33). In many cases, when screened positive for a condition, the person is referred for additional tests and procedures, many of which might be invasive. They will also be enrolled in unnecessary programmes of treatment.

The flipside of this is that some will not be picked up by the screening tool when they do, in fact, have all the warning signs of the condition being targeted. Such cases are referred to as false negatives. That means individuals will not receive further investigation, nor will they receive the treatment that might prevent or delay the onset of the condition.

As with most things, there is an issue of cost, be it in terms of money or emotion. Given the reasonably high rates of false positives, people are receiving interventions for reasonably mild forms of depression. They are unlikely to gain much from the treatment. Because the depression is mild, it will most likely disappear without any intervention. Although not harmful to that individual, they receive a level of care that someone in more dire need would benefit from. This is important in our current state, where funding is restricted and resources are rare (34).

From a more philosophical perspective, there is some concern levelled at the overuse of screening tools. This concern is steeped in a fear that they encourage a reductionist approach to care. In other words, they distract the clinician from considering the broader picture, focusing down on discrete bodily and psychological symptoms without necessarily considering the social and environmental components that might equally be pertinent to that individual (35). In other words, there is a need in all cases to consider the biological, psychological, social, and environmental factors.

Now that we have examined the accuracy of screening tools, the next step is to look in detail at how depression is codified. Many consider the *Diagnostic and*

Statistical Manual of Mental Disorders, or DSM for short, to be the go-to manual for making an accurate diagnosis. Because of that, and since the new version of the ICD—*International Statistical Classification of Diseases and Related Health Problems*—will not be officially presented until after I have submitted my manuscript, I have listed the various diagnoses of depression as they appear in the most recent DSM, the DSM-5 (19).

Diagnosis

Both the ICD and DSM are designed to provide clinicians with a formal, reliable system for diagnosis. The ICD, developed by the World Health Organization, encapsulates a holistic approach to health and well-being. It is not just concerned with mental health issues but rather health in a more general sense and is a vital resource for those in epidemiology and health management. The DSM is concerned solely with mental health. The current edition, the DSM-5, appeared in 2013. The latest iteration of the ICD, the ICD-11, will be presented to Member States of the WHO later this year, to supplant the ICD-10 by the beginning of 2022 (36).

In most cases, the main features of depressive disorders are as described earlier, namely a predominance of low mood combined with an absence of positive mood in conjunction with a variety of symptoms. The DSM-5 lists disruptive mood dysregulation disorder, major depressive disorder, persistent depressive disorder, premenstrual dysphoric disorder, substance/medication-induced depressive disorder, depressive disorder due to another medical condition, other specified depressive disorder, and unspecified depressive disorder.

In the more severe cases of major depression, the individual shows either marked physical slowing or heightened agitation, referred to as psychomotor retardation and agitation, respectively. In these more severe cases, a person does not derive pleasure from any life event that usually elicits positive emotions. In this sense, they are in a state of perpetual anhedonia. Somatic symptoms are largely to the fore here. As we will see shortly, in opposition to the weight gains seen in those with atypical depression, weight loss and a general lack of appetite are the norm. Sleep is significantly reduced. The usual pattern is that people tend to wake early and not be able to return to sleep. There are variations throughout the day, with the severity of depression being worse in the morning, a situation known as diurnal variation.

In such cases, a person may also experience symptoms of psychosis in the form of hallucinations and delusions. The nature of these hallucinations and delusions reflect the negative nature of the depression, with self-blame featuring heavily. However, other content may appear that is unrelated to the depression (37). Because the symptoms do not always necessarily reflect the depressed mood state of the individual and instead resemble the types of florid psychosis seen in schizophrenia, accurate diagnosis can be difficult.

Unipolar–bipolar

Up until relatively recently—by that, I mean up to and including the DSM-II (38)—depressive illness was generally classified under the Kraeplinian title, manic-depressive illness. This was distinguished from what he referred to as dementia praecox, a condition now known as schizophrenia (39). There were exceptions based on the frequency of depressive periods, namely involutional melancholia, psychotic-depressive reaction, and depressive neurosis.

It is now clear that unipolar and bipolar disorders are distinct entities. Unipolar disorder is a mood disorder associated with long stretches of depression. Bipolar disorder describes a condition where there are alternative cycles of depression and mania. This was previously described as manic depression. When looking at the age of onset, it is clearly earlier in bipolar disorder (40). There seems to be a more substantial genetic basis for bipolar disorder as well (41).

Endogenous depression and reactive depression

From time to time, you may come across the terms endogenous depression and reactive depression. This dichotomous view was prevalent in psychiatry at the turn of the twentieth century, an interpretation at odds with our assumption that most conditions are on a sliding scale of severity. According to this conceptualization of depression, the endogenous form is the more severe. In contrast, reactive depression is less debilitating and specifically tied to an event that acted as a trigger (42). The terms stuck, mainly because they seemed to capture differences in how the two forms responded to treatment. Endogenous depression appeared to be more responsive to drug therapies. The main argument for a unitary view of depression came from Akiskal and McKinney. They argued that, despite the origins, there is a standard neurophysiological profile to depression (43).

Subthreshold depressive symptoms

It is generally accepted that the lives of individuals who show symptoms of depression below those set by either the DSM or ICD can still be negatively affected if they persist over time. These are referred to as subthreshold depressive symptoms (44). A person may have this condition if they exhibit one symptom of depression but with insufficient evidence of other related symptoms to meet a positive diagnosis of depression. The symptoms would be considered persistent if they existed despite low-level forms of intervention.

Seasonal affective disorder

Seasonal affective disorder (SAD) is associated with a lowered mood and a general lack of energy. It is most prevalent in young females. It is almost exclusively associated with the dark days of the winter months. However, SAD is now sub-sumed under the diagnosis of recurring major depression with a seasonal pattern (19). These seasonal fluctuations are thought to be the by-product of a combination of a reduction in serotonin levels and a rise in melatonin, which together results in lowered mood and excessive tiredness, respectively, forcing out of synchrony the body's natural circadian rhythm.

DSM-5 criteria

Table 2.1 presents the various forms of depression categorized in the latest edition of the DSM, the DSM-5 (19). Several changes from the DSM-IV occurred in the DSM-5. The diagnosis of disruptive mood dysregulation disorder was added to reduce the risk for overdiagnosis of bipolar disorder in children. The diagnosis of persistent depressive disorder (dysthymia) is also new and had its origins in the DSM-IV's chronic major depression and dysthymia. Premenstrual dysphoric disor-der is now placed in the main body of the DSM-5. The subsequent sections follow the diagnoses closely as set out in the DSM-5.

Assessment

Having spent some time detailing the development of depression and the process of making an accurate diagnosis, it is time now to turn to an examination of how we assess depression in different contexts. In this section, we shall look at some of the measures used, some of which have been adapted to meet the needs of other age groups or cultures. Depression means different things to different people. The way it manifests varies depending on your age. The experience of depression is also distinct in different cultures.

Measuring depression

When evaluating depression, as with any other condition, it is crucial to ensure a sufficiently holistic assessment is made. It should never be just a matter of how many symptoms a person exhibits at a particular time. Of vital importance to the overall picture is the extent of functional impairment the person is experiencing (44).

In line with expanding conceptions of what depression is, myriad tools can as-sess it clinically. By a large margin, the majority of the measures available are self-report in nature. However, there do exist assessment tools that require independent rating by a trained clinician. An example of a clinician-administered assessment is the Structured Clinical Interview for DSM Disorders. As its name indicates, the criteria here are based on those outlined in the DSM. Most of these measures as-sess depression in general, whereas some are specific to certain demographics (45). Specific measures will be discussed shortly.

Table 2.1 DSM-5 Categories for Depressive Disorders

Diagnosis	Features	Prevalence	Additional information
Disruptive mood dysregulation disorder	The main feature of disruptive mood dysregulation disorder is a constant state of extreme irritability. This is characterized by outpourings of anger and a persistent mood of annoyance. This diagnosis is used for children up to the age of 12. It has been linked to the development of unipolar depression in adulthood	Rates of this condition are higher in school-age children who are male. Onset for this condition must occur before the age of 10. How the symptoms associated with this condition manifest will change as the child grows older. Children diagnosed with this condition are at a higher risk of developing unipolar depression and anxiety when they reach adulthood. Males are the predominant sex associated with this diagnosis	Because of the raised levels of aggression and functional consequences of the condition, it is crucial to monitor for suicidal behaviour. Because of the inability to tolerate frustration, performance at school tends to suffer markedly. Friendships are also rife with problems
Major depressive disorder	The main symptoms associated with major depressive disorder are depressed mood, an inability to derive pleasure from activities, weight loss, sleep disturbances, psychomotor agitation/retardation, fatigue, feeling worthless or guilty, cognitive difficulties, and repetitive thoughts about death. Five or more of these symptoms need to be present during two weeks to meet this diagnosis. They have to indicate a significant change in that person's usual level of functioning. Also, there needs to be evidence	Prevalence is higher in 18–29-year-olds than those over the age of 60. There are up to three times higher rates in females where onset is during adolescence. Although major depressive disorder can develop at any age, onset is increasingly likely with puberty. Peak rates occur in people in their 20s. Still, others find they experience their first depressive episode in later life. There is much evidence that rates of major depressive disorder are higher among females.	Neuroticism is a significant risk factor for major depressive disorder. This is linked to a poorer ability to deal with life stressors. There is a higher risk of developing this form of depression if you are a first-degree family member of someone else with the condition. In fact, in some cases, the risk is four times higher. Genetic heritability accounts for 40 per cent of cases. In terms of other influencers, there are many. These include other disorders, such as substance misuse and anxiety, as well as other medical conditions.

(Continued)

Table 2.1 (Continued)

Diagnosis	Features	Prevalence	Additional information
	that the symptoms are causing impairment across various domains of a person's life, such as work or relationships with others. Other causes of these symptoms must be ruled out, such as an existing medical condition or substance misuse. To meet this diagnosis, the person should not have experienced an episode of mania or hypermania		There are apparent cultural differences in the way major depressive disorder manifests. In the majority of countries, depression often goes without detection in primary care. For many cultures, the main presenting symptoms are somatic complaints, particularly difficulties falling asleep at night and lacking energy. There is no conclusive evidence to suggest that either symptoms or response to treatment differ in the two sexes. What does appear to vary is the risk of suicide, which is higher in women, but fewer numbers of completed suicides. The risk of suicide is present throughout a depressive episode. The risk is higher for those who have attempted suicide in the past. However, it is not the case that completed suicides are necessarily preceded by suicide attempts. Males are at higher risk of completed suicides, as are single people or those living on their own.

Persistent depressive disorder (dysthymia)

This diagnosis is characterized by a depressed mood that generally predominates throughout the day for most days. To meet the criteria for this diagnosis, the preponderance of a depressed mood must have been apparent for at least two years in adults. A person may have a dual diagnosis of persistent depressive disorder and major depressive disorder if they meet the criteria for both. The mood for this condition is described as primarily sad. People may find their appetite affected, experience sleep problems, feel fatigued, have low self-esteem, find it difficult to concentrate, and feel hopeless. The person would not have been without these symptoms for more than two months to meet this diagnosis. Because the nature of this condition is chronic, and the person has not experienced any change since the symptoms first manifested early on in life, their condition may not be reported because nothing obvious has changed. They have always been like that.

The figure for prevalence in the United States is around 0.5 per cent for persistent depressive disorder. The onset of this condition often occurs at a young age. Its development is described as insidious in the sense that it would appear always to have been present, with no defining event leading to a marked change in behaviour. By its nature, persistent depressive disorder is chronic. The pattern of persistent depressive disorder and borderline personality disorder developing among those diagnosed with both conditions suggests a common mechanism at play.

More unsatisfactory outcomes are associated with high levels of neuroticism, more severe symptoms, poor overall functioning, and the co-occurrence of anxiety disorders or conduct disorder. When looking at environmental risk factors, experiencing the loss of a parent or separation during childhood is significant here. In terms of heredity, those with this condition tend to also have a parent or sibling with the condition. There are also several neurological markers linked to persistent depressive disorder, including differences in the structure and functioning of the prefrontal cortex, anterior cingulate, amygdala, and hippocampus.

(Continued)

Table 2.1 (Continued)

Diagnosis	Features	Prevalence	Additional information
Premenstrual dysphoric disorder	The number and severity of symptoms in premenstrual dysphoric disorder coincide with changes during the menstrual cycle. Symptoms include mood swings, irritability, hopelessness, and tension. In addition, there is a lack of interest in usual activities, difficulty concentrating, lethargy, craving for a particular food, sleep disturbances (hypersomnia or insomnia), feeling out of control, and physical sensations, such as muscle pain and breast tenderness. These symptoms result in a great deal of distress, with all areas affected by a person's life. Five or more of these symptoms should be apparent in the week leading up to the onset of menses – the discharge of blood and mucosal tissue from the uterus, described as menstrual flow. Symptoms improve with the start of menses and all but disappear post-menses.	Although estimates vary considerably, partly due to the concern of reporting accuracy, 12-month prevalence is around 1.3 per cent for those who show functional impairment with no evidence of comorbidity. There can be an onset of this condition any time following menarche, a woman's first menstrual period. For those approaching menopause –when menstruation stops and oestrogen and progesterone drops – symptoms can worsen. These then cease following menopause. However, hormone replacement therapy can result in the re-occurrence of symptoms.	Several environmental factors are associated with this condition. Stress is a major factor, as is a history of interpersonal trauma such as physical or sexual abuse, and sociocultural aspects of the female gender role, including the level of education, reproductive, and lifestyle factors (48). There is a lack of clarity about the role of genetics here. When looking at things that affect this condition, there is evidence that those who take oral contraceptives report fewer symptoms of premenstrual dysphoric disorder. Premenstrual dysphoric disorder has been reported in many countries, although there is uncertainty if occurrences differ across cultures. How symptoms are expressed and the pattern of help-seeking behaviour will likely change across various cultures.

	The characteristic features of premenstrual dysphoric disorder are extreme mood lability, irritability, dysphoria, and anxiety, all of which coincide with the premenstrual phase of the menstrual cycle and again disappear after menses. The person must be symptom-free once the menstrual period begins. Although rare, some have reported delusions and hallucinations during the late luteal phase of the menstrual cycle, when the corpus luteum forms in the ovary, secreting both progesterone and oestrogen, leading to a thickening of the womb's lining in preparation for a fertilized ovum.	
Substance/ medication-induced depressive disorder	The prime characteristic is a predominant, persistent depressed mood. It is essential that these mood changes occur during or after substance intoxication or following medication. Drugs associated with this condition include alcohol, hallucinogens, amphetamine, cocaine, among	Based on US figures, the lifetime occurrence of this condition is 0.26 per cent. The depressive disorder must be directly linked back to a drug for a diagnosis of substance/medication-induced depressive disorder to be made. Symptoms disappear once the drug has been withdrawn.	A history of major depressive disorder is a significant risk factor for this condition, as is psychosocial stressors. Based on US data, there does appear to be a bias towards males from low-income backgrounds to be diagnosed with this condition. There was evidence of substance

(Continued)

Table 2.1 (Continued)

Diagnosis	Features	Prevalence	Additional information
	others. Prescribed medications also implicated include steroids, levodopa, and chemotherapeutic drugs.		use disorder in their family and a series of stressful life events leading up to substance misuse in many cases. Blood or urine samples can be analysed to provide evidence of the specific substance of misuse. This can then be used to help with the definitive diagnosis. The emergence of suicidal thoughts often coincides with the first use of a drug or medication.
Other diagnoses	*Depressive disorder due to another medical condition* The all-encompassing depressed mood is directly linked to a medical condition. In terms of diagnosing this condition, it is helpful to take note of the pattern of symptoms in conjunction with changes in the medical condition, specifically concerning changing the severity of symptoms and subsequent remission. There are several medical conditions where there is a known association with depression. These include stroke, Huntington's disease, Parkinson's disease, multiple sclerosis, and traumatic brain injury. *Other specified depressive disorder* This diagnosis is made if the symptoms do not meet the requirements for any of the above classifications of depression. Specific reasons identified by clinicians when making this diagnosis are recurrent brief depression, short-duration depressive episode (4–13 days), and depressive episode with insufficient symptoms. *Unspecified depressive disorder* As with the above condition, this diagnosis is used where symptoms do not meet the requirements of any of the other DSM diagnoses. The unspecified nomenclature here is used when the clinicians do not specify a reason for the diagnosis. This might be because there is not enough time to make a more specific diagnosis.		

Sex differences

As one might expect, men and women express depression in slightly different ways. The focus for men tends to be more on functional problems, such as difficulty concentrating and maintaining attention, and its impact on their ability to work. Among men, depression may be masked by a range of other behaviours. These include excessive alcohol consumption, as well as an increased tendency towards anger and violence.

When you look at how depression manifests in women, there is a tendency to focus on emotional issues. To some extent, this makes it a lot easier to diagnose depression, especially as women tend to be more willing to seek help than men. There seems to be a greater variety of symptoms reported by women, including feelings of pain, mental torment, panic, and phobia.

On the whole, people are more accepting and sympathetic towards women who are depressed as opposed to men (46), no doubt symptomatic of hidden gender stereotypes. This reflects society's reinforcement of depression in women but its rejection of it in men. The outcome is that men rely on alcohol to help deal with their depression.

Population-specific measures

The vast majority of measures of depression have been designed with a general, non-specific audience in mind. Well, this is not entirely true. In most cases, it would be reasonable to say that the general, non-specific audience in mind is of Western origin. However, it is essential to consider the population-specific nature of depression, thus necessitating a specialized tool (47). In this sense, some measures are used to assess depression in different age groups and cultures. The Kimberley Indigenous Cognitive Assessment of Depression (KICA-dep) was developed to be a culturally sensitive measure of depression for Indigenous Australians (48). In this, as in other examples, items have been reworded to reflect the cultural norms of that society. It is more than a matter of merely translating a tool into another language.

Age-specific measures

In Chapter 8, we shall be considering how depression affects individuals across the whole lifespan. The previous section was concerned with measures developed to be used in specific populations. For the purpose of this section, we will consider measures of depression designed with a particular age group in mind. Such measures are essential in ensuring the language used is appropriate, and that relevant symptoms and behaviours are captured by the items (49).

An example of a measure aimed solely at children is the Children's Depression Inventory 2 (CDI 2; (50)). It can be used for children aged 7–17 years. Information is gathered from the children themselves alongside assessments by parents and teachers. At the other end of the age range, we have the Geriatric Depression

Scale (GDS-30) (51). This was developed with older adults in mind. Each question is answered dichotomously, with "yes" or "no" answers. This simple scale allows this measure to be used effectively in cases where there are varying degrees of cognitive impairment.

Symptom severity

Of course, depression measures are not used solely as a diagnostic aid. For many reasons, both academics and clinicians require measures that accurately assess the severity of symptoms at varying time points in patients. In most cases, such measures are used to see if a specific treatment strategy is working. Does symptoms severity drop over time, for example? In many cases, these are self-report scales, such as the Beck Depression Inventory (52). However, they can be administered by a clinician, as in the case of the Hamilton Rating Scale for Depression (53).

Comorbidity

The coexistence of another condition and depression can present problems for generic measures of depression (54). In a few instances, specific measures have been developed for a significant coexisting psychiatric or medical condition. A much-used example is the Hospital Anxiety and Depression Scale (54). The purpose of this scale is to assess both symptoms of anxiety and depression without the confound of other physical symptoms. The Depression in the Medically Ill Scale (55) focused on cognitive elements to better detect depression with a coexisting medical condition. An example of a scale that targets a health condition explicitly is the Cardiac Depression Scale (56), and so is a more suitable measure of outcome for this patient group. When looking at comorbidity with another psychiatric disorder, the Calgary Depression Scale for Schizophrenia (57) accurately distinguished symptoms of depression from the negative and positive symptoms of schizophrenia. The Screening Assessment of Depression—Polarity (58) is a way to reduce the likelihood of misdiagnosing someone as experiencing unipolar depression while actually in the depressive phase of bipolar disorder.

Wider impact

Until recently, figures estimating the effects of disease were determined by how many people died each year in each condition. Rankings of mortality rates then fed into public health policies to combat the impact of these conditions. Due to its very nature, such reports overlooked mental health conditions. Fortunately, thinking on this issue has changed. The World Health Organization now assesses the level of disability alongside mortality (59). A new metric was introduced, the Disability Adjusted Life Year (DALY) (60). This figure quantifies premature death and disability by calculating the number of years lost or taken up by these factors. The main upshot of this change in focus is that depression is now seen as a significant health concern facing the entire planet. In fact, depression was the leading cause of concern among all non-fatal conditions, and fourth overall when one included fatal conditions (60).

Not only does depression rob people of any quality of life, but it is also a significant economic burden (61). Depression is costly not only in terms of the amount of time a person spends off work, but also it is a pricey endeavour to treat the condition considering the ubiquitous nature of the diagnosis. Figures based on data from the Office of National Statistics in the UK estimate direct costs of treatment to be around £370 million (62). Troublingly, 84 per cent of that cost was accounted for by the prescribing of antidepressant medication. Even more concerning was the estimate of indirect costs associated with depression—lost productivity that is borne by employers, society, and the family—with an estimate of £8 billion in terms of the prevalence of depression (morbidity costs), and £562 million for costs related to loss of life as the result of depression (mortality costs). However, a more recent study, one that attempted to project figures into the future, produced different statistics, most notably concerning the cost incurred by the prescribing of drugs. In this study, antidepressant medication represented only 1 per cent of the total costs. At the same time, hospital care accounted for over half (63).

What is clear is the reality that indirect costs outstrip costs incurred by healthcare services. By far, the most significant here are losses in both productivity and employment (62).

Having described the psychological symptoms associated with depression in detail, it is essential to consider the broader implications of this condition. Depression affects all aspects of a person's life, including relationships with friends and family and work. This is often accompanied by a substantial loss in earnings, which negatively affects family and relationships. It also impacts a person's ability to obtain employment in the future, with links to higher rates of unemployment (64). Many factors can lead some people with depression to become increasingly dependent on benefits to assist them in their lives. Taken together, all these elements contribute further to eroding a person's sense of self-worth and belief in their ability to change the situation. If it persists, marked impairments in social functioning are likely to develop.

Physical health is also greatly affected, and as a result, so is a person's life expectancy in some instances. We shall explore the impact of depression on physical health in more detail in Chapter 6. Depression aggravates many of the symptoms associated with medical complaints. It also impacts the outcome; in many cases, depression negatively affects the success of a person's response to a particular treatment regimen. Because depression has been shown to influence the outcome, for some conditions, such as coronary heart disease, this can have profound effects, increasing the risk of death in some instances (65, 66).

Depression also influences mortality as a result of its link with suicide. Around two-thirds of death by suicide is linked in some way to depression. The connection is even stronger in individuals with depression who also have to contend with a severe physical health condition (72). In Chapter 8, we shall look at strategies to help prevent suicide.

On top of all this, there is the stigma associated with depression, and mental health conditions in general, for the individual to contend with (67). Often, the public's impression of depression is that people with the condition are unstable and disturbed (25). Among other things, this general attitude likely explains why people with depression are reticent to seek help, be it from family and friends, or indeed professionals (68).

The bigger picture

When making a potential diagnosis of depression, the clinician needs to consider other elements that might feed into the bigger picture. We shall look soon at the impact of culture, highlighting the need to be aware of variations in terms of how depression is perceived and reported. There are many other things to consider when assessing someone for a mental health condition. Being aware of any underlying cognitive impairment is crucial, particularly knowing whether the person has a learning disability (45). In such cases, additional support will be needed. For example, it may be necessary to modify how an intervention is provided and the agreed duration of any treatment packages. Suppose a person has problems with language or communication, and they are suspected to be experiencing depression. In that case, a helpful tool is the Distress Thermometer (69), a single-item scale that elicits distress experienced during the past week (70). Alternatively, asking the person's family or their carer about their behaviour can elicit the information needed.

Culture

There is much evidence to show cultural differences regarding the prevalence of a range of mental health conditions, including depression (71). For example, depression seems higher among women from black and minority ethnic (BME) communities (72). How a condition manifests is dependent on cultural values and expectations, as are perceived sources of support.

The prominence of depression differs significantly across diverse cultures. The highest figures are found in Europe, North America, and Australia, whereas rates are lower in East Asia (73). Therefore, the role of culture is essential in trying to understand more about the relationship between our biology and the world in which we live. There appears to be something inherently amiss in some societies to account for the relatively high rates of depression. On the flip side, something is fundamentally right about other cultures. Is it, then, the case that some societies experience more stress than others, or is it a matter of under-reporting or over-reporting of depressive symptoms in specific sectors?

The way symptoms manifest varies across different cultures. In the United Kingdom and the United States, it is right to say that depression is primarily indicated by a prominent lowered mood and general lack of interest in life. For other cultures, such as certain Mediterranean societies, headache and nervousness are the initial warning signs. In contrast, fatigue is the main one in Asia (45, 74).

Striving for the positive

Chentsova Dutton (73) presents a good overview of the literature, albeit focusing on comparing and contrasting North American and East Asian cultures. This divide reflects the bulk of the amassed literature. In the West, there is a focus on developing and maintaining a healthy emotional life. We feel good about who we are. It is an area over which we exert personal control (75). The growing demand for books on happiness provides a testament to this. Western ideals about striving for a successful life often fit uncomfortably with the Eastern origins of many of these self-help books.

In many cases, therein lies the basis of much of our inner turmoil: the distinction between seeking pleasure and obtaining true happiness. Holding positive beliefs about self and future does help buffer us against the *Sturm und Drang* of daily life. An inability to achieve this is inevitably indicative of failure and so feeds a depressogenic style of thinking.

Such striving for the positive needs to be tempered with a sense of reality. There is nothing wrong with holding such drives and motivations. Still, equally, we must be able to deal with situations when things do not go as planned, when, for whatever reason, barriers are erected in front of us. Failure is an all-too-frequent aspect of our daily lives. Not being able to meet our own goals will likely result in a torrent of negative emotions that, for someone prone to depression, will result in an escalating spiral of negativity.

As already seen, there are apparent cultural differences in terms of rates of depression in East Asian cultures. When looking at how depression is reported in these societies, less emphasis is placed on communicating feelings of happiness and optimism when asked to complete standard indices of depression (76). There are higher levels of self-criticism in addition to this (77). Nonetheless, depression is not as rife. One argument that has been proposed is that, because there is more openness about an individual's own limitations, people are more resilient to negative information about the self. Failing to meet expectations is generally seen as being due to inadequate exertion on behalf of the individual concerned (78). Because of this, there is a dogged determination to rise to the challenge rather than retreat. Because such feelings and behaviour do not contravene societal norms, people do not feel ashamed, which would be the default Western response when faced with similar situations.

Self and others

Within the West, we strive for individuality and self-rule. As is increasingly apparent, we like to be in charge of all of life's choices, even our own death. Our goals and objectives permeate all strata, including those of whom we befriend. In our modern world, people follow the path dictated by their career aspirations. In many cases, this involves moving further and further away from their roots, away from family and childhood friends. In this sense, it has been argued that relationships centre around colleagues and neighbours rather than friends in the real sense of the word (73). As a result, relationships reflect current goals. Throughout life, our plans change, and as a result, so do our social networks. There is an inherent lack of consistency that undermines stability.

In contrast to this individualistic ethos, East Asian and Eastern European cultures follow a more collectivistic pattern (73). In such societies, there are strong bonds with family. People tend to remain in relatively close proximity, thereby maintaining a physical and psychological connection. Success or failure in others is experienced at a level comparable to a person's reaction to events in their own life, a situation far removed from the norm in Western societies.

With depression, such close harmony may be a double-edged sword. Being so intermeshed in the emotional lives of one another can lead to turmoil when a relationship within the group breaks down. Contrary to this, the sense of overwhelming support and empathy experienced in collectivist societies can act to buffer against the stress of life and may ameliorate symptoms commonly associated with depression (79, 80).

Contrasting this to a person's sense of self in individualistic societies, here sense of self is context-specific. There is a compartmentalizing of self that is tied to particular roles. In other words, our understanding of who we are at work differs from how we see ourselves when with friends. Disharmony in one situation does not, as a result, necessarily lead to disruption in other spheres of our mental life. Such inherent flexibility in our perception of self may help in minimizing the impact of significant life stressors. Such complexity of self may provide a mental *cordon sanitaire* that helps buffer against depression (81).

Expressing feelings

In Chapter 6, we shall focus on depression across the lifespan. One of the problems with diagnosing depression in older adults is how they describe their ailments. Generally, depression is viewed as a mental health condition. In this sense, the main focus is on the internalized torment people experience. However, there are also physical manifestations of depression. Most people, including clinicians, are primed to respond to the changes in mood associated with depression, not necessarily the bodily sensations. It is because of this that depression often goes undetected among older adults. They talk about somatic complaints rather than emotions.

The distinction between the body and emotion in relation to depression is central to some vital cultural differences. As with older adults, there is a tendency among certain cultures—Asian and Middle Eastern, among others—to refer to bodily complaints rather than thoughts and feelings. The DSM (19) demands specific changes in mood and overall mental well-being to fulfil a diagnosis of major depressive disorder. Reports of headaches and fatigue are unlikely to ring the appropriate alarm bells, so a positive diagnosis of depression will not be made.

Communicating emotional upset is, in some cultures, discouraged, especially to those who are strangers. In many cases, extended rapport does not exist between

GPs and their patients (82). Patients might even feel it unsuitable to discuss emotional problems with their doctor (83). This might lead to a focus on somatic complaints rather than feelings and emotions (73).

Appropriate measures

We have examined some of the cultural differences that should be considered when talking about depression. Because of this, there is a real need to ensure sensitivity to the diverse needs of various ethnic and religious groups. This impacts all levels of care. It includes an obligation to ensure assessments are culturally sensitive, that explanations provided take into consideration a person's specific beliefs and attitudes, and thus feeding into the review of appropriate treatment plans (44).

At a pragmatic level, measures of depression should be translated into appropriate languages such that they do not lose any of their subtlety and sensitivity. In addition, culturally specific measures must be seen to reflect the construct of depression experienced by the target community (49). Even though there is an awareness of this, most screening tools employed across the board were validated using white populations. Because of that, adequate resources need to be allocated to validating culturally specific tools so that they are available when required. The NICE guidelines on depression (28) provides an excellent overview of some of the available tools, along with an assessment of their accuracy (Section 5.2.9).

Before moving on, a better understanding of the needs of different cultures is one thing. Ensuring that existing measures are sensitive to how symptoms are expressed is another. However, the entire foundation of mental health research is based chiefly on Western contexts. This includes recommendations for drug treatments and psychological therapies (84, 85). Thus, we need to be sensitive to how distress in other cultural groups can be better eased.

Summary

Much has been presented around the diagnosis and assessment of depression in this chapter. We started by looking at how depression develops and identified key risk factors associated with the condition. There followed a detailed section on the different diagnostic categories as presented in the current edition of the DSM. Assessment tools were then discussed, with a particular emphasis on making sure that appropriate measures are selected depending on who is being evaluated. The point here is that different age groups and people from different cultures need measures sensitive to how depression will manifest.

On top of that, the presence of a comorbid physical or mental health condition brings its own set of complications. So specific measures have been developed to help with the diagnosis of depression in these circumstances. The chapter draws to a close by taking a look at the bigger picture, in other words, the economic impact of depression and the effect of different cultures. In the previous chapter, we talked about the loss of the individual when discussing the impact of diagnostic labels and how we must hold onto the sense of the person as unique, not merely an embodied cluster of symptoms. Here in this chapter, there is a similar theme reflected in the need to ensure diagnoses and assessments are sensitive to the values and expectations of the individual. A person's culture is an essential part of who they are, and cultures differ in terms of how depression manifests. Again, holding onto the concept of individuality is critical for accurate assessment and diagnosis.

References

1 World Health Organization. Depression 2017. Available from: www.who.int/mediacentre/factsheets/fs369/en/.
2 World Health Organization. Depression. World Health Organization; 2019 [01/06/2019]. Available from: www.who.int/en/news-room/fact-sheets/detail/depression.
3 Reddy MS. Depression: The disorder and the burden. Indian J Psychol Med. 2010;32(1):1–2.
4 Katon W, Schulberg H. Epidemiology of depression in primary care. Gen Hosp Psychiatry. 1992;14(4):237–247.
5 Risch N, Herrell R, Lehner T, Liang KY, Eaves L, Hoh J, et al. Interaction between the serotonin transporter gene (5-HTTLPR), stressful life events, and risk of depression: A meta-analysis. JAMA. 2009;301(23):2462–2471.
6 Collishaw S, Hammerton G, Mahedy L, Sellers R, Owen MJ, Craddock N, et al. Mental health resilience in the adolescent offspring of parents with depression: A prospective longitudinal study. Lancet Psychiat. 2016;3(1):49–57.
7 Singleton N, Bumpstead R, O'Brien M, Lee A, Meltzer H. Psychiatric morbidity among adults living in private households, 2000. Int Rev Psychiat. 2003;15(1–2):65–73.
8 Harris T. Introduction to the work of George Brown. Where inner and outer worlds meet: Psychosocial research in the tradition of George W Brown. Br J Psychiat. 2000:1–52.
9 Hyde CL, Nagle MW, Tian C, Chen X, Paciga SA, Wendland JR, et al. Identification of 15 genetic loci associated with risk of major depression in individuals of European descent. Nat Gen. 2016;48:1031–1036.
10 Health NIOM. Depression 2016. Available from: www.nimh.nih.gov/health/topics/depression/index.shtml.
11 Kendler KS, Gardner C, Neale M, Prescott C. Genetic risk factors for major depression in men and women: Similar or different heritabilities and same or partly distinct genes? Psychol Med. 2001;31(4):605–616.
12 Fava M, Kendler KS. Major depressive disorder. Neuron. 2000;28(2):335–341.
13 Hamman C, Henry R, Daley S. Depression and sensitization to stressors among young women as a function of childhood adversity. J Consult Clin Psychol. 2000;68:782–787.
14 Nuechterlein KH, Dawson ME. A heuristic vulnerability/stress model of schizophrenic episodes. Schizophr Bull. 1984;10(2):300.
15 Harris T, Brown GW, Robinson R. Befriending as an intervention for chronic depression among women in an inner city. 1: Randomised controlled trial. Br J Psychiat. 1999;174(3):219–224.
16 Kupfer DJ. Long-term treatment of depression. J Clin Psychiatry. 1991;52:28–34.
17 Giles DE, Jarrett RB, Biggs MM, Guzick DS, Rush AJ. Clinical predictors of recurrence in depression. Am J Psychiatry. 1989;146(6):764–767.
18 Mitchell AJ, Subramaniam H. Prognosis of depression in old age compared to middle age: A systematic review of comparative studies. Am J Psychiatry. 2005;162(9):1588–1601.

19 American Psychiatric Association. Diagnostic and statistical manual of mental disorders: DSM-5. 5th ed. Washington, DC: American Psychiatric Association; 2013.
20 Rodin I, Thompson C. Seasonal affective disorder. Adv Psychiatr Treat. 1997;3(6): 352–359.
21 Magnusson A, Partonen T. The diagnosis, symptomatology, and epidemiology of seasonal affective disorder. CNS Spectr. 2005;10(8):625–634.
22 National Institute for Health and Care Excellence. Depression: The treatment and management of depression in adults (update). NICE Clinical Guideline. October 2009;90(23):24.
23 Andrews G, Jenkins R. Management of mental disorders. Sydney: World Health Organization Collaborating Centre for Mental Health and Substance Abuse; 1999.
24 Meltzer PB, Brugha T, Farrell M, Jenkins R, Lewis G, The reluctance to seek treatment for neurotic disorders. J Ment Heal. 2000;9(3):319–327.
25 Priest RG, Vize C, Roberts A, Roberts M, Tylee A. Lay people's attitudes to treatment of depression: Results of opinion poll for Defeat Depression Campaign just before its launch. BMJ. 1996;313(7061):858–859.
26 Kisely S, Gater R, Goldberg DP. Results from the Manchester Centre. In: Üstün TB, Sartorius N, editors. Mental illness in general health care: An international study. Chichester: John Wiley & Sons; 1995, pp. 175–191.
27 Rabins PV. Barriers to diagnosis and treatment of depression in elderly patients. Am J Geriatr Psychiatry. 1996;4(4 Suppl.).
28 Üstün TB, Sartorius N. Mental illness in general health care: An international study. Chichester: John Wiley & Sons; 1995.
29 Goldberg D, Huxley P. Mental illness in the community: The pathway to psychiatric care. Int J Rehabil Res. 1983;6(1):127.
30 Burroughs H, Lovell K, Morley M, Baldwin R, Burns A, Chew-Graham C. 'Justifiable depression': How primary care professionals and patients view late-life depression? A qualitative study. Fam Pract. 2006;23(3):369–377.
31 Stegenga JA. Medical nihilism. 1st ed. Oxford: Oxford University Press; 2018.
32 Peckham CS, Dezateux C. Issues underlying the evaluation of screening programmes. Br Med Bull. 1998;54(4):767–778.
33 Marteau TM. Psychological costs of screening. BMJ. 1989;299(6698):527.
34 Palmer SC, Coyne JC. Screening for depression in medical care: Pitfalls, alternatives, and revised priorities. J Psychosom Res. 2003;54(4):279–287.
35 Dowrick C. Beyond depression: A new approach to understanding and management. Oxford: Oxford University Press; 2009.
36 World Health Organization. WHO releases new International Classification of Diseases (ICD 11) 2018. Available from: www.who.int/news-room/detail/18-06-2018-who-releases-new-international-classification-of-diseases-(icd-11).
37 Project TP, Andrews G. Management of mental disorders. World Health Organization Collaborating Centre for Mental Health and Substance Abuse; 2000.
38 American Psychiatric Association. Committee on nomenclature and S. Diagnostic and statistical manual of mental disorders. 2nd ed. Washington: American Psychiatric Association; 1968.
39 Wagner AL, Rehm LP, Ivens-Tundal C. Mood disorders: Unipolar and bipolar. In: Sutker PB, Adams HE, editors. Comprehensive handbook of psychopathology. 3rd ed. Dordrecht, The Netherlands: Springer Science+Business Media; 2004.
40 Burke KC, Burke JD, Jr., Regier DA, Rae DS. Age at onset of selected mental disorders in five community populations. Arch Gen Psychiatry. 1990;47(6):511–518.

41   Allen MG. Twin studies of affective illness. Arch. Gen. Psychiatry. 1976;33(12): 1476–1478.
42   Gaddy MA. Endogenous and reactive depression. In: Ingram RE, editor. The international encyclopedia of depression. Springer Publishing Company; 2009.
43   Akiskal HS, McKinney WT. Depressive disorders: Toward a unified hypothesis: Clinical, experimental, genetic, biochemical, and neurophysiological data are integrated. Sci. 1973;182(4107):20–29.
44   Excellence NIfC. Depression in adults: Recognition and management. NICE Guidelines [CG90]. 2009.
45   Nezu AM, Nezu CM. Assessment of depression. In: Ingram RE, editor. The international encyclopedia of depression. Springer Publishing Company; 2009.
46   Hammen CL, Peters SD. Differential responses to male and female depressive reactions. J Consult Clin Psychol. 1977;45(6):994–1001.
47   Nezu AM, Nezu CM, Friedman J, Lee M. Assessment of depression among mental health and medical patient populations. In: Gotlib IH, Hammen CL, editors. Handbook of depression. 2nd ed. ed. New York; London: Guilford Press; 2010. pp. 44–68.
48   Almeida OP, Flicker L, Fenner S, Smith K, Hyde Z, Atkinson D, et al. The Kimberley assessment of depression of older Indigenous Australians: Prevalence of depressive disorders, risk factors and validation of the KICA-dep scale. PLoS One. 2014;9(4):e94983.
49   Nezu CM, Nezu AM. Assessment of depression. In: Ingram RE, editor. The international encyclopedia of depression. New York; London: Springer; 2009.
50   Kovacs M. Children's depression inventory 2 (CDI 2). Pearson; 2010.
51   Yesavage JA, Brink TL, Rose TL, Lum O, Huang V, Adey M, et al. Development and validation of a geriatric depression screening scale: A preliminary report. J Psychiatr Res. 1982;17(1):37–49.
52   Beck AT, Steer RA, Brown GK. Beck depression inventory-II. San Antonio. 1996;78(2): 490–498.
53   Miller IW, Bishop S, Norman WH, Maddever H. The modified Hamilton rating scale for depression: Reliability and validity. Psychiatry Res. 1985;14(2):131–142.
54   Zigmond AS, Snaith RP. The hospital anxiety and depression scale. Acta Psychiatr Scand. 1983;67(6):361–370.
55   Parker G, Hilton T, Bains J, Hadzi-Pavlovic D. Cognitive-based measures screening for depression in the medically ill: The DMI-10 and the DMI-18. Acta Psychiatr Scand. 2002;105(6):419–426.
56   Hare DL, Davis CR. Cardiac Depression Scale: Validation of a new depression scale for cardiac patients. J Psychosom Res. 1996;40(4):379–386.
57   Addington D, Addington J, Maticka-Tyndale E. Assessing depression in schizophrenia: The Calgary depression scale. Br J Psychiatry. 1993.
58   Solomon DA, Leon AC, Maser JD, Truman CJ, Coryell W, Endicott J, et al. Distinguishing bipolar major depression from unipolar major depression with the screening assessment of depression-polarity (SAD-P). J Clin Psychiatry. 2006;67(3):434–442.
59   Murray CJL, Lopez A. The global burden of disease: A comprehensive assessment of mortality and disability from diseases, injuries, and risk factors in 1990 and projected to 2020. Boston, MA: Harvard School of Public Health on behalf of the World Health Organization and the World Bank; 1996.
60   Organization WH. Reducing risks, promoting healthy life. Geneva: World Health Organization; 2002.

61 Ustun TB, Ayuso-Mateos JL, Chatterji S, Mathers C, Murray CJ. Global burden of depressive disorders in the year 2000. Br J Psychiatry. 2004;184:386–392.

62 Thomas CM, Morris S. Cost of depression among adults in England in 2000. Br J Psychiatry. 2003;183(6):514–519.

63 McCrone PR, Dhanasiri S, Patel A, Knapp M, Lawton-Smith S. Paying the price: The cost of mental health care in England to 2026. King's Fund; 2008.

64 Psychiatrists RCo. Mental health and work. Royal College of Psychiatrists; 2008. Available from: https://assets.publishing.service.gov.uk/government/uploads/system/uploads/attachment_data/file/212266/hwwb-mental-health-and-work.pdf.

65 Cassano P, Fava M. Depression and public health: An overview. J Psychosom Res. 2002;53(4):849–857.

66 Nicholson A, Kuper H, Hemingway H. Depression as an aetiologic and prognostic factor in coronary heart disease: A meta-analysis of 6362 events among 146 538 participants in 54 observational studies. Eur Heart J. 2006;27(23):2763–2774.

67 Sartorius N. Eines der letzten Hindernisse einer verbesserten psychiatrischen Versorgung: Das Stigma psychischer Erkrankungen. Neuropsychiatrie-Munchen-Deisenhofen. 2002;16(1/2):5–10.

68 Bridges K, Goldberg D. Somatic presentation of depressive illness in primary care. J R Coll Gen Pract Occas Pap. 1987(36):9.

69 Roth AJ, Kornblith AB, Batel-Copel L, Peabody E, Scher HI, Holland JC. Rapid screening for psychologic distress in men with prostate carcinoma. Cancer. 1998;82(10):1904–1908.

70 Roth AJ, Kornblith AB, Batel-Copel L, Peabody E, Scher HI, Holland JC. Rapid screening for psychologic distress in men with prostate carcinoma: A pilot study. Can Interdiscip Int J Am Can Soc. 1998;82(10):1904–1908.

71 Bhui K, Bhugra D, Goldberg D, Dunn G, Desai M. Cultural influences on the prevalence of common mental disorder, general practitioners' assessments and help-seeking among Punjabi and English people visiting their general practitioner. Psychol Med. 2001;31(5):815–825.

72 Creed F, Tomenson B, Riste L. Prevalence of anxiety and depressive illness and help seeking behaviour in African Caribbeans and white Europeans: Two phase general population survey. 1999.

73 Chentsova Dutton Y. Culture and depression. In: Ingram RE, editor. The international encyclopedia of depression. New York; London: Springer; 2009.

74 Association AP, Association AP. Diagnostic and statistical manual of mental disorders, Revised 4th ed. Washington, DC: Author; 2000.

75 Heine SJ. Self as cultural product: An examination of East Asian and North American selves. J Pers. 2001;69(6):881–906.

76 Yen S, Robins CJ, Lin N. A cross-cultural comparison of depressive symptom manifestation: China and the United States. J Consult Clin Psychol. 2000;68(6):993–999.

77 Saint Arnault D, Sakamoto S, Moriwaki A. The association between negative self-descriptions and depressive symptomology: Does culture make a difference? Arch Psychiatr Nurs. 2005;19(2):93–100.

78 Heine SJ, Lehman DR, Ide E, Leung C, Kitayama S, Takata T, et al. Divergent consequences of success and failure in Japan and north America: An investigation of self-improving motivations and malleable selves. J Pers Soc Psychol. 2001;81(4):599–615.

79   Calvete E, Connor-Smith JK. Perceived social support, coping, and symptoms of distress in American and Spanish students. Anxiety Stress Coping. 2006;19(1):47–65.

80   Plant EA, Sachs-Ericsson N. Racial and ethnic differences in depression: The roles of social support and meeting basic needs. J Consult Clin Psychol. 2004;72(1):41–52.

81   Koch EJ, Shepperd JA. Is self-complexity linked to better coping? A review of the literature. J Pers. 2004;72(4):727–760.

82   Simon GE, VonKorff M, Piccinelli M, Fullerton C, Ormel J. An international study of the relation between somatic symptoms and depression. N Engl J Med. 1999;341(18):1329–1335.

83   Burr J, Chapman T. Contextualising experiences of depression in women from South Asian communities: A discursive approach. Sociol Health Illn. 2004;26(4):433–452.

84   Lin K-M. Biological differences in depression and anxiety across races and ethnic groups. J Clin Psychiatry. 2001;62:13–19; discussion 20–21.

85   Lawrence V, Murray J, Banerjee S, Turner S, Sangha K, Byng R, et al. Concepts and causation of depression: A cross-cultural study of the beliefs of older adults. Gerontologist. 2006;46(1):23–32.

Chapter 3

Models of depression

Biological model

Genetics

Genetics does seem to play a significant role in depression. Familial risk is higher in those who develop depression early on (1). Precisely what the mechanism is here is not yet clear. There seems to be a proneness to suffer hardship and a tendency to become depressed (2). Several factors have been identified as potentially mediating this genetic susceptibility in individuals. These include how one responds to stressful situations, among other things. This, then, is a classic example of gene–environment interaction.

Of interest here is the general finding that depression is recurrent in nature. This means that people are more likely to experience a subsequent depressive event in the future. There is evidence to show that subsequent episodes of depression are less dependent on the presence of environmental stressors (3).

Endocrine models

Hypothalamic–pituitary–adrenal axis

The hypothalamic–pituitary–adrenal axis, the HPA axis for short, mediates the body's response to stressful events. It seems to be particularly important in depression. This is because around half of those diagnosed with depression show hypercortisolemia; high cortisol levels, in other words. This is due to both an over-secretion of the hormone itself and a reduction in the negative feedback received by the hypothalamus and pituitary that normally regulates its levels.

Some studies have produced findings that suggest elevated levels of cortisol play a causative role in depression. This is because reducing levels of the hormone results in a raising in mood (4). Also, antidepressants act to resolve issues with the negative feedback loop (5). High cortisol levels are also implicated in changes in 5-hydroxytryptamine (5-HT) neurotransmission, a neurotransmitter intimately linked to depression, more commonly referred to as serotonin.

DOI:10.4324/9781315688879-3

Chronically raised levels of cortisol lead to structural changes, namely atrophy within the hippocampus. Such changes have also been shown in depression (6). One explanation for this is neurotoxicity, but other accounts propose a reduction in the formation of new nerve cells or atrophy of the dendrites. Indeed, one explanation of how antidepressants work is their role in increasing neurogenesis within the hippocampus (7).

We also know that events occurring during one's childhood can result in someone developing depression. Again, the HPA axis is implicated here. Such early stressors alter the body's response to stress, thus providing a potential explanation for heightened vulnerability to depression later in life (8).

Assessing levels of cortisol is rife with problems as, by its very nature, cortisol levels fluctuate throughout the day and also change depending on the level of experienced stress. It has been suggested that the link between neuroendocrine disturbance and depression can be explained by abnormal levels of the central neurotransmitter, noradrenaline. Noradrenaline suppresses hypothalamic corticotropin-releasing hormone (CRH), thus resulting in a reduction in the amount of pituitary adrenocorticotropic hormone (ACTH) secreted by the pituitary gland. This leads to lower levels of cortisol being emitted by the adrenal glands. The converse of this, where there is a deficiency of noradrenaline in the central nervous system, is an increase in symptoms of depression and increased cortisol levels (9).

The dexamethasone suppression test (DST) is used to assess depression. Dexamethasone causes the pituitary gland to secrete less ACTH. Following an injection of dexamethasone, changes in the levels of cortisol can be measured. One would expect plasma cortisol levels to drop accordingly, but this fails to occur in a proportion of individuals with depression.

Evidence suggests that people with depression who also show an abnormal DST respond better to antidepressants. Non-suppression of DST is linked to poorer outcomes following cognitive therapy (10). It is also associated with an increased risk of suicide (11). Once symptoms improve, abnormalities in the DST response disappear (9). However, this effect is not specific to depression. A variant of this test is more successful at delineating those with or without depression (12).

Hypothalamic–pituitary–thyroid axis

Disruption in thyroid function can result in marked changes in mood. Those who experience hypothyroidism show symptoms comparable to depression, as in some cases do those with hyperthyroidism. Thyroid dysfunction is undoubtedly observed in depression for some. There is evidence that adding thyroid hormone to an ordinary course of treatment potentiates the effect of the antidepressant medication (13). Evidence exists that low levels of triiodothyronine, or T3, a thyroid hormone, are linked to a longer time to recurrence of depression (14). T3 is also associated with increased rates of neurogenesis within the hippocampus (15).

Dehydroepiandrosterone

Dehydroepiandrosterone, or DHEA, is believed to counteract high levels of cortisol. Indeed, previous evidence indicates that a high level of cortisol is bad. However, the negative impact of such high levels may be ameliorated if there are also concomitant high levels of DHEA. In this sense, the ratio of cortisol to DHEA might be more appropriate in terms of the onset of depression (16). There is some evidence that administering DHEA could be a form of antidepressant treatment (17) as it reduces the impact of cortisol.

Neurochemical models

The main focus of biological models of depression is varying deficiencies in crucial neurotransmitters. They are referred to as the monoamine theories of depression and, as such, relate to catecholamines, noradrenaline, dopamine, and serotonin (18). The monoamine hypothesis of depression grew out of the finding that the drug reserpine caused depression. This was due to monoamine depletion. Antidepressants, on the other hand, inhibit monoamine reuptake. The analysis showed lower monoamine metabolites in the cerebrospinal fluid of those with depression, suggesting a deficiency at monoaminergic synaptic sites of several critical neurotransmitters, namely noradrenaline, dopamine, and serotonin. Drugs used to treat depression will be explored in more detail in Chapter 9. These drugs generally work by increasing levels of essential neurotransmitters either by blocking reuptake or by inhibiting their breakdown. Although the emphasis has been on reversing the depletion of noradrenaline and serotonin in depression, it is clear that this is not the complete picture as other diagnoses are associated with reductions in the same neurochemicals (19). There is growing evidence that acetylcholine and gamma-aminobutyric acid (GABA) are also implicated.

Serotonin

Serotonin is involved in several bodily processes. These include the regulation of sleep and the consumption of food, among other things. It is also linked to the control of impulsive behaviour. Those who have an imbalance of serotonin tend to experience depression. However, such imbalance is also associated with obsessive-compulsive disorder and panic disorder.

The serotonin hypothesis of depression has been a prevalent theory in psychology (20). One major piece of evidence is the lack of tryptophan evident in those with depression. Tryptophan, an amino acid, is a precursor of serotonin, 5-hydroxytryptamine, or 5-HT for short. The enzyme tryptophan hydroxylase (TPH) is involved in the initial step of synthesizing 5-HT. How serotonin itself is metabolized also differs, such that absorption, or uptake, is reduced. One way to test the relationship with depression is to use the tryptophan depletion (TD) paradigm. This involves giving a person various amino acids, although excluding tryptophan in this mixture. Plasma levels of tryptophan quickly drop. Because of that, the synthesis of serotonin decreases. For healthy individuals, who have no history of depression, this drop in tryptophan levels does not have any marked effect on mood. This is not the case for those experiencing a remission from depression and no longer taking medication. In such cases, it has the effect of inducing a resurgence of depression-like symptoms (21).

Noradrenaline

Noradrenaline is associated with situations that require an individual to be alert and ready for action. We know that noradrenaline is vital for effective cognitive functioning. It is one of the neurotransmitters boosted by caffeine, thereby contributing to the cognitive-enhancing effects of drinks such as coffee and tea (22, 23).

Levels of noradrenaline are also affected by depression. Some antidepressants work by preventing the reuptake—absorption of a secreted neurotransmitter by the synaptic bouton—of noradrenaline (24). Evidence of noradrenergic dysfunction comes from studies showing a lowered growth hormone response to clonidine and desipramine, both of which are α_2 receptor agonists (24). In healthy individuals, such α_2 agonists increase the release of growth hormone. A comparably diminished response is retained even when a person is in remission from depression, so it might be the case that this is a potential trait marker for depression. Patients who are treatment-resistant show lower levels of noradrenaline and dopamine originating from the brain (25).

Dopamine

Dopamine is implicated in both motor and mental activities. Concerning cognition, it is intrinsically linked to motivation. Similarly to that described earlier, there seems to be a reduced growth hormone response to the dopamine agonist apomorphine (25). The drug bupropion shows antidepressant properties and works by reducing the reuptake of dopamine (24).

Acetylcholine

There is an increased growth hormone response to the pyridostigmine challenge. Pyridostigmine, an anticholinesterase drug, releases growth hormone by reducing the inhibitory effect of somatostatin. This hormone regulates a range of physiological and hormonal functions. Further evidence of cholinergic dysfunction comes from the observation that those with depression have shorter sleep latency—the time taken to fall asleep—and more extended periods of REM sleep—a period of the sleep cycle associated with the storage of memories and learning—both of which are indicative of increased cholinergic activation. This increased activity in the cholinergic neurotransmitter system, in conjunction with reduced levels of noradrenaline—the cholinergic-adrenergic balance theory of depression—are thought to be behind depression (26). This theory postulates that each mood state results from some balance between central acetylcholine and noradrenaline levels in areas of the brain responsible for regulating affect. Depression is thought to result from higher levels of acetylcholine (27).

Gamma-aminobutyric acid

Baclofen-induced growth hormone release differentiates those who have depression from healthy participants. In depression, the growth hormone response is reduced. This indicates a lowered response of γ-aminobutyric acid (GABA) receptors in this patient group (28).

Interaction between different neurotransmitter systems

Although most drugs specifically target a particular neurotransmitter system, there is also the likelihood that other systems will be affected down the line. Serotonin is a good example. Linked to this is the suggestion that multiple neurotransmitter systems are implicated in depression. This can be seen in different clustering of symptoms. In other words, apathy indicates low levels of noradrenaline, whereas sleep disruption is likely due to a deficit in serotonin (24). Because of this, models of depression that specify a single neurotransmitter tend to be flawed (29).

Neuroimaging accounts

Evidence is accumulating that there are structural changes in the brains of those diagnosed with depression. Indeed, there is ample evidence from both imaging studies and post-mortem examination that there is a reduction in the size of critical areas, including the frontal lobes, hippocampus, thalamus, and basal ganglia (30). Amygdala volume changes in those taking antidepressant medication compared to those who are not (31). In order, these are regions of the brain associated with many activities, including control of thought processes, learning and memory, regulation of sleep, mood regulation, and the processing of emotions.

When looking at scans of older adults with depression, there is a widening of the sulci—the grooves you see in the cortex—combined with the enlargement of the ventricles—cavities containing cerebrospinal fluid. There is an argument that, in some cases, the lowered mood associated with depression is exacerbated by the presence of cerebrovascular disease—a condition referred to as vascular depression (32). Magnetic resonance imaging (MRI) scans show a link between white matter lesions—primarily due to ischaemia—and more severe depressive symptoms (33, 34).

Having looked at changes picked up by structural scans, functional imaging also highlights some fundamental differences in people with depression. Although functional scans do not measure neural activity *per se*, they track changes that can be viewed as a proxy of such action. By measuring glucose metabolism or blood flow—both of which indicate neural activity—it is possible to compare the brain function of those with depression with non-depressed individuals. Studies of this nature have identified reduced activation of the frontal lobes—hypofrontality—and a reduction in the activity in the basal ganglia (35).

Findings from imaging studies have also provided evidence to explain the emotion processing difficulties associated with depression. For instance, when presented with a range of different stimuli, there is increased activity in both the anterior cingulate and prefrontal regions—areas associated with emotion regulation—when people with depression are shown negatively toned material, and the opposite effect when presented with positive items (36). This increased activity is sustained in those with depression. In healthy controls, heightened activity to negative material reduces as the person adapts to the aversive stimuli. This does not happen in depression, so it may suggest increased rumination about the negative aspects of the situation (37). There also seems to be a heightened amygdala response when perceiving negative emotions in others and a similar reverse effect to that seen previously for positive emotions (38).

Inflammation models

Explanations of depression based on increased levels of inflammation are gaining support (7, 39). Evidence of this comes from heightened levels of C-reactive protein (CRP). This is indicative of an inflammatory response. In support of this theory is the finding that depression-like symptoms can be induced following the administration of pro-inflammatory drugs (40). Of interest, in particular, is the finding that levels of inflammatory biomarkers are higher in those who do not respond to antidepressant medication (24). Indeed, there is evidence to suggest that anti-inflammatories can be effective in treating depression in such cases (41).

It is unclear what the cause of the inflammation is here. One argument is that it is a response to depression whereas it might be a response to some underlying trauma that increases the individual's risk for depression (42). There is likely a link between poor health associated with depression and inflammation.

Immune system

The immune system of someone with depression is weakened. This is due to a protracted period of stress. The body is unable to sustain the level of preparedness elicited by stress. We shall see shortly that the typical inflammatory response to acute stress essential for removing pathogens and assisting healing becomes chronic and systemic (43).

Depression is often experienced by those who have received a diagnosis of a chronic condition. Examples include, but are by no means limited to, diabetes, musculoskeletal conditions, coronary heart disease, cancer, and neurodegenerative disorders. As we shall see in Chapter 5, depression exacerbates the symptoms associated with such medical conditions. Depression is also noted to have a negative effect on the outcomes of such individuals. Because of this, it is of fundamental importance to better understand the mechanism(s) whereby depression exerts such effects. The link with immune system function is just one such explanation.

There is much evidence now of the impact of psychological reactions on immune system function. Indeed, the field of psychoneuroimmunology—a study of the interactions between psychological states, the nervous system, and the immune system—is increasingly acknowledged to be of fundamental importance when examining the effects of conditions and the treatment thereof.

The two-way communication between the immune system and the central nervous system is via cytokines. Cytokines—proteins involved in cellular communications—regulate immunological response. The body's immune response can be either non-specific or specific in nature. All foreign bodies entering the body are met by the non-specific response. This is the most adaptive form of responding immediately, as all invading bodies are treated similarly. No previous exposure to a specific pathogen is needed to produce the appropriate response. Inflammation forms part of this first line of defence. Inflammation occurs in response to either tissue damage or infection. The inflammatory response is controlled by proinflammatory cytokines. The presence of these cytokines acts to draw immune cells to the site of injury. More on cytokines in the next section.

I started this section by saying how depression is linked to a range of different conditions. It is also true to say that inflammation is also standard across many of the same conditions. The essence of the inflammatory response is to help protect the body from further infection and assist in the repair process. However, things can go awry. Instead of the inflammatory response being directed to invading bodies, it can be targeted at the body's own tissue. Of course, although I say invading organisms, this does not necessarily have to be the case. Indeed, inflammation is associated with atherosclerotic plaques. The degree of inflammation is a good predictor of the risk of a heart attack (44). It is believed to play a substantive role in many non-infectious conditions resulting in disability or death.

The link here with depression centres around long-term inflammation that goes unchecked. Studies have shown levels of proinflammatory cytokines, C-reactive protein, and IL-6 to be higher in those with depression (45, 46) and higher levels of white blood cells involved in the inflammatory response (47). Evidence points to higher levels of inflammation in depression, indicative of the non-specific immune response. In contrast, the specific immune response is weaker (48).

It is yet far from clear what the mechanisms are here. It might not be the case that depression directly causes changes in immune response or that inflammation occurs before a specific episode of depression. However, it could be that inflammation, when it does happen, exacerbates the symptoms of depression experienced (48).

Cytokines

As seen in the previous section, cytokines are a vital component of the inflammatory response. They are proteins that enable the transmission of signals across the cell membrane. The presence of immune cells at the site either of infection or damage results in various cytokines that then regulate the inflammatory response. There does appear to be a clear link between depression and cytokines. Indeed, proinflammatory cytokines result in depression-like symptoms and behaviour in otherwise healthy individuals. Similar outcomes occur in those given cytokine immunotherapy as a treatment for an underlying medical condition (49).

Cytokines are associated with a range of adaptive behaviours that promote recovery, referred to as sickness behaviour (50). Such responses include excessive daytime sleeping and withdrawal from the presence of others, among other things (51, 52). Interestingly, many of the symptoms of sickness behaviour mirror those of depression.

Levels of various biochemical markers of inflammation are higher in those who have received a diagnosis of depression (53). The evidence at the moment does not allow for any claims concerning causality since studies are largely cross-sectional (54).

Environmental models

Biological predisposition is rarely sufficient on its own to cause a disease or illness. An appropriate environmental trigger is needed. This is referred to as the vulnerability-stress model.

Vulnerability-stress models

The literature on depression is fraught with competing explanations for the causes of the condition. However, we are far from being able to claim with any degree of certainty an overarching answer. Because of this, some have argued that accounts of depression that incorporate both the biological and psychosocial aspects of the condition may offer the best chance of providing clarification on this issue (55). In other words, these models take account of both individual susceptibility to a condition (referred to as the diathesis or vulnerability) and life events or circumstances implicated in its aetiology (stress factors). This is the premise behind diathesis-stress/vulnerability-stress models (55).

The presence of life stressors is a given in cases of depression. However, being exposed to specific stressors does not mean that a person will develop depression. We all face trying situations at various points in our lives, but we do not all experience depression. This is where individual vulnerabilities come into play. Some are more prone to develop certain conditions given exposure to the right stressor, often through genetic susceptibility or maladaptive modes of thinking.

There are variations in these vulnerability-stress models. One version is the risk-resilience model. The argument here is that, in addition to particular vulnerabilities, each individual also has protective factors that they can draw upon, such as specific competencies, strengths, and resilience (55). In this case, whether a person develops depression is dependent on the balance between a person's vulnerability to it—which can be numerous—and the protective factors they have in place.

Another variant of these models is the vulnerability-transactional stress model (56). The premise of this model is that, although vulnerabilities may be traits in some cases, such as a genetic predisposition, it may not always be the case. Indeed, vulnerability based on maladaptive cognitive processing is open to change (55). Therefore, vulnerability is different at separate points in time within a person's individual life course.

Interpersonal models of depression

Underpinning this approach is the belief that depression is the result of problems with our interactions with others. This model suggests that a person develops a negative view of themselves based solely on how others perceive them (57), an argument that is reminiscent of the "looking glass self" (58). Some also argue for the centrality of attachment theory here. They maintain that we all have an in-built need to feel connected with others (59). People become vulnerable to depression when these needs are not met earlier in life.

It is the tendency to misinterpret the behaviour of others that helps maintain depression. This is because, although support from others may be sought, doubts begin to grow about how genuine the person is being. The net result of this constant barrage of questioning about their honesty is that the people offering support begin to withdraw. This sparks an even greater demand for assurance that their needs are being understood. This pattern of behaving becomes increasingly dysfunctional, resulting in even more emotional turmoil.

Psychological models

Perhaps an appropriate place to start is with Freud's classic, *Mourning and Melancholia* (60). In this paper, Freud argues that melancholia—for him, the most severe form of depression—results from a person's reaction to loss. The self-reproach symptoms that characterize melancholia are displaced emotions that originate in our feelings towards a loved one. When the object of one's affections is lost, because the person has internalized the object of their affection, it is not the world that feels empty, but themselves (61).

The idea that there is a depressive personality underpins many of these theories. The work of Blatt makes distinctions between anaclitic depression and introjected depression, or in other words, depression resulting from either dependency or self-criticism (62). The former results from a loss early in life, whereas the latter occurs because of negative evaluations of self that have grown out of the negative behaviour of others.

Beck talked instead of sociotropic depression and autonomous depression (63). Sense of self for sociotropic individuals is based on relationships with others, with interpersonal conflict leading to depression. For autonomous individuals, a sense of who they are is reliant on their personal achievements. Any loss of status increases the likelihood of depression developing.

We shall explore some of these approaches in more detail, beginning with psychodynamic models of depression.

Psychodynamic models

To begin with, it is important to note that psychodynamic theory is not a unified approach but rather one that consists of a range of conceptualizations about the various conditions and how they should be treated (64). This is true for a great deal of what comes under the topic area of psychology to varying extents. We often refer to terms as if they relate to particular things. Words or phrases such as depression, dementia, psychotherapy, cognitive therapy, and so on are used to refer to some well-defined entity. This is clearly not the case. For the vast majority, such words or phrases are nothing more than umbrella terms that are a shorthand for a range of conditions and/or concepts. Clearly, the use of umbrella terms serves a purpose, allowing people to communicate ideas efficiently. However, it is always important to be cognizant that, in doing so, some of the individual characteristics or nuances of the topic under discussion are in danger of being ignored, however unintentional this might be.

Within the remit of psychodynamic models fall ego psychology, attachment theory, and many others. It is certainly not within the scope of this book to cover all forms of individual approaches subsumed under each overarching theory or model. So, having made a point of drawing attention to the potential pitfalls of using umbrella terms, I shall retreat under its protective folds and merely relay some of the shared themes of the various forms of psychodynamic models.

Intrinsic to these models is the concept of self-esteem, specifically how low self-esteem can feed many fires of self-doubt. Anger is also prevalent here, especially in terms of the level of guilt people often experience. There is also the challenge to balance the need for the support and approval of others against the sanctity of the self. All of these processes are intertwined.

Freud was the first to lay out a psychodynamic account of depression. In *Mourning and Melancholia* (65), Freud argued that a person is more vulnerable to depression later in life if they had experienced loss as a child. This work was necessary from several perspectives, not least in its weighing up the differences between experiences of those who are mourning against those who experience depression. An important distinction made by Freud was the realization that, whereas mourning results from a tangible loss, depression may occur without any such trigger. Instead, the loss often experienced by those with depression is more metaphysical in nature, relating not to the loss of a person, for example, but instead to self-esteem. The feelings of disapproval and condemnation against the self are the results of internally focused anger.

Developing Freud's work, later writers, such as Klein, increasingly emphasized the centrality of internalization and projection to our behaviour. Internalization refers to the process of creating internal representations of our experiences, especially with other people. These internal depictions may or may not be accurate representations of reality. By projection, we mean the striving to find in other people emotions that are not consciously accessible in the self, states that are deemed unbearable, and in doing so, evoking in the self the appropriate feelings—feelings that could not be expressed directly, without this conduit—in response to the other person's behaviour.

The two processes operate in tandem. Through projection, we induce others to experience feelings that are inaccessible to one's conscious self, with the result that one's own internalization of who that person is begins to change, becoming more warped and inaccurate with time. Mistaken assumptions about other people become with time increasingly ingrained as a result of this. Indeed, the recipient of the projections begins to behave in a manner that is in keeping with these false beliefs. The net result of all this is a growing uncertainty towards those we care about. Klein refers to this as the depressive position, an attitude that is comparable to what we describe as depressive realism, the argument that depression brings with it a tendency to see the world and our place in it as it truly is, unspoiled by the false hopes and expectations of the eternal optimist.

There was a move away from seeing depression rooted in loss or dependency, instead advocating the tension experienced when there is discord between our hopes, desires, and the stark reality of the situation. Depression may then result from feeling unable to do anything to change the trauma that one is faced with. The work of Bibring (66) in the Fifties presaged the later work of Seligman with his learned helplessness account of depression (67).

Blatt (68) argued for the interplay between nurturing relationships and maintaining a stable sense of self. Both are mutually reinforcing but likewise can be mutually disruptive. Long-lasting, positive relationships with others support our sense of who we are. This bolstered sense of self leads us to develop such relationships further. This can quite quickly go awry. Two forms of depression are thought to arise from a breakdown in relations with others. Dependent depression—sometimes referred to as anaclitic depression—is associated with feeling abandoned by the person one is dependent on. Blatt also proposes a self-critical depression—introjective depression—that is steeped in guilt and a sense of failure.

Kernberg (69) talks about a depressive personality where the characteristics describe a person dependent on others and lacking the ability to adequately express anger. When anger is vented, they experience intense guilt, and this translates into depression. There is a sense of inevitability here. Through feelings of dependency, an over-idealized image of others is developed. Given that people are unlikely to live up to such flawless standards, the person inevitably experiences disappointment and anger at their idol. Depression follows close on the heels of these emotions. Because of the overwhelming sense of dependency on others, needs tend not to be communicated adequately due to fear that others will abandon them. This feeds the flames of anger that builds up, increasing the likelihood of an outburst with its ensuing feelings of guilt and depression.

Reinforcement models

A reinforcement model is a behavioural approach. Ferster (70) argued that loss in one's life is tantamount to the loss of essential sources of reinforcement. Loss of such sources leads to a general reorganization of behaviour. In a similar vein, Lewinsohn and colleagues (71) argue that lowered mood and withdrawal occurs when one no longer receives sufficient reinforcement from critical areas in one's life. Hopelessness soon follows on from this. Lack of support may happen in several ways. A person may be in a situation where they have lost a particular source of reinforcement or find themselves in a situation where reinforcement provided is inadequate.

In some cases, it might be that the individual concerned cannot fully realize the available potential for reinforcement. A third possibility is that a person is not able to garner satisfaction even though it is available. In this sense, depression from a behaviourist perspective might result from the loss of a loved one, being in a less-than-loving relationship, having poor social skills, or being highly anxious.

One of the main features of depression is the propensity towards self-fulfilling prophecy. The nature of the behaviour fuelled by depression is that it elicits responses from others that reinforce the current trajectory. In other words, other people encourage depressive behaviour further by showing concern for the individual. However, although others may dole out sympathy in the initial stages, such support is soon replaced by a cold shoulder. The result is that an original source of reinforcement is no longer present.

Treatment from this perspective should be based on identifying sources of reinforcement and encouraging engagement with these sources, improving interpersonal skills and anxiety desensitization (72). Improving a person's self-awareness is an essential mediating factor in this process (73).

Social skills models

Several perspectives have held poor social skills as being a significant contributor to depression, thereby arguing that depression is interpersonal in nature (74). One approach that I have used repeatedly in my own research is that of social problem-solving. Poor social problem-solving skills are intrinsically linked to depression (75–77).

Learned helplessness model

Seligman's (78) model of learned helplessness developed from his work with dogs, noting their response when exposed to electric shocks from which they could either escape or not. Dogs that were unable to avoid being shocked became passive and withdrawn. However, when allowed to escape shocks as the result of a contingent behaviour, outcomes improved.

It was later claimed that how we explain behaviours and outcome is essential in determining who will be more likely to develop depression following a particular series of events (79). Those more vulnerable tend to explain away adverse outcomes as being caused by established and pervasive aspects of our character. In contrast, positive effects result from changeable and specific events in our environment. This reflects an idiosyncratic attributional style that reinforces depressogenic thinking. Self-esteem is affected (internal attribution), and the duration and pervasiveness of the depression are determined by both the stable and global attributions that people make. Of course, having a particular attributional style does not mean a person will automatically become depressed (80). Still, it has been suggested that those who feel hopeless due to helplessness are more likely to develop depression.

Nolen-Hoeksema (81) argues that a person's cognitive response to adverse events contributes to sex differences. Those who ruminate about the causes and potential outcomes of an event experience extended periods of depression. This is in direct contrast to those who instead use various strategies to refocus the mind. Women are more prone to a ruminative style. In contrast, men are more likely to use a diversionary technique.

Self-control model

The notion of self-control concerns an individual's ability to be in charge of their own behaviour. The self-control model (82) argues that depressed individuals selectively attend to adverse events, focus on immediate costs, are incredibly exacting of themselves, make depressogenic attributions, and cannot self-reward, instead exhibiting a tendency towards self-castigation.

Cognitive models

The foremost exponent of the cognitive model of depression is Beck (83). The premise of this approach is that depression is characterized by a negative cognitive triad comprising a negative view of self, the world, and one's future. Their experience is relayed through schema—internalized cognitive representations—that produce this maladaptive way of thinking. The type of distorted thinking identified by this model includes believing negative events are caused by oneself (arbitrary inference), focusing on the negative (selective abstraction), as well as an overestimation of negative outcomes and under-estimation of positive ones (magnification and minimization) (84). In this sense, a person continually responds to their interpretation and expectations rather than the event itself. In other words, there is a disconnect with objective reality. Such schema-based misinterpretation manifest as negative automatic thoughts. As a result, the person is unaware that the manner in which they are interpreting life is being hijacked. Underlying these automatic thoughts is an inescapable sense of loss.

Beck's approach underlies the cognitive approach to therapy for depression (85). The main goal of cognitive therapy is to actively challenge instances of maladaptive thinking. The individual builds up strategies to deal better with any future situation that might prove stressful.

Thinking in depression is associated with many cognitive distortions. In other words, the way information is processed and understood fails to match the reality of the situation. Beck (83) talked about distortion by commission, which means that internal biases re-colour neutral or positively toned information into negative. Whereas this refers to cognitive distortions of attended to information, another error results from selective inattention. Distortion by omission describes the situation where an individual does not acknowledge positive information and instead focuses only on the negative.

Self-focused attention

Self-focused attention is described as a person's awareness of their physical and psychological self based upon their own processing of the information generated by the body. This experience is distinct from information gleaned from the outside world (86). Lewinsohn incorporated such ideas into a revised version of the model (87). This concept also forms part of the self-regulatory perseveration model (88). This argues that disruptions to a person's life that are viewed as being pivotal in terms of their sense of self-worth will lead to a heightened level of self-focused attention. This then becomes the primary mode of operation and eats away at self-esteem and contributes to negative mood states. Future negative events merely act to increase the level of self-focus. When a positive life event is experienced, individuals with depression are thought not to benefit from the occasion because, perversely, the level of self-focus is lessened. By no means is self-focused attention unique to depression but is instead present across a range of mental health conditions (86).

Broaden-and-build theory

It is important to remember that depression is about prolonged lowered mood and a lack of ability to derive pleasure from activities, referred to as anhedonia. In this sense, a lack of positive emotions is a defining characteristic of depression. Our ability to experience fun and feel contentment help buffer us against the all-to-frequent curveballs that life throws at us in our daily lives. Indeed, there are links between positive emotions and resilience. A resilient person can draw upon positive emotions when faced with a challenging situation (89). When this rebalancing no longer happens, our mental lives take a downward turn (90, 91).

One argument for the importance of positive emotions is that they encourage flexibility and increased creativity (92). An individual can create a very personal and wide-ranging catalogue of responses to different situations based on personal resources of varied nature—cognitive, psychological, social, physical—which help buffer an individual against pressures from future adverse events (93). This is referred to as the broaden-and-build theory.

Therefore, those who do not enjoy positive emotional experiences are deprived of the experiences that will help compile this self-protective repertoire. In addition to this, when a person experiences depression, their perceived options for any given situation appear greatly diminished. Such narrowing of attention can lead only to an escalation of negative emotion.

From the perspective that a lack of positive emotions is a significant issue in depression, there is evidence to show meditation that emphasizes compassionate feelings—loving-kindness meditation—can seem to help individuals experience positive emotions and, in that sense, build up resources that will help them better deal with future threatening situations (94). An increase in such resources led to a reduction in depressive symptoms.

Along a similar line, Seligman and colleagues (95) showed that an intervention that boosted positive emotions alongside promoting an individual's sense of meaning in life—positive psychotherapy—also had a significant positive effect on depressive symptoms.

Hope is seen as a central component in all therapy, especially within psychotherapy (96). In other words, it is essential that clients feel they have the power to help improve their own lives. This sense of empowerment may feed into the wider focus of attention associated with the broaden-and-build theory described earlier. As seen, this will help individuals develop vital personal resources that can be to hand when faced with a future situation that is upsetting.

Rumination

Rumination refers to a pattern of behaviour characterized by repetitive cogitation on mental anguish and the perceived causes (97, 98). It described the process rather than reflecting any content. In this sense, rumination can be best described as a form of perseveration, a type of mental rigidity where a person is trapped within a closed-loop of processing, unresponsive to any change in circumstances. This manner of responding is passive and does eventuate in attempts to address any of the concerns.

A ruminative style is closely linked to both the development and maintenance of depression (99). Exploring rumination in more depth leads to identifying two underlying factors (100). One aspect is a sense of brooding and refers to negative thinking about one's behaviour and situation. On the other hand, pondering is a more general style of thinking. It calls to mind a more exploratory and rational approach to distress. Therefore, it may not be surprising to note that brooding is more predictive of depression than pondering (100).

In depression, a ruminative style will lead to negative thinking about the past, present, and future. A consequence of this thinking pattern means that any attempt to change the situation will be met with uncertainty, with any plan formed being far from ideal as a solution. Another unfortunate consequence of depression is that friends and family slowly begin to back away. This happens because someone prone to rumination tends to be unpredictable in their emotions while at the same time being extremely demanding of the support of others (99).

Cognitive vulnerability

In an earlier section, we talked about vulnerability-stress models, often referred to as diathesis-stress. The diathesis, or specific vulnerability, can be a genetic predisposition to a condition. When a person is exposed to an appropriate stressor, they will develop the condition, whereas someone without the specific vulnerability will not. We often think that diathesis refers to some biological component, but that is not necessarily the case. Diathesis can also be thought of in terms of cognitive vulnerabilities. A person may not be experiencing depression but, on exposure to the right (or perhaps that should be the wrong) stressor, an inherent maladaptive style of processing information will lead to depression. Similarly, someone who does not have such depressogenic processing patterns will not experience the downward spiral into depression (101). A negative mood will instead be present but without the escalation.

Cognitive reactivity

So far, we have explored the role of negative thinking in all its forms, leading to and maintaining depression. However, Segal and Ingram (102) illustrated there was no longer evidence for this way of thinking once a person recovered from their current episode. It is not clear how such depressogenic thinking could, in fact, play a causal role in depression (103). However, the critical thing to consider here is that it is unlikely that such predispositions to think in specific ways will manifest unless they find themselves in a personally challenging situation. In other words, there is an underlying pattern of behaviour that is elicited given the appropriate stressor, a pattern that can be described as cognitive reactivity (104).

Evolutionary theories

Taken at face value, it might appear that the symptoms we usually associate with depression are not the most advantageous in terms of survival. The characteristic lack of motivation, of drive. The disturbances of mood and affect. These are indeed entirely negative in terms of well-being. From an evolutionary perspective, maybe not. There are various accounts for why depression and other mental health conditions might be explained from an evolutionary point of view. A lack of interest in the environment, withdrawal from others, among other behaviours, could be adaptive if one were in the wild, separated from one's parent(s) or group. By adopting this response, an individual is not emitting apparent signals of distress, nor are they presenting themselves as an easy target for any predator that may be lurking about. They would also not be expending unnecessary energy. The physical acts of isolation and withdrawal may be seen as a mirror of one's mental landscape. People describe feeling alone and shut off (105).

Other reactions include a submissive attitude and a loss of confidence. These are often experienced in the context of some downfall, be it physical or mental. Gilbert (106) argues that two models can explain these behaviours: those relating to entrapment models and those described as attachment theory. Both can be argued to link directly to emotion regulation.

One important thing to consider here is a person's sense of control over the stressor. According to the arrested defences model, if threatened and there is a will to fight against the situation, a person will experience stress (107). This is because the fight or flight response that served us so well in our past is often inappropriate and is prevented from taking over our behaviour. This can lead to the suppression of anger or feelings of entrapment. Indeed, some have described depression as a desire to escape but feeling trapped (108).

Attachment theory appears to permeate the entire field of psychology. It concerns the belief that our interactions with those who cared for us early in life shape the person we become and determine how we develop and sustain relationships with others. Bowlby (109) referred to working models, mental representations of the world, and those in it. It also encapsulated our sense of self. We learn to develop ways to keep in close contact with our primary caregiver to derive a sense of security and emotional and physical comfort. On separation, an infant is at risk of displaying a range of protest-despair responses to the situation. The infant actively searches for their caregiver, communicating distress to bring about reunion. This is described as protest behaviour (110). If this is not successful, a child switches to a pattern of responding called despair, a form of behavioural deactivation (110). Sitting still and waiting for the caregiver to return is a good strategy in terms of adaptive behaviour. Engaging too long in protest behaviour will only attract unwanted attention that may threaten the infant's safety.

Gilbert argues many evolutionary accounts reflect emotion regulation at some level. The way we respond still reflect the needs and demands of our earliest ancestors. Gilbert argues that there is a need to translate these approaches into something resembling a biopsychosocial model (111) to better understand the origins of the behaviours we have been talking about here in this chapter.

Summary

There is extensive literature on the psychological origins of depression that encompasses all manifestations of thought. These include early psychodynamic models through to contemporary accounts that are firmly rooted in cognitive neuroscience. Much is made of recent research exploring the potential biological aspects of depression. In particular, there is a great deal of research at the moment looking at the role of inflammation in several conditions, including, as we have seen, depression. As one would expect, the models presented in this chapter underpin the wide variety of treatment options available for those with depression. These will be examined in Chapters 7 and 8. One of the main things to remember when looking for causes of depression is that it is rarely one thing in isolation. Instead, the vulnerability-stress models argue that it is a combination of biological and psychological predispositions alongside specific environmental triggers that result in depression. It is also important to remember that the variety of contributing factors will differ for each individual who experiences depression. Because of that, we must not generalize the reasons for and subsequent management of depression for people with the condition.

References

1   Hirschfield RMA, Weissman MM. Risk factors for major depression and bipolar disorder. In: Davis KL, editor. Neuropsychopharmacology: The fifth generation of progress: An official publication of the American College of Neuropsychopharmacology. Philadelphia, PA; London: Lippincott/Williams & Wilkins; 2002, pp. 1017–1025.

2   Kendler KS, Karkowski-Shuman L. Stressful life events and genetic liability to major depression: Genetic control of exposure to the environment? Psychol Med. 1997; 27(3):539–547.

3   Kendler KS, Thornton LM, Gardner CO. Genetic risk, number of previous depressive episodes, and stressful life events in predicting onset of major depression. Am J Psychiatry. 2001;158(4):582–586.

4   Murphy BEP. Antiglucocorticoid therapies in major depression: A review. Psychoneuroendocrinology. 1997;22:S125–S32.

5   Pariante CM. The glucocorticoid receptor: Part of the solution or part of the problem? J Psychopharmacol. 2006;20(4_suppl):79–84.

6   Sheline YI, Minyun MA. Structural and functional imaging of affective disorders. In: Davis KL, editor. Neuropsychopharmacology: The fifth generation of progress: An official publication of the American College of Neuropsychopharmacology. Philadelphia, PA; London: Lippincott/Williams & Wilkins; 2002, pp. 1065–1080.

7   Anacker C, Zunszain PA, Cattaneo A, Carvalho LA, Garabedian MJ, Thuret S, et al. Antidepressants increase human hippocampal neurogenesis by activating the glucocorticoid receptor. Mol Psychiatry. 2011;16(7):738.

8   Heim C, Newport DJ, Heit S, Graham YP, Wilcox M, Bonsall R, et al. Pituitary-adrenal and autonomic responses to stress in women after sexual and physical abuse in childhood. JAMA. 2000;284(5):592–597.

9   Hayes P, Ettigi P. Dexamethasone suppression test in diagnosis of depressive illness. Clin Pharm. 1983;2(6):538–545.

10 Thase ME. Hypothalamic-pituitary-adrenocortical activity and response to cognitive behavior therapy in unmedicated, hospitalized depressed patients. Am J Psychiatry. 1996;153(7):886.

11 Coryell W, Schlesser M. The dexamethasone suppression test and suicide prediction. Am J Psychiatry. 2001;158(5):748–753.

12 Heuser I, Yassouridis A, Holsboer F. The combined dexamethasone/CRH test: A refined laboratory test for psychiatric disorders. J Psychiatr Res. 1994;28(4):341–356.

13 Altshuler LL, Bauer M, Frye MA, Gitlin MJ, Mintz J, Szuba MP, et al. Does thyroid supplementation accelerate tricyclic antidepressant response? A review and meta-analysis of the literature. Am J Psychiatry. 2001;158(10):1617–1622.

14 Joffe RT, Marriott M. Thyroid hormone levels and recurrence of major depression. Am J Psychiatry. 2000;157(10):1689–1691.

15 Eitan R, Landshut G, Lifschytz T, Einstein O, Ben-Hur T, Lerer B. The thyroid hormone, triiodothyronine, enhances fluoxetine-induced neurogenesis in rats: Possible role in antidepressant-augmenting properties. Int J Neuropsychopharmacol. 2010;13(5):553–561.

16 Markopoulou K, Papadopoulos A, Juruena MF, Poon L, Pariante CM, Cleare AJ. The ratio of cortisol/DHEA in treatment resistant depression. Psychoneuroendocrinology. 2009;34(1):19–26.

17 Wolkowitz OM, Reus VI, Keebler A, Nelson N, Friedland M, Brizendine L, et al. Double-blind treatment of major depression with dehydroepiandrosterone. Am J Psychiatry. 1999;156(4):646–649.

18 Wagner AL, Rehm LP, Ivens-Tundal C. Mood disorders: Unipolar and bipolar. In: Sutker PB, Adams HE, editors. Comprehensive handbook of psychopathology. 3rd ed. Dordrecht: Springer Science + Business Media; 2004.

19 Thase ME, Frank E, Kupfer DJ. Biological processes in major depression. In: Beckham EEE, Leber WRE, editors. Handbook of depression: Treatment, assessment, and research. Dorsey Press; 1985, pp. 816–913.

20 Maes M, Meltzer HY, D'Hondt P, Cosyns P, Blockx P. Effects of serotonin precursors on the negative feedback effects of glucocorticoids on hypothalamic-pituitary-adrenal axis function in depression. Psychoneuroendocrinology. 1995;20(2):149–167.

21 Reilly J, McTavish S, Young A. Rapid depletion of plasma tryptophan: A review of studies and experimental methodology. J Psychopharmacol. 1997;11(4):381–392.

22 Christopher G, Sutherland D, Smith A. Effects of caffeine in non-withdrawn volunteers. Hum Psychopharmacol. 2005;20(1):47–53.

23 Smith AP, Christopher G, Sutherland D. Acute effects of caffeine on attention: A comparison of non-consumers and withdrawn consumers. J Psychopharmacol. 2013;27(1):77–83.

24 Cleare AJ, Rane LJ. Biological models of unipolar depression. In: Power M, editor. The Wiley-Blackwell handbook of mood disorders. John Wiley & Sons; 2013, pp. 39–68.

25 Schatzberg AF, Garlow SJ, Nemeroff CB. Molecular and cellular mechanisms in depression. In: Neuropsychopharmacology: The fifth generation of progress: An official publication of the American College of Neuropsychopharmacology. Philadelphia; London: Lippincott/Williams & Wilkins; 2002, pp. 1039–1050.

26 Janowsky DS, Overstreet DH. The role of acetylcholine mechanisms in mood disorders. In: Davis KL, editor. Neuropsychopharmacology: The fifth generation of progress: An official publication of the American College of Neuropsychopharmacology. Philadelphia; London: Lippincott/Williams & Wilkins; 2002, pp. 945–956.

27 Janowsky D, Davis J, El-Yousef MK, Sekerke HJ. A cholinergic-adrenergic hypothesis of mania and depression. Lancet. 1972;300(7778):632–635.

28 O'Flynn K, Dinan TG. Baclofen-induced growth hormone release in major depression: Relationship to dexamethasone suppression test result. Am J Psychiatry. 1993;150(11):1728.

29 Cowen PJ, Browning M. What has serotonin to do with depression? World Psychiatry. 2015;14(2):158.

30 Kempton MJ, Salvador Z, Munafò MR, Geddes JR, Simmons A, Frangou S, et al. Structural neuroimaging studies in major depressive disorder: Meta-analysis and comparison with bipolar disorder. Arch Gen Psychiatry. 2011;68(7):675–690.

31 Hamilton JP, Siemer M, Gotlib IH. Amygdala volume in major depressive disorder: A meta-analysis of magnetic resonance imaging studies. Mol Psychiat. 2008;13(11):993.

32 Alexopoulos GS. Depression in the elderly. Lancet. 2005;365(9475):1961–1970.

33 Thomas AJ, O'Brien JT, Davis S, Ballard C, Barber R, Kalaria RN, et al. Ischemic basis for deep white matter hyperintensities in major depression: A neuropathological study. Arch Gen Psychiatry. 2002;59(9):785–792.

34 Cees De Groot J, De Leeuw FE, Oudkerk M, Van Gijn J, Hofman A, Jolles J, et al. Cerebral white matter lesions and cognitive function: The Rotterdam Scan Study. Ann Neurol. 2000;47(2):145–151.

35 Fu CH, Walsh ND, Drevets WC. Neuroimaging studies of mood disorders: Euroimaging studies of disorders. In: Fu, CHY, Walsh, ND, Drevets, WC. Neuroimaging in Psychiatry. CRC Press; 2003, pp. 139–178.

36   Elliott R, Rubinsztein JS, Sahakian BJ, Dolan RJ. The neural basis of mood-congruent processing biases in depression. Arch Gen Psychiatry. 2002;59(7):597–604.

37   Dedovic K, Slavich GM, Muscatell KA, Irwin MR, Eisenberger NI. Dorsal anterior cingulate cortex responses to repeated social evaluative feedback in young women with and without a history of depression. Front Behav Neurosci. 2016;10:64.

38   Fu CH, Williams SC, Cleare AJ, Brammer MJ, Walsh ND, Kim J, et al. Attenuation of the neural response to sad faces in major depression by antidepressant treatment: A prospective, event-related functional magnetic resonance imaging study. Arch Gen Psychiatry. 2004;61(9):877–889.

39   Leonard BE. The concept of depression as a dysfunction of the immune system. In: Depression: From psychopathology to pharmacotherapy. Vol. 27. Karger Publishers; 2010, pp. 53–71.

40   Capuron L, Miller AH. Cytokines and psychopathology: Lessons from interferon-α. Biol Psychiatry. 2004;56(11):819–824.

41   Nery FG, Monkul ES, Hatch JP, Fonseca M, Zunta-Soares GB, Frey BN, et al. Celecoxib as an adjunct in the treatment of depressive or mixed episodes of bipolar disorder: A double-blind, randomized, placebo-controlled study. Hum Psychopharmacol. 2008;23(2):87–94.

42   Danese A, Moffitt TE, Pariante CM, Ambler A, Poulton R, Caspi A. Elevated inflammation levels in depressed adults with a history of childhood maltreatment. Arch Gen Psychiatry. 2008;65(4):409–415.

43   Morey JN, Boggero IA, Scott AB, Segerstrom SC. Current directions in stress and human immune function. Curr Opin Psychol. 2015;5:13–17.

44   Libby P. Atherosclerosis: The new view. Sci Am. 2002;286(5):46–55.

45   Miller GE, Stetler CA, Carney RM, Freedland KE, Banks WA. Clinical depression and inflammatory risk markers for coronary heart disease. Am J Cardiol. 2002;90(12):1279–1283.

46   Zorrilla EP, Luborsky L, McKay JR, Rosenthal R, Houldin A, Tax A, et al. The relationship of depression and stressors to immunological assays: A meta-analytic review. Brain Behav Immun. 2001;15(3):199–226.

47   Herbert TB, Cohen S. Depression and immunity: A meta-analytic review. Psychol Bull. 1993;113(3):472.

48   Stetler C. Immune system. In: Ingram RE, editor. The international encyclopedia of depression. New York; London: Springer Publishing Company; 2009.

49   Pollak Y, Yirmiya R. Cytokine-induced changes in mood and behaviour: Implications for 'depression due to a general medical condition', immunotherapy and antidepressive treatment. Int J Neuropsychopharmacol. 2002;5(4):389–399.

50   Hart BL. Biological basis of the behavior of sick animals. Neurosci Biobehav Rev. 1988;12(2):123–137.

51   Dantzer R, O'Connor JC, Freund GG, Johnson RW, Kelley KW. From inflammation to sickness and depression: When the immune system subjugates the brain. Nat Rev Neurosci. 2008;9(1):46.

52   Maier SF, Watkins LR. Cytokines for psychologists: Implications of bidirectional immune-to-brain communication for understanding behavior, mood, and cognition. Psychol Rev. 1998;105(1):83.

53   Raison CL, Capuron L, Miller AH. Cytokines sing the blues: Inflammation and the pathogenesis of depression. Trends Immunol. 2006;27(1):24–31.

54 Szigethy E, Low CA. Cytokines. In: Ingram RE, editor. The international encyclopedia of depression. New York; London: Springer Publishing Company; 2009.
55 Hankin B, Abela JR. Diatheses stress models of depression. In: Ingram RE, editor. The international encyclopedia of depression. New York; London: Springer Publishing Company; 2009.
56 Hankin BL, Abramson LY. Development of gender differences in depression: An elaborated cognitive vulnerability—transactional stress theory. Psychol Bull. 2001;127(6):773.
57 Sacco WP. A social-cognitive model of interpersonal processes in depression. In: Joiner TE, Coyne JC, editors. The interactional nature of depression: Advances in interpersonal approaches. American Psychological Association; 1999, pp. 329–362.
58 Cooley CH. Human nature and the social order. Routledge; 2017.
59 Hammen C. The emergence of an interpersonal approach to depression. In: Joiner TE, Coyne JC, editors. The interactional nature of depression: Advances in interpersonal approaches. American Psychological Association; 1999, pp. 21–35.
60 Freud S, Phillips A. On murder, mourning and melancholia. London: Penguin; 2005.
61 Wagner A, Eagle M. Depression (Freud). In: Skelton RM, editor. The Edinburgh international encyclopedia of psychoanalysis. Edinburgh: Edinburgh University Press; 2006.
62 Blatt SJ. Levels of object representation in anaclitic and introjective depression. Psychoanal Study Child. 1974;29:107–157.
63 Beck AT. Cognitive therapy of depression. The Guilford Press; 1979(1985).
64 Levy KN, Wasserman RH. Psychodynamic model of depression. In: Ingram RE, editor. The international encyclopedia of depression. New York; London: Springer Publishing Company; 2009.
65 Freud S. Mourning and melancholia. The standard edition of the complete psychological works of Sigmund Freud, volume XIV (1914–1916): On the history of the psychoanalytic movement, papers on metapsychology and other works; 1957, pp. 237–258.
66 Bibring E. The mechanism of depression. In: Greenacre P, editor. Affective disorders; psychoanalytic contributions to their study; 1953, pp. 13–48.
67 Seligman ME. Learned helplessness. Ann Rev Med. 1972;23(1):407–412.
68 Blatt SJ. Levels of object representation in anaclitic and introjective depression. Psychoanal Study Child. 1974;29(1):107–157.
69 Kernberg OF. Psychopathic, paranoid and depressive transferences. Int J Psychoanal. 1992;73(1):13.
70 Ferster CB. A functional analysis of depression. Am Psychol. 1973;28(10):857–870.
71 Lewinsohn PM, Biglan A, Zeiss AM. Behavioral treatment of depression. In: Davidson PO, editor. Behavioral management of anxiety, depression, and pain: Based on 1975 Banff International Conference papers. New York: Brunner/Mazel; 1976, pp. 91–146.
72 Lewinsohn PM. The coping with depression course: A psychoeducational intervention for unipolar depression. Eugene, OR: Castalia Pub. Co.; 1984.
73 Lewinsohn PM, Hoberman H, Teri L, Hautzinger M. An integrative theory of depression. In: Reiss S, Bootzin RR, editors. Theoretical issues in behavior therapy. Orlando: Academic Press; 1985.
74 Joiner T, Jr., Coyne JC. The interactional nature of depression: Advances in interpersonal approaches. Washington, DC; London: American Psychological Association; 1999.

75 Nezu AM, Nezu CM, Perri MG. Problem-solving therapy for depression. Wiley; 1989.
76 Christopher G, Thomas M. Social problem solving in chronic fatigue syndrome: Preliminary findings. Stress Heal. 2009;25(2):161–169.
77 McMurran M, Christopher G. Social problem solving, anxiety, and depression in adult male prisoners. Legal Criminol Psychol. 2009;14(1):101–107.
78 Seligman MEP. Helplessness: On depression, development, and death. San Francisco: W. H. Freeman; New York: Trade Distributor, Scribner; 1975.
79 Abramson LY, Seligman ME, Teasdale JD. Learned helplessness in humans: Critique and reformulation. J Abnorm Psychol. 1978;87(1):49–74.
80 Abramson LY, Alloy LB, Metalsky GI. The cognitive diathesis-stress theories of depression: Toward an adequate evaluation of the theories' validities. In: Alloy LB, editor. Cognitive processes in depression. New York: Guilford Press; 1987, pp. 3–30.
81 Nolen-Hoeksema S. Sex differences in unipolar depression: Evidence and theory. Psychol Bull. 1987;101(2):259–282.
82 Fuchs CZ, Rehm LP. A self-control behavior therapy program for depression. J Consult Clin Psychol. 1977;45(2):206–215.
83 Beck AT, Alford BA. Depression: Causes and treatments. 2nd ed. Philadelphia, PA.: University of Pennsylvania Press; Bristol: University Presses Marketing [distributor]; 2008.
84 Beck AT. Thinking and depression. I. Idiosyncratic content and cognitive distortions. Arch Gen Psychiatry. 1963;9:324–333.
85 Beck AT. Cognitive therapy of depression. Guilford Press; 1979.
86 Ingram RE. Self-focused attention in clinical disorders: Review and a conceptual model. Psychol Bull. 1990;107(2):156–176.
87 Lewinsohn P. A behavioral approach to depression. In: Coyne JC, editor. Essential papers on depression. New York; London: New York University Press; 1986.
88 Pyszczynski T, Greenberg J. Self-regulatory perseveration and the depressive self-focusing style: A self-awareness theory of reactive depression. Psychol Bull. 1987; 102(1):122–138.
89 Fredrickson BL, Tugade MM, Waugh CE, Larkin GR. What good are positive emotions in crises? A prospective study of resilience and emotions following the terrorist attacks on the United States on September 11th, 2001. J Pers Soc Psychol. 2003;84(2):365–376.
90 Fredrickson BL, Losada MF. Positive affect and the complex dynamics of human flourishing. Am Psychol. 2005;60(7):678–686.
91 Schwartz RM, Reynolds CF, III, Thase ME, Frank E, Fasiczka AL, Haaga DA. Optimal and normal affect balance in psychotherapy of major depression: Evaluation of the balanced states of mind model. Behav Cogn Psychother. 2002;30(4):439–450.
92 Fredrickson BL. The role of positive emotions in positive psychology. The broaden-and-build theory of positive emotions. Am Psychol. 2001;56(3):218–226.
93 Coffey KA, Fredrickson B. Positive emotion dysregulation. In: Ingram RE, editor. The international encyclopedia of depression. New York; London: Springer; 2009.
94 Fredrickson BL, Cohn MA, Coffey KA, Pek J, Finkel SM. Open hearts build lives: Positive emotions, induced through loving-kindness meditation, build consequential personal resources. J Pers Soc Psychol. 2008;95(5):1045–1062.
95 Seligman ME, Rashid T, Parks AC. Positive psychotherapy. Am Psychol. 2006;61(8): 774–788.
96 Snyder CR, Michael ST, Cheavens JS. Hope as a psychotherapeutic foundation of common factors, placebos, and expectancies. In: Hubble ML, Duncan BL, Miller SD, editors. The heart & soul of change: What works in therapy. Washington, DC; London: American Psychological Association; 1999, pp. 179–200.

97   Nolen-Hoeksema S. Responses to depression and their effects on the duration of depressive episodes. J Abnorm Psychol. 1991;100(4):569–582.

98   Nolen-Hoeksema S. Rumination. In: Ingram RE, editor. The international encyclopedia of depression. New York; London: Springer; 2009.

99   Nolen-Hoeksema S, Wisco BE, Lyubomirsky S. Rethinking rumination. Pers Psychol Sci. 2008;3(5):400–424.

100   Treynor W, Gonzalez R, Nolen-Hoeksema S. Rumination reconsidered: A psychometric analysis. Cognit Ther Res. 2003;27(3):247–259.

101   Ingram RE. Cognitive vulnerability. In: Ingram RE, editor. The international encyclopedia of depression. New York; London: Springer Publishing Company; 2009.

102   Segal ZV, Ingram RE. Mood priming and construct activation in tests of cognitive vulnerability to unipolar depression. Clin Psychol Rev. 1994;14(7):663–695.

103   Barnett PA, Gotlib IH. Psychosocial functioning and depression: Distinguishing among antecedents, concomitants, and consequences. Psychol Bull. 1988;104(1):97–126.

104   Ingram RE. Cognitive reactivity. In: Ingram RE, editor. The international encyclopedia of depression. New York; London: Springer; 2009.

105   Gilbert P. Evolution. In: Ingram RE, editor. The international encyclopedia of depression. New York; London: Springer Publishing Company; 2009.

106   Gilbert P. Psychotherapy and counselling for depression. Sage; 2007.

107   Gilbert P. Depression and stress: A biopsychosocial exploration of evolved functions and mechanisms. Stress. 2001;4(2):121–135.

108   Gilbert P, Allan S. The role of defeat and entrapment (arrested flight) in depression: An exploration of an evolutionary view. Psychol Med. 1998;28(3):585–598.

109   Bowlby J. Separation: Anger and anxiety. Attachment and loss, Vol. 2. London: Hogarth; 1973.

110   Gilbert P. Evolution and depression: Issues and implications. Psychol Med. 2006; 36(3):287–297.

111   Gilbert P. Depression: A biopsychosocial, integrative and evolutionary approach. In: Power M, editor. Mood disorders: A handbook of science and practice. John Wiley & Sons; 2004.

Chapter 4

The cognitive neuropsychology perspective

Basic cognitive processes

Before we can look at the more advanced cognitive processes, we first need to identify some of the more fundamental operations that occur as they underpin all the higher-order functions we will describe shortly. Before we can process and control information, we need first to attend accurately to it.

Attention

Attention, or more specifically problems experienced maintaining attention, is a real problem for all of us. We are constantly bombarded with a variety of distractions that interrupt our train of thought. Multi-tasking is the norm these days. We rarely focus our undivided attention on one solitary activity. It is more likely that, whatever we do, our smartphone is within arm's reach. This is the primary source of interruption for most of us in our lives, along with the computer and the tablet, that is. How many times in the day do we hear the notification tone heralding a new text message or email, a news bulletin, and so on? Quite aside from that, there are few now who will sit quietly to watch a programme. Instead, eyes flit from the television screen to that of their smartphone and back. However, an essential part of our daily functioning is maintaining focus on an activity regardless of what is going on around us.

It is clear from this that attention is limited. We only have finite resources to allocate to tasks in the present moment. When you think about the multitude of sensations that manifest each moment of our lives, it is evident that it would be impossible to attend to and process everything. This is where attention comes into play. Attention allows us to focus on only those items essential to whatever our current goal is. At least, that is how it should be. We shall see that this does not always happen, and the result is quite catastrophic.

The aim here is not to provide a history and overview of the attention literature. Many excellent texts do that already (1). I, too, offer an account of attention in Chapter 2 of my book, *The Psychology of Ageing: From Mind to Society* (2). Attention and other related functions are severely affected by depression (3, 4). Indeed,

DOI:10.4324/9781315688879-4

this was the basis for my PhD. In a subsequent chapter (Chapter 9), we shall also see that an in-depth understanding of attention lends itself to specific forms of intervention to improve the lot of individuals with depression.

Having just said that I will not provide an overview of theories of attention, it is essential to briefly explain some of the key ideas in cognitive psychology and cognitive neuroscience as it will aid understanding why problems are experienced and how specific therapies work.

Automatic and controlled processing

Underlying Beck's cognitive theory of depression (see Chapter 3) is the concept of negative automatic thoughts (5). The presence of intrusive thoughts vies for a person's attention (6). This constant distraction interferes with the person's ability to perform everyday activities (3).

The concept of automaticity within cognitive psychology refers to processes with no conscious intervention or awareness and minimal or no likelihood of control. On the other hand, intended behaviour is effortful, requiring attention and constant monitoring (6). Typically, more than one activity can occur automatically. Because no conscious awareness is needed, interference between activities is minimal, so there are no adverse effects. Consciously driven behaviour is effortful, so there are restrictions due to capacity limitations of the individual (7).

We are all aware of automatic behaviours in our everyday lives. A practical example to illustrate some of these ideas is driving. When we become experienced drivers, we carry out multiple activities simultaneously without actually thinking about them. They have become routinized and only intrude into our consciousness when things go awry. When something happens out-of-the-blue, we find ourselves diverting our attention to this new source of vital information. In the case of driving, it might be that the satellite navigation system has alerted us to traffic ahead and is suggesting an alternative route. We need to choose whether to accept the alternative way or continue forward as planned and blindly ignore the all-knowing satnav at our peril. In such cases, we are using controlled processing—as well as a desire to be bloody-minded in this instance—to make a conscious decision. In this sense, controlled processing occurs when conscious attention is needed. Because of this, we are restricted to performing limited numbers of activities at any single point in time to ensure accuracy. With time and repetition, such activities demand less-and-less attention and may indeed become automatic. Just recall your first experience of trying to juggle steering the car, indicating left or right or both, checking mirrors, braking, avoiding collisions, and, well, the list goes on. Yet, as we know, practice makes each of us the world's best driver.

When looking at these processes in depression, it is clear that there are marked problems starting activities and then keeping track of one's progress (8). These issues are indicative of difficulties with executive control. We will come back to executive functions later; indeed, they will be the focus of much of this chapter. By executive function, we mean a range of cognitive processes that deal with the way we focus our attention, process and integrate data, prevent distraction, monitor our current behaviour, and many other discrete yet ultimately related activities. This inability to control how attention is allocated explains why individuals with depression experience major problems directing their attention away from negative thoughts and images, and in doing so, perpetuating a cycle of maladaptive thinking.

While it is firmly established that there are problems with executive functioning in those with depression, the impact of depression on more automatic forms of processing is less well-established. The argument has generally been that automatic processing is more affected by anxiety than depression. In the case of anxiety, there is a bias in processing material perceived as threatening (7). Indeed, this is something my research focused on (3).

Vulnerability to triggers

For many, depression occurs in response to a particularly stressful event or a series of events. It is also evident when reviewing the research that those who have experienced depression in their past tend to be more vulnerable to future episodes. This is because they are operating at a heightened alert for potentially stressful events in their environment. In such cases, relatively minor events can be sufficient to trigger another depressive episode. Under any other circumstance, these events may have been brushed aside and so have relatively minor significance on the individual's behaviour.

Bring to mind a time when you have felt relatively low. Things do not seem to be going the way you would like. We have all had such moments. I have experienced many moments like that during the writing of this book. Think now about what happened at these times. I am sure that, during these phases, we started to bring to mind other occasions in our lives when things began to go wrong. We may even start to see links between the past and the present, a sense that it is all happening again and we have no control over events. This escalation of negativity is due to how memories are stored and recalled in the brain. We also know that similar things happen during happy times. When we are happy, we tend to think about other joyful occasions in our life. There is a strong sense that mood is reinforced through such processes. So, why does this happen?

In a highly influential paper, Segal and colleagues proffered an explanation of why certain people are prone to depression (9). Depression is associated with repeated activation of negative memories. Memories are deeply interconnected mental entities. Cues in the environment that activate certain aspects of a memory (e.g. a particular song) lead to the reactivation of the entire memory structure (e.g. a birthday party during which the music was played). In this sense, it could be argued that only very subtle cues are needed to dredge up negative memories from a person's past and reinforce their current depressed mood. This process is called sensitization (9) and refers to the lowered threshold for activation of negative memories. In addition to depressogenic memories being more easily activated, it is also apparent that the person with depression has little control over this process. Because they cannot inhibit the activation of these memories, the person experiencing them is caught in a downward spiral.

This can be explained by looking at how memories are maintained and activated. We know that depression results in the activation of memories associated with current and past depressive episodes. We also know that, with each activation of a specific memory, memory traces strengthen. Given sufficient interconnection between traces, activation of one memory element will lead to the activation of related links. In the case of depression, exposure to minor cues related to a previous negative experience can quickly activate other corresponding memory traces. These then act to reinforce the negative mood. This process is described as kindling (10). A related process is that of sensitization (10). With repeated activation of memory traces, the threshold required for activation reduces. Because of that, memories can be triggered more easily on exposure to related stressors. One consequence of this is that this escalation of negative recollection is much harder to stop (11).

Higher-order cognitive processes

Having looked at some of the more low-level cognitive processes, we turn our attention to more complex operations. Some of the difficulties experienced by those with depression reflect a deficit in executive control mechanisms. In other words, due to the competing demands imposed by the task at hand, on top of the internally driven thought intrusions, poor executive control makes it more challenging, or indeed impossible, to direct action appropriately, resulting in the inevitable errors and slips of action seen in depression. However, there is more to it than this. My own research shows that depression leads to a global deficit in working memory. Working memory refers to the limited capacity workspace that underpins the vast majority of our behaviour, allowing us to temporarily store and actively manipulate different information streams. There are also links between working memory and our long-term memory stores. Executive control (or executive function, depending on your field) is part of this overall process. Evidence shows that the subsidiary processes linked to working memory operation are also adversely affected by depression (3).

Working memory and depression

What is working memory?

My PhD was centred on exploring working memory in people with depression and anxiety. I talk a lot in this chapter about executive function. This is part of working memory. This is neither the time nor place to enter into a long discussion about what is meant by working memory. I will say that there are different models, and each has a different take on what processes occur as part of their conceptualization. For the purpose of this chapter, I will briefly present an overview of the most prominent model, the one associated with Alan Baddeley.

The original model was proposed in 1974 in a groundbreaking paper by Baddeley and Hitch (12). Two systems deal with the temporary storage of auditory and visual-spatial information, the phonological loop and visuospatial sketch pad, respectively. The central executive is involved in a range of discrete yet overlapping functions, described as fractionation. The executive is engaged when one task is prioritized over another, when time-sharing is needed to carry out two or more activities simultaneously, and when you need to block out distracting sounds to better focus on the task at hand (13). There are several other operations, but this provides a taste of what the central executive does and why it is so vital to everything we take for granted in our lives.

How is working memory affected by depression?

Until I carried out my research, there had been little interest in what happened to working memory in depression. The published research focused exclusively on consciously controlled operations, namely those driven by the central executive. There was nothing about how working memory as a whole was affected. The paper that inspired me in my research was published by Channon and colleagues (14). When comparing those with depression with a control group, depression did not affect how auditory or visuospatial information was stored. It only appeared as if the central executive operation was affected, but not for all such tasks. However, several issues presented themselves on closer examination, and I was determined to address these in my research.

I wanted to ensure that whatever I found in terms of working memory impairment could be explicitly attributed to depression. To achieve that, alongside a depression group, I recruited a group diagnosed with an anxiety disorder. Anxiety also impairs working memory. Having the two groups allowed me to compare them in terms of their profiles of impairment.

My findings were different from those previously reported in the literature. Contrary to earlier studies, I found that the results showed depression to be associated with impairments across all components of working memory. For those with anxiety, the deficits were more focused. It was clear that depression impairs performance on tasks where automatic processing predominates. Previously, it had been thought that only tasks requiring controlled or conscious attention were affected (3).

One of the things I did was manipulate the level of difficulty of the various tasks. In other words, people performed the task under standard instructions initially, then again with an additional cognitive load. Participants were instructed to engage in suppression activity during the task, such as repeating "the" at a steady rate or counting backwards from 99.

It was clear that those in the depression group found performing tasks under standard instructions difficult. I argued that this was because they were already conducting a dual-task due to negative automatic thoughts characteristic of the condition. In other words, these were vying for the finite cognitive resources we all have.

One of the most exciting findings from this study was evidence of what I referred to as a "substitution effect." This was where the accuracy of the depression group improved as the task demands increased. This would at first seem counterintuitive. On scouring the literature, I noticed that a similar effect had been observed previously in a paper by Krames and MacDonald (15). However, I hasten to add this is not the same MacDonald who was my PhD supervisor. Looking back even further, Foulds published a paper in 1952 that again shows something comparable (16). Both these papers used entirely different tasks and experimental setups. Still, nonetheless, the effects they observed were relevant to what I found.

So, why was this the case? Why, in fact, did performance in a group that showed deficits in working memory functioning actually improve with increasing task demands? I argued that the types of negative thoughts that pervade states of depression are highly demanding of cognitive resources. This is why they show impairment on standard conditions of the tasks presented. As I mentioned previously, the presence of these negative thoughts acted so that these individuals were, in effect, operating under dual-task conditions as they were processing the negative thoughts and trying to carry out the memory activity.

When the task demands increased, I proposed that these task-irrelevant thoughts were displaced by task-relevant processing. In other words, the cognitively challenging memory task was allocated greater priority. Also, I argued that there was a clear improvement in performance because task-relevant processing is less demanding of that individual's attention than maintaining negative thoughts associated with their depression.

These findings emphasized the profound effect depression has on day-to-day functioning, one that was largely ignored by clinicians at the time due to a lack of experimental evidence, although patients were only too aware of these problems. The tests used in this study proved to be sensitive measures that could differentiate successfully between the performance profiles of depression and anxiety compared to a healthy control group.

Aside from the experimental study that I just reported, I also conducted a series of interviews with in-patients diagnosed with depression. Attending to and processing intrusive thoughts appears to be fundamental to maintaining a depressed mood (17). Negative automatic thoughts surface unbidden, intruding into conscious awareness. Thoughts and images are generally repetitive and negatively toned. People find it difficult to sustain concentration when such thoughts are present. This hinders day-to-day functioning. In Watts and Sharrock's study (18), difficulties reported included concentrating on television programmes, reading, and having conversations. Patients complained that they were prevented from doing what everyone else takes for granted. Patients did not see the problems they faced in terms of the effect of depression on general functioning. Instead, loss of mental power was held responsible. Consequently, they did not believe that functioning would return to normal in remission, which compounded their already pessimistic view of the future.

It has been proposed that deficits associated with depression are primarily due to an internal struggle that splits attention between the current task activity and the demands imposed by the continual stream of task-irrelevant cognitions (19): a situation analogous to performing dual-task activities (15). Watts, MacLeod, and Morris (20) identified two forms of concentration lapses in depression: (1) the presence of task-irrelevant thoughts, what they term "mind wandering"; (2) blanking, which occurs when no schemata are competing for selection. Deficits occur because of a combination of reduced processing resources and inefficiency in the way they are allocated to activities (21).

From the interviews I conducted, it was clear that working memory deficits constitute a significant portion of the problems people face from depression. Both attention and memory problems accounted for a reasonable proportion of participants' responses. Participants complained of an inability to retain information for short periods. They also reported lapses in attention which disrupted the performance of activities. There were also problems associated with switching from one activity to another.

This supports the literature which shows that depression is associated with the inefficiency in allocating attentional resources: an activity where the central executive plays a significant role (22).

High levels of distractibility to both internal and external stimuli, classic symptoms of depression, were also reported, which coincided with reports that patients found it difficult to concentrate due to thought intrusion. Patients reported frequently experiencing confusion as being prevalent when depressed, where attention is being split between numerous activities. This has obvious implications in day-to-day functioning, such as concentrating at work, following conversation, and maintaining interest in hobbies.

Patients reported substantial problems with memory, and in particular working memory. Evidence of this included problems with articulatory rehearsal (e.g. retaining verbal information for short periods), visuospatial short-term memory (e.g. remembering where keys were left), and concurrent processing (e.g. reading while surrounded by people talking).

Difficulties were expressed when there were lists of tasks to complete, with some activities being of greater importance than others. Previous research has shown that depressed individuals adopt unrealistic goals when given tasks to perform (23). The patients interviewed in this study reported difficulty assigning priority to certain tasks over others, which made them feel frustrated. The central executive is thought to adopt a prominent role during such activity as prioritization which requires a great deal of planning and coordination (24).

Because of repeated memory errors and numerous memory failures, patients tended to rely upon *aide memoires*. This is a strategy whereby the environment is manipulated to prompt the individual to remember what they have to do (25). Varieties of mnemonic techniques were reported, including the use of wall-planners, Post-Its, and placing to-be-remembered items in strategic locations. In two instances, interviewees talked of using music as a self-imposed distracter against internally generated negative thoughts. It was acknowledged that automatic thoughts tended to be available for conscious inspection. Listening to music helped distract the individual from any thought intrusions, which made it easier for the person to concentrate on a given task.

There is a great deal of evidence in both interviews and questionnaire data to support findings of working memory and attentional deficits in depression (3, 14) and their impact on everyday activities. Some areas that warrant further investigation include the impact of intrusive thoughts as interference, the strategies developed to overcome these intrusions, and the processing of orally presented material in everyday interactions. Each of these has severe implications for a person's day-to-day functioning. Defining the problem and then devising a strategy to eliminate, or at least contain, the problem would greatly benefit the person concerned.

It would appear then that working memory should be considered when investigating cognitive deficits during depression. Difficulty concentrating is evidenced by both mind wandering and negative thoughts. Patients reported having problems with remembering to do things at particular times and remembering things that have already occurred. An area where the impact is strong is language skills, in both the production and understanding of speech. These and other operations involving working memory are assumed to play essential roles in our day-to-day lives. We should note that the sort of experiences reported by patients is not merely consequences of depression; such memory failures are frustrating, for example, and may actually influence the course of depressive disorder (26). A deficit in any of these areas needs to be considered when assessing and treating patients exhibiting depressive symptomatology.

There are clear implications here in terms of treatment. For example, interventions such as cognitive behavioural therapy are highly demanding of mental resources. It requires people to test their assumptions and monitor and evaluate outcomes, among other things. It is challenging for someone with depression, and even more so when one factors in the types of cognitive impairments they experience.

Before moving on, I would like to share one of those rare moments in academia when you suddenly become aware that your research has been singled out by colleagues in your field. Still, up until the moment of realization, you had been unaware. This happened to me a few years back now. I had just received an inspection copy of a new textbook that I planned to use for my module. It was the latest edition of the well-respected Matlin text, *Cognitive Psychology* (27). Given my field was working memory, naturally, I opened the book at the appropriate chapter and started to flick through the pages. Near the end of the chapter, I experienced one of those mental double-take moments. Did my eyes deceive me? Was that my name? Tentatively adjusting my gaze, I found that, indeed, my name was mentioned, and not just that, the entire section focused on the paper I have just been talking about. A silent scream rippled through me. I quickly read the section to make sure my article was not being ripped to shreds. It was not. We academics are a paranoid lot. I had a feeling comparable to the one I used to get as a child on Christmas morning. The feeling stayed with me for days afterwards. So did the self-induced headache of much excitement. It was a wonderful experience. It meant so much, especially given that a considerable proportion of an academic's life is spent writing articles or grant applications that have taken months to prepare and submit and then waiting many weeks only to find it criticized and/or rejected. Mind you, it is still the best job in the world regardless. I am incredibly fortunate to conduct the research that I do and then write about it. Each publication or grant success gives a thrill, but nothing like the sheer joy I have just described. I shall temporarily stop being self-indulgent. Possibly . . .

Dysexecutive syndrome

I have talked repeatedly about executive functions and shall continue to do so. This is because much of what we do requires such operations that fall under the umbrella of executive control. There is a large and growing literature on the impairments of executive function. Over the years, such difficulties have been given different names, although they broadly refer to the same or similar things.

Dysexecutive syndrome refers to symptoms that reflect some damage to or fault in the frontal lobes. It was a term first coined by Alan Baddeley (28) to move away from terms based on location—previously frontal lobe syndrome—to ones describing functional impairment. Although impairment in frontal lobe functioning is at the root of these problems, a term not based on localization allows for the fact that other brain areas are implicated as well. The frontal lobes have connections throughout the brain, enabling the dynamic interchange of information we rely on.

The difficulties experienced can be cognitive and/or emotional depending on the site of damage: in this case, predominantly dorsal (top) and/or ventral (bottom), respectively (29). We know that damage to the frontal lobes manifest as problems planning and initiating behaviours, coordinating actions, and inhibiting irrelevant information. Rylander (30) perfectly described the condition as follows;

> [D]isturbed attention, increased distractibility, a difficulty in grasping the whole of a complicated state of affairs . . . well able to work along old routine lines . . . (but) . . . cannot learn to master new types of tasks . . . (and) in new situations . . . (the patient is) at a loss.

Language may also be affected, such as poor fluency or a tendency to wander off-topic. A person may continue to respond fixedly even though the situation has changed, a behaviour known as perseveration. They may also report memories that are entirely made up, the result of confabulation (31).

Depression-executive dysfunction syndrome

In Chapter 6, the focus will be on depression across the lifespan. Part of this chapter will focus on depression in older adults. Depression, as we know, often occurs as a response to declining health. This is especially pertinent as we grow older.

However, as we are currently concentrating on neurocognitive accounts of depression, it is appropriate to spend some time examining an account that focuses on executive dysfunction and its link to depression among older adults.

As seen, executive dysfunction is associated with problems concerning the initiation, modification, and inhibition of behaviour. All of these symptoms are prevalent in depression, especially among the older adult population (32). Depression among older adults is more often than not mixed up with a host of health-related conditions. Sometimes this occurs within the context of neurological changes. Indeed, rates of depression are high among those diagnosed with Alzheimer's disease, Parkinson's disease, Huntington's disease, and other such conditions. Other structural changes have been linked to depression in this age group. One example is the presence of white matter hyperintensity within subcortical structures. Areas of hyperintensity picked up using magnetic resonance imaging (MRI) are the consequence of lesions resulting from ischaemia caused by stroke or haemorrhaging. The upshot of this is varying degrees of cognitive decline. One aspect of cognition particularly impaired is executive function. This led to the identification of a discrete condition, depression-executive dysfunction syndrome (33).

Depression among older adults is often characterized by problems initiating a behaviour, being unable to interrupt ongoing activity and a decline in the ability to inhibit specific actions. There is evidence to suggest that such impairments remain even after depressive symptoms have been addressed. The argument here is that these deficits reflect neurological changes within the frontostriatal pathway, the neural circuitry involved in a range of motor, cognitive, and behavioural operations, specifically those involving executive functions. Alexopoulos (34) argues that deficits in functioning within this pathway are intrinsically linked to depression.

The level of functional impairment observed in those with depression with concomitant executive dysfunction is higher than those without pronounced cognitive deficits (34). In this subgroup, levels of psychomotor retardation are higher, as is the loss of general engagement and interest in life (apathy). Also, such patients have less insight into their condition.

From a treatment perspective, depression-executive dysfunction syndrome is associated with poorer outcomes when prescribed antidepressants (35). There are also higher rates of relapse in this subgroup.

Metacognition

This section will focus on self-regulation, although in doing so, I will still be continuing with the theme of executive function. First, we shall explore the concept of metacognition and examine why it is vital for controlling our behaviour. We shall look at models of depression where the emphasis is on the control of attentional processes, specifically the control and regulation of emotional responses, and, in doing so, I shall weave in the literature on emotional intelligence. We will finish with a look at the problems faced by those who cannot identify how they or others are feeling. Firstly, though, metacognition.

Metacognition is a complex process but can be best explained as monitoring and controlling our thinking and behaviour. It is a mechanism for overseeing our cognitive operations. Interest in metacognitive processes has expanded hugely over the last couple of decades or so and covers a vast range of topics that include tip-of-the-tongue phenomena, learning and comprehension, as well as emotion regulation.

We are all highly successful at doing several complex activities simultaneously in our daily lives, and we are also very good at remembering to do things at a specific time or when in a particular place. Inevitably, errors creep in at various points. At these junctures, we become aware that something has gone strangely wrong. This is an example of metacognitive processes making us aware that we have failed at some level. This interruption of ongoing behaviour is a vital component of self-monitoring. It allows us to reflect on what is happening, cogitate on what we intended to do, and then makes the necessary adjustments, all relatively seamlessly. Our ability to monitor our thoughts and feelings is pivotal to all forms of self-regulation. It is to this that we now turn to.

Self-regulation

Central to theories of self-regulation are goals. Goals are the way we represent in our minds some desired state. Such goals vary in terms of how challenging they are, how specific the end state is, and how close in proximity the goal state is. These are referred to as quantitative dimensions (36). In addition to this, chosen future goal states can be a representation of either things to work towards or things to avoid, personal aspirations or obligations (37), or something to be attained or confirmed (38), and so vary qualitatively (39).

Because these are goal states, a person can appraise the situation to gauge whether or not they have been achieved. Any shortfall in attaining a goal is met with anguish and may either spur the person on or leave them feeling the situation is futile, only too aware of the gulf between reality and the desired state. Depression is likely where the discrepancy is perceived to be significant. Where there is little to prevent the person from achieving the desired state, individuals will demonstrate persistence (40). An important determiner as to whether someone persists in a chosen course of action or not is how confident they are that they will be able to achieve it. Judgment of a lack of self-efficacy—a person's belief that they can carry out the intended action—more than likely will lead to lowered mood and stagnation (41).

When applying this approach to depression, one can see that individuals with depression tend to set goals that are difficult to achieve (42). There appears to be a tendency towards perfectionism in depression that exacerbates the situation (43). On top of this, the goals adopted tend to be less well-defined than those of individuals who are not depressed (44), thereby increasing the likelihood of working towards unattainable objectives. At a higher level, many of the goals held by individuals with depression tend to conflict with one another, and as a result, cause more confusion for the individual trying to make sense of the situation (45). As already indicated, a personal feeling that a particular goal or set of goals is not being met will likely lead to depression (37).

It is interesting to note that self-evaluation of performance lacks accuracy when looking at successes (46). Being highly critical of successes will feed into the belief that the individual is failing to meet their goals, accentuating depression. However, the reverse is true when looking instead at performance failures. This is in keeping with the concept of depressive realism (47). Most accounts of depression argue that the person with this condition does not have an accurate view of the world. This is because underlying this view is a series of maladaptive beliefs and assumptions. The concept of depressive realism flips this on its head and argues that they have a much more accurate idea of reality. The foundation for this claim is that it is supposedly "normal" individuals who engage in distorting reality, colouring all activity in a self-enhancing manner (48).

Cognitive attentional syndrome

Wells and Matthews (49) argued that underpinning a range of psychological conditions is a propensity for persistent worry and rumination resistant to conscious control, a situation they refer to as cognitive attentional syndrome. At the root of this syndrome are two general metacognitive beliefs. One belief system is referred to as positive and manifest as ways of thinking that reinforce the maladaptive thinking style. Other views are negative and reflect the uncontrollable nature of this way of thinking. More of this in a moment. What is primarily transient in most people is amplified and maintained by the cognitive attentional syndrome in those who ruminate excessively. This way of thinking is sustained over time because the worry and rumination focus on information that dissuades individuals from challenging these assumptions. In fact, a sense of threat is heightened in this self-perpetuating cycle.

Metacognitive model of depression

Wells and Matthew's (49) work led to the development of the metacognitive model of depression (50). In depression, a negative thought or belief is triggered by an event. This then leads to rumination as a way to try to deal with the situation. In other words, the person believes that if they spend long enough analysing their thoughts, they will find a way to solve the problem. This is what Wells and Matthews (49) refer to as a positive metacognitive belief. On top of that, as mentioned in the previous section, there are negative metacognitive beliefs that act to prolong the depression. An example here would be that the person feels they have no control over their thoughts. A combination of the two leads to the sense of hopelessness experienced by those with depression.

Over time, with recurrent depression, individuals become more sensitive to events that might precipitate another episode. Such threat-monitoring strategies (51) make the person hypersensitive to minutiae both externally and internally that under normal circumstances would go unnoticed, but here are pounced upon, thereby precipitating another period of depression.

Treatment based on this approach aims to eradicate the maladaptive way attention is allocated. The primary method for achieving this is attention training to exhort more control over one's thought processes, intending to modify underlying beliefs. Positive assumptions about the benefits of rumination are challenged (see Chapter 8).

Having explored in some detail explanations of depression linked to self-regulation, with a particular focus on attention control, the next part of this chapter will now examine emotion regulation. I will be referring to various cognitive mechanisms as these are central to controlling and harnessing emotions. Cognitive control and monitoring mechanisms also help explain how problems arise, resulting in maladaptive responses and an escalation in negative emotion.

Emotion regulation

What is emotion regulation?

We rely on our ability to regulate emotions almost every minute of every day. It is what enables us to achieve what we want to without any significant transgressions. Yes, we face obstacles constantly, but we deal with them. The only outward sign that something more is going on below the surface is a subdued muttering as you go about your duties.

Emotion regulation, then, is all about what emotions we experience and when and how they are expressed (52). My current work on nostalgia is one way of harnessing the power of emotion regulation. Focusing on personal memories that are positive and self-reinforcing boosts a person's belief in themselves (53). This is emotion regulation as we are explicitly tapping into a private resource—a nostalgic memory—and deploying it to help us feel better at a suitable time.

Inevitably, at some point in our day, something will happen that will rile us. For most of us, it might be surprising to know that such feelings can occur at work. Yes, I know, difficult to believe. Bear with me. Yes, I know it is the lowest form of wit.

That grant application you had spent months working on. You submitted it a while back. In between sips of coffee, you glance at your screen and notice a new email. It is from the funder. You immediately experience a desire to do anything other than open the email, but you do. You might receive a pleasant surprise, however, all too often . . .

So, what do you do when you see you have not been successful. Do you scream? Do you bellow a naughty word like "turnips" at the computer? Do you run up and down your corridor like someone possessed? Yes, you do. That is not emotion regulation.

Generally, I shall be referring to intrinsic emotion regulation. This is self-regulation of emotion. There are instances where we regulate the emotions of others, and this is referred to as extrinsic regulation. Many situations demand that both happen at the same time. The types of processes used in regulating emotion may be consciously driven or hidden: explicit versus implicit, in other words (54). A third feature is the impact of emotion regulation on the emotional dynamics of the situation. In other words, how does a person's response differ from an unregulated reaction?

The role of emotion in our lives

There has been much academic debate over the centuries about the role of emotion; more specifically, do emotions lend a unique perspective when performing activities in our daily lives, or are they merely an unwanted intrusion.

For Damasio, emotions are essential (55). He argued that a life devoid of emotion is peppered by terrible mistakes. His work with people who have suffered damage to the frontal lobes shows how central emotion is when making decisions. If we experience a strong negative emotion about a decision we consider, we know not to pursue it. Damasio describes the importance of such somatic markers to the way we all make decisions.

On the contrary, others have argued that emotions can be troublesome. People often experience emotions that are out of kilter with the situation in which they find themselves facing. Emotions may manifest at an inconvenient or inappropriate time, presenting with an unsolicited force (56).

The upshot then is that, whether one's view of emotion is predominantly positive or negative, they nonetheless occur, in many cases unbidden. The only strategy we have is to regulate them, and in doing so, harness their energy to our advantage rather than be overwhelmed by their intensity.

What of valence?

When we think of emotion regulation, we naturally think about reigning in negative emotions. This is because we tend to view negative emotions as being disruptive and harmful. Of course, it is not just negative emotions that need regulating. Positive emotions can also be a source of disturbance. An over-ebullient outpouring can be as equally disruptive as a swathe of melancholy in certain situations (57).

Turning up and turning down emotion

Just as we suppose that only negative emotions need to be controlled, we also tend to assume that regulation of emotion means downplaying or eliminating these reactions. This is clearly not the case. From a clinical point of view, it might undoubtedly be the case that much focus is given to reducing the impact of negative emotions, or conversely extreme positive emotions, to redress the emotional balance of people's lives disturbed by such an emotional roller coaster. However, when considering the world through a non-clinical lens, when we think about our own lives, we reflect for a moment on times when we have made the conscious decision to ramp up a positive response to achieve some particular end. I am sure you can bring to mind instances where you did not do this but wished you had to maintain or extend the pleasure you felt.

To some extent, given the constant demands imposed on us, many of which are of our own choosing, we do need to make time for life's pleasures. We may not have time—how often do you hear that phrase?—to seek out new things, but we do have within our power to prolong fleeting moments of pleasure that occur in myriad forms every day in our lives. I can think of many such missed opportunities in my own daily existence. The short walk from the car park to the building where my office is located invariably gives me golden opportunities to delight in small wonders. The smell of freshly mown grass. The rustling made by a rotund and beautifully formed Robin on the bank. The glory of a vivid sunrise or sunset. Fleeting moments that are all-too-often dismissed out of hand, only to be replaced by thoughts of the backlog of email that needs to be trawled through, or the next deadline to meet, or all the other stress-inducing minutiae of our daily work lives. Instead of relishing such unbidden moments of delight, we immediately turn our attention to the many to-be-completed activities that fill our mental in-boxes.

I appear to be proselytizing the joys of a mindful existence. Indeed, I am. This is partly out of angst from an awareness of the disparity between this desired state and the all-too-frequent frugality of my own mental existence. However, the concept of emotion regulation is at the core of a well-balanced life. A life well-lived.

Emotional intelligence

The idea that emotional responses need to be regulated is not a new one. Ancient Greek philosophers were only too aware of this. Here we shall turn our attention to mechanisms that help us do this. One of the key concepts here is that of emotional intelligence. Much like resilience, the notion of emotional intelligence is much discussed. It appears to be ubiquitous. As in many such cases, there is the risk that its importance will become masked by its general overuse. Indeed, there is an entire industry focused on marketing courses that promise to increase emotional intelligence. There are many popular science books out there on the topic. So, what do we mean by emotional intelligence?

How does emotional intelligence differ from emotion regulation?

Having just talked about emotion regulation, and before I embark on exploring emotional intelligence, I need to be clear about the distinction. On the surface, they may seem to refer to the same thing. They do, sort of, but with clear differences in their focus. As a result, they have developed largely in isolation from each other. Emotion regulation, as we have seen, focuses on how someone manages their emotions. On the other hand, emotional intelligence looks at individual differences to identify who can make the most of their emotional responses. An interesting paper by Peña-Sarrionandia and colleagues (58, 59) explores how these constructs could be integrated.

What is emotional intelligence?

Emotional intelligence refers to individual differences in how people can acknowledge, process, and use emotions. It has its origins in Thorndike's notion of social intelligence (60), which was all about how well we can understand the behaviour of others. The work of Gardner is a more immediate precursor, with his notion of intrapersonal and interpersonal intelligence (61) reflecting a person's ability to understand their own emotions and those of other people. The construct was properly defined by Salovey and Mayer in 1990 (62), before being popularized by Goleman with his book, *Emotional Intelligence: Why It Can Matter More than IQ* (63), first published in 1995. Models of emotional intelligence (EI) generally fall into two categories: ability EI or trait EI.

Ability models see emotional intelligence as something that should be measured like any other intelligence, namely by testing a person's performance (64). Trait models differ and instead see emotional intelligence as different facets of an individual's personality, and so it is assessed using self-report measures in the same way as personality types are determined (65). Of course, both approaches can be complementary in the sense that together they consider a person's capacity to deal effectively with emotions and the tendency to make use of those skills (66).

One might argue that individual differences in emotional intelligence are best reflected by the concept of trait EI. One indicator of how successfully a person translates their emotional intelligence into practice is how much distress they experience when faced with a difficult situation. One generally finds that those with higher emotional intelligence tend to experience less emotional reactivity to such events (67).

High emotional intelligence

When considering the impact of emotional intelligence in a real-life setting, much demonstrates its potential to protect individuals from stressors of varying kinds. Levels of depression are lower, and satisfaction with life is higher (68). When looking at the adverse effects of stress among undergraduates, those high in emotional intelligence manifest fewer physical and psychological symptoms of stress during examination periods (67). Similarly, high levels of emotional intelligence seem to protect nurses from experiencing burnout (69). Also, people with high emotional intelligence tend to enjoy more harmonious relationships with others (70).

Some of the reasoning to explain such positive effects include that people high in emotional intelligence are better able to manage stress when it is experienced, primarily by experiencing lower levels of distress and drawing on more adaptive ways of responding in these situations.

Emotion dysregulation

Having espoused the importance of emotion regulation, it is vital to consider the consequences of emotion dysregulation. We have seen that emotion regulation is adaptive. However, an inability to effectively regulate emotion—emotion dysregulation—results in largely maladaptive behaviour. Poor emotion regulation impacts across all domains of a person's life, eroding relationships and one's health, to name but two (71). The effect of emotion dysregulation is no more apparent than when one looks at the various diagnoses presented in the DSM (72).

Thinking about those everyday occurrences when, for example, something irritates or upsets us. Still, instead of shouting or crying, we suppress our responses such that they meet the acceptable norms of the situation in which we find ourselves. Obviously, some of us are better at keeping a lid on our emotions than others. Indeed, there is a lot of individual differences associated with emotional intelligence (73).

When a person reacts, possibly quite justifiably, with raw emotion to a situation, there is more than a slight chance their natural response will exacerbate the problem. An unguarded remark that had unintentional repercussions now escalates into a full-blown argument. Where does one go from there? Life is stressful enough without contributing to the burden in this way. Emotional intelligence is a concept that allows us to account for such individual variation in one's ability to deal with such situations.

We also know that it is not just about how we regulate our own emotions but also how we manage the emotions experienced by others. A good example here is talking to others when one is feeling concerned or upset about something. This might be talking to a trusted colleague about an issue at work. Talking to others is meant to be a source of comfort. However, enlisting the help or support of others should come with a health warning. I am sure you have experienced a situation where you have started talking about a specific problem that you needed advice on, only to find that, rather quickly, the topic of the conversation may be similar, but the protagonist has changed. The conversation is no longer about your dilemma. Rather, it has switched to a similar issue experienced by the person you are trying to garner support from. Sometimes this is beneficial in the sense that you know someone else has experienced a spookily similar situation. In the majority of cases, that is the intention of your friendly interlocutor. More often than not, however, although that may have been the intention of the person concerned, one experiences a degree of frustration. The conversation should be about *your* problem in the present, not *their* problem from the past. It might also be the case, and I am sure you can also think of instances where this has happened, that you seek friendly support when you are upset, only to find that the person from whom you are hoping to elicit the support has also become upset, more upset than you, in fact. Your distress has caused them to feel distressed. Instead of feeling a sense of relief, you now feel even more upset purely due to their reactive distress. This is not a good situation to be in. So, always be aware of how a person might respond to your plight. An empathic response is good. An overinflated emotional outpouring is not. The same goes for you. Ensure that, should you ever be called upon to offer kind words, ensure that you regulate your emotional response in a manner appropriate to the needs of the person eliciting the support.

Poor emotional intelligence

Studies have shown that individuals high in emotional intelligence experience fewer issues with mental health (74). The converse is also true. Low levels of emotional intelligence mean that you are at the beck and call of various powerful and often competing emotions. Your emotional life is in turmoil. An inability to regulate unwanted emotional states is clearly linked to a range of conditions, including depression (75).

Underlying mechanisms of emotional intelligence

Thus far, we have looked at emotion regulation and the role emotional intelligence plays in all this. However, we have not yet considered how this happens. In other words, what mechanisms underlie the set of competencies that we call emotional intelligence. As one might expect, there are competing theories posited offering up explanations based on the way situations are appraised, the types of coping strategies initiated, and the automatic manner in which emotional stimuli is processed (66).

Trait EI

When looking at trait EI, one explanation is that how a situation is appraised is all-important. Once evaluated, an assessment of one's capacity to deal with the problem determines the outcome (76). Trait EI has also been implicated in selecting the appropriate coping strategy to deal with a situation. Coping strategies are often dichotomized into adaptive and maladaptive strategies. Adaptive strategies are usually associated with a rational, problem-focused approach. In contrast, maladaptive strategies are associated with an emotion-focused approach. Indeed, emotional intelligence is related to adaptive approaches to coping (77).

This link between emotional intelligence and coping strategies directly relates to my own work on social problem-solving. I have shown a strong relationship between adaptive social problem-solving behaviour and high levels of emotional intelligence (78). In such situations, people see problems as challenges to overcome and are adept at compensating and adjusting behaviour to fit the situation. High emotional intelligence was associated with a rational approach to solving problem situations, one characterized by perseverance and seeing the case from the perspective of the person or persons involved.

We shall explore social problem-solving shortly and look at how it can be harnessed as an intervention in Chapter 7. To explore the mechanisms at work here, it is essential to consider whether coping strategies mediate emotional intelligence and positive outcomes.

Specificity of emotion regulation

An additional crucial point is that studies often talk about emotion as if it is a single entity. However, this is clearly not the case. When looking at the underlying neurophysiology, different emotions are linked to separate systems. As a case in point, anger is subserved by a different neural structure to that underlining fear (79). From an emotional intelligence point of view, we cannot assume that all emotions can be dealt with equally effectively because one has high emotional intelligence. To some extent, everyone has their Achilles heel.

We know that those who have high levels of emotional intelligence tend to respond better to unpleasant situations. They tend to look for positive elements to focus upon, actively engage in mood repair by bringing to mind happy thoughts or memories, reason about what needs to be done, and more accurately place the problem they are experiencing in perspective (66, 76). However, it also appears that trait EI leads to more adaptive responses to a range of emotions. In this sense, it does seem that high emotional intelligence is associated with success in regulating a variety of different reactions, and not just those specific to one particular context (66). High emotional intelligence helps a person deal effectively with negative emotions and helps sustain and harness positive mood states. This study also showed that the positive outcomes associated with high emotional intelligence cannot be explained by a relative lack of emotional reactivity. Instead, those who have high emotional intelligence are more likely to not only select an appropriate strategy but also carry out that strategy. This means they are more likely to experience positive emotions and less likely to experience negative emotion. Their analysis showed that emotional intelligence (trait EI) mediated the outcome. Strategy choice explained their tendency to experience more positive and less negative emotion (66).

Problem-focused versus emotion-focused coping

As a caveat here, one should remember that, although problem-focused coping is seen generally as being the ideal response in any given situation, and emotion-focused coping is to be avoided at all cost, it is not as simple as that. Maybe, in the majority of cases, this assumed taxonomy of coping might hold true. However, there are certain situations where the reverse is the case. The appropriateness of these two approaches largely rests on how the problem situation is perceived. Suppose there is some degree of personal control over the situation. In that case, a problem-focused approach is likely to be the preferred choice. This is because how we approach the problem will likely change, reduce, or eliminate the original source of the stress entirely.

However, there are some situations where we have no personal control over events. In such cases, no amount of problem-solving will have the slightest impact on the source of stress. To do so would be to engage in a futile, energy-sapping activity. In these situations, the best form of coping is to divert our energy to deal with something we can control, namely our emotional response to the stressor. In such cases, an emotion-focused approach is, therefore, more adaptive. If we can control our thoughts and feelings, then the impact of the stressor might be lessened, even though it is still present.

We also know that some stressors, whether we have the power to exert control over them or not, are transient. In other words, if we bide our time, they will just dissipate. I am sure we can all think of examples of such cases. However, just how insightful we are at the time of such stress varies greatly. We are all too often primed to respond to every form of stressor we encounter, mostly successfully. It is important to reflect on the extent to which some of these stressors actually necessitated a response. Would they have just gone away? Did we expend needless energy?

In some cases, the answer would be "yes" to both. Holding back, then, is an important skill to harness. Inhibiting the default response to always respond. Being aware of our desire to jump in feet first without taking time to consider whether it is, in fact, appropriate to react or not.

Consider the upshot of all this. When we respond to stressors that are mere flash-in-the-pan events, we end up creating more stress. We make a crisis where one would not have occurred had we merely held back. Bring to mind a time when you have read an email from a colleague and have been incensed by its inherent message. To address the injustice you feel, you set about writing a pithy response. This leads to an answer to your reply. The original author explains that your interpretation was not how they intended the email to be read. However, this apparent justification of the original slight merely fuels you to write another email, this time copying in line managers and so on and so forth. The situation has escalated out of hand very quickly. Clearly, I have never engaged in such behaviour. . ... I cannot help but bring to mind Ed Reardon here, the hapless writer who is consumed with biting volleys against perceived injustices every day. The Radio 4 comedy is a perfect satire on contemporary life and the ideal antidote. Hearing one of his rants on the phone to some unfortunate, only to be cut-off mid flow with the response, "Hello, hello, no gone," echoes in my mind.

The rapid escalation of adverse events is merely facilitated by improvements in technology. The tyranny of email chains is a bane of many of our lives, and not just at work. The desire to "just quickly check my email" means that the divide between work and home life is eroded beyond recognition. You only have to extend the focus to other forms of electronic communication to see how the same processes and outcomes are repeated *ad infinitum* every hour of every day. Would this have happened in the day of pen-and-paper and physical in-boxes? I know there is always a fondness to think back to less technologically advanced times when life was simpler and less stressful. Still, the answer, in this case, is probably a resounding "'no." There was more time to iron things out amicably then, preventing the unnecessary escalation that has become just part-and-parcel of daily life or daily strife if you feel particularly jaded. Did you not hear people declaiming that they will "just quickly drive to work to check my pigeonhole"? Certainly not. Our fetishization of technology has led us to a very dark place, one in which we need to muster all our energies to avoid being sucked into its deepest recesses. However, every cloud has a silver lining and all that. Where would we be without Angst-ridden Avians or whatever the current in vogue game is?

Of course, achieving this mastery of restraint is easier said than done. It is worth considering the writings of the Stoic philosophers, emphasizing self-control, resilience, and focusing on the moment. It is perhaps interesting to note that the literature on problem-solving behaviour among older adults shows something comparable. Older adults often hold off responding, preferring to adopt a more considered approach to dealing with stress (80). This brings to mind a quotation from Marcus Aurelius: "Chasing what can't be done is madness" (81, 5.17).

Before moving on, we should consider this within the framework of the biopsychosocial model: some are born stressed (*bio*), some achieve stress (*psycho*), and some have stress thrust upon them (*social*).

Alexithymia

What is alexithymia?

Much of my research refers to alexithymia. There are strong parallels with the research just discussed on emotion regulation and emotional intelligence. The term *alexithymia* was first used in 1972 by Sifneos within the context of therapy to describe people who could not express how they felt and could not engage in mental visualization and fantasies (82). From a therapeutic perspective, the patient or client cannot engage in symbolic thinking—the use of abstract concepts—to better identify and explore their feelings and desires. Given this, it may be no surprise that this patient group often failed to describe dreams (83). As a result, the thought processes in this group of individuals tend to be pragmatic, prosaic, and almost entirely focused on external events.

In combination, all this means that people who score high on alexithymia find it extremely difficult to recognize and describe how they are feeling. They are unable to map changes in bodily responses to specific emotional states. Others have described such individuals as lacking any indication that they experience emotion. They are not able to feel empathy towards others. The characteristics that I have just described have been linked to a range of conditions, including depression, psychosomatic disorders, and personality disorders, among others (78, 84).

Alexithymia and depression

The prevalence of alexithymia in the general population is around 13–19 per cent (85, 86). Some studies have shown the prevalence of alexithymia to be significantly higher in people with depression, with rates of roughly 32 per cent (87).

There is a debate about whether alexithymia and depression are distinct constructs or whether they overlap (88, 89). Indeed, there is evidence to indicate alexithymia may be a risk factor for depression (90).

Long-term memory and depression

Before ending this chapter, we should consider how other forms of memory are affected by depression. In particular, long-term memory. Indeed, an understanding of emotion regulation helps explain how such memories are affected by depression.

Mood-congruent encoding

When looking at the literature in this area, it is crucial to distinguish between the terms affect, emotion, and mood. This is something we defined in Chapter 1. One of the things we know to be associated with depression is that our mood determines what we encode from our environment and what we retrieve from our memory stores. This is called mood-congruent processing.

We can learn material better if it is consistent with our current mood. This is mood-congruent encoding (91). The explanation for this is that when a person's mood matches the material they are attempting to learn, they process the content to a higher level, forming more elaborative links. This means that, when asked to recall the information, the memory traces are more integrated, so recall is better (92).

Mood-congruent memory

We also know that people are better able to remember information when their mood at retrieval matched when the material was learned. This is called mood-congruent memory bias (93). However, such effects have not consistently been replicated (94). The effect seems to be strongest for real-life events as opposed to artificially contrived scenarios (95). The likely explanation is that there is a clear link between a person's mood and the event itself in actual situations. In other words, there is a perceived causal relationship (96). It is also more evident if the material presented is related explicitly to the self (97).

Such biases in recall occur due to the amygdala's involvement in the processes carried out by the hippocampus and orbitofrontal cortex. The amygdala is vital for the rapid detection of emotional information and generating an emotional response. We shall return to the amygdala a little later as it is pivotal in all that we discuss. Memory is improved in line with increases in amygdala response. There is a more substantial effect for material that is directly linked to the self because content that is perceived to be personally meaningful is processed more intensely, thereby forming more elaborate memory traces (98). In fact, there is evidence to show such emotional reactivity to be linked to cognitive vulnerability to depression (99) (see Chapter 3).

Autobiographical memory

For many, our long-term memories define who we are. They provide us with a sense of self. There is one type of memory in particular that is pivotal here, and that is autobiographical memory. These memories are made up of two distinct components: memories of specific events in our lives—called episodic memories—and essential facts about our life—referred to as semantic memory (100).

There is a great deal of literature out there showing how such memories are affected by depression. Studies have shown that people with depression tend to remember over-general autobiographical memories. In other words, they lack specificity because they do not reference a uniquely personal event in their lives (101). Interestingly, increased specificity of autobiographical recall significantly predicted those who then recovered from depression (102).

An explanation of why this occurs links to emotion regulation. Because specific autobiographical memories may be feared since they could be highly negative, a person may avoid distress by bringing to mind non-specific memories where the potential impact on the person is minimized (103).

Studies have also been carried out that looked at the structure of autobiographical memories in people with depression. Dalgleish and colleagues (104) were asked to list the most critical periods in their life. These are referred to as life chapters and denote episodes in their life that have deep personal meaning. People generally identified around ten such periods. When asked to apply descriptors to these life chapters, it might not be surprising to learn that people who were depressed selected more negative terms by which to describe these stages compared to healthy controls. They also had a less integrated sense of self. A person who has not experienced depression has a highly integrated self that combines positive and negative aspects and resolves any resulting incongruity. In someone with depression, this does not happen, resulting in compartmentalization, with different chapters in a person's life being viewed as either positive or negative.

It may be argued that the lack of specificity helps to stop people from overthinking about events in their lives that could invoke negative emotions (105). This blotting out of the specific could be seen as habitual and not imposing any conscious demands on the person. That being the case, it would likely be in operation all the time regardless of the emotional nature of the material. This ensures certain events are not recalled. To do so would require active thought suppression.

Before leaving this chapter, this final section concerns a structure referred to repeatedly in this chapter and elsewhere: the amygdala.

The amygdala

The amygdala—from the Latin *Amygdalus*, meaning almond—is involved at all levels of an emotional response, from detection to reaction and beyond. It is situated in the limbic region of the brain. It comprises several nuclei linked to specific parts of the brain and subserving discrete functions (106).

As indicated earlier, it underpins our ability to recognize and respond to emotional situations. Stimuli are assessed for salience, threat, or reward levels on entering the basolateral region of the amygdala, referred to as the input region (106). This happens due to this region receiving information from sensory input, the hippocampus—involved in memory retrieval—and the association cortex—areas of the brain where thinking and reasoning occur. Outgoing information is sent to the orbitofrontal cortex, hippocampus, and striatum, influencing memory formation and behavioural responses.

The central nucleus of the amygdala is the main output region. Activation in the basolateral area disinhibits neurons in the central nucleus. Because of that, it is pivotal in determining how we react emotionally to events, manifesting as fear or anxiety (106). This region is connected to many other parts of the brain, including the hypothalamus (involved in the control of the autonomic nervous system, which serves a homeostatic function), nucleus ambiguus (motor neurons involved in regulating heart rate), and the facial motor nucleus (which innervate muscles in the face to produce different expressions).

The amygdala is particularly adept at reacting to environmental stimuli that are far from obvious—such as poor lighting—or occur fleetingly, so too quick to be registered consciously. As we have seen, it also reacts to emotive images, words, and so on. The intensity of its response depends on the emotional value of the stimulus and the person's current state of mind.

Having already talked in some depth about emotion regulation, from a neuroanatomical perspective, such processes involve cortical dampening, or inhibition, of the amygdala. This is driven mainly by the ventromedial prefrontal cortex and the orbital prefrontal cortex (107).

As might be expected, then, the amygdala plays a central role in depression. Increased amygdala activity helps maintain a negative mood due to the increased sensitivity to adverse environmental events. In addition to continuous overactivation, amygdala reactivity is also higher in depression (106), particularly faces and elements in the environment that are not the focus of conscious attention (108). Experiencing negative thoughts help to sustain this increased level of amygdala activation. As a result, this leads to continued rumination, so prolonging the depressed mood still further.

Summary

One of the main characteristics of depression is a profound impairment in cognitive functioning. This chapter has focused on problems with attention and executive function to a large extent and long-term memory. We also explored self-regulation and emotion regulation. In this section, we looked at how our thoughts and feelings can be harnessed to improve functioning. However, we also saw how poorly regulated emotions can have a disastrous effect. Importantly, we saw how cognition and emotion are intertwined. It is clear then how maladaptive thought processes can quickly lead to a self-perpetuating cycle of emotional turmoil and eventual depression. Examining the cognitive deficits associated with depression was the focus of my research at the start of my career. One of the things that struck me from my findings and those of other studies was how problems with attention and working memory impact almost every zone of daily functioning. How everyday tasks, even the simplest ones, have become dual tasks, with the demands of the activity competing with the internal monologue that requires more and more of our mental energy. On top of this, when you consider the sheer intellectual effort necessitated by many psychological treatments, such as cognitive behavioural therapy, there needs to be greater awareness of the impairments experienced by people with this condition. The principles and exercises associated with many therapies require motivation and perseverance, two things severely lacking in depression. We shall be turning our attention to treatment shortly.

References

1 Styles EA. The psychology of attention. 2nd ed. Hove: Psychology; 2005.
2 Christopher G. The psychology of ageing: From mind to society. Basingstoke: Palgrave Macmillan; 2014.
3 Christopher G, MacDonald J. The impact of clinical depression on working memory. Cogn Neuropsychiatry. 2005;10(5):379–399.
4 Ingram RE. Self-focused attention in clinical disorders: Review and a conceptual model. Psychol Bull. 1990;107(2):156–176.
5 Beck AT. Cognitive therapy and the emotional disorders. New York: International Universities Press; 1976.
6 Hartlage S, Alloy LB, Vázquez C, Dykman B. Automatic and effortful processing in depression. Psychol Bull. 1993;113(2):247.
7 Vázquez C, Hernangómez L. Automatic and controlled processing in depression. In: Ingram RE, editor. The international encyclopedia of depression. New York; London: Springer; 2009.
8 Hartlage S, Alloy LB, Vazquez C, Dykman B. Automatic and effortful processing in depression. Psychol Bull. 1993;113(2):247–278.
9 Segal ZV, Williams JM, Teasdale JD, Gemar M. A cognitive science perspective on kindling and episode sensitization in recurrent affective disorder. Psychol Med. 1996;26(2):371–380.
10 Segal ZV, Williams J, Teasdale J, Gemar M. A cognitive science perspective on kindling and episode sensitization in recurrent affective disorder. Psychol Med. 1996;26(2):371–380.
11 Monroe SM, Harkness KL. Life stress, the "kindling" hypothesis, and the recurrence of depression: Considerations from a life stress perspective. Psychol Rev. 2005; 112(2):417.
12 Baddeley AD, Hitch GJ. Working memory. In: Bower GA, editor. Recent advances in learning and motivation. Vol. 8. New York: Academic Press; 1974, pp. 47–90.
13 Baddeley A. Exploring the central executive. Q J Exp Psychol. 1996;49(1):5–28.
14 Channon S, Baker JE, Robertson MM. Working memory in clinical depression: An experimental study. Psychol Med. 1993;23(1):87–91.
15 Krames L, MacDonald M. Distraction and depressive cognitions. Cognit Ther Res. 1985;9(5):561–573.
16 Foulds G. Temperamental differences in maze performance. Part II. The effect of distraction and of electroconvulsive therapy on psychomotor retardation. Br J Psychol. 1952;43(1):33.
17 Anderson JR. The architecture of cognition. Psychology Press; 2013.
18 Watts FN, Sharrock R. Description and measurement of concentration problems in depressed patients. Psychol Med. 1985;15(2):317–326.

19   Teasdale JD, Proctor L, Lloyd CA, Baddeley AD. Working memory and stimulus-independent thought: Effects of memory load and presentation rate. Eur J Cogn Psychol. 1993;5(4):417–433.

20   Watts FN, MacLeod AK, Morris L. A remedial strategy for memory and concentration problems in depressed patients. Cognit Ther Res. 1988;12(2):185–193.

21   Watts, FN. Problems of memory and concentration. In: C. G. Costello CG, editors. Symptoms of depression. New York; Chichester: John Wiley & Sons; 1993, pp. 113–140.

22   Nuechterlein KH, Dawson ME. Information processing and attentional functioning in the developmental course of schizophrenic disorders. Schizophr Bull. 1984;10(2):160–203.

23   Kuhl J, Helle P. Motivational and volitional determinants of depression: The degenerated-intention hypothesis. J Abnorm Psychol. 1986;95(3):247.

24   Baddeley ADE. Working memory. Oxford: Clarendon; 1986.

25   Harris JE. Memory aids people use: Two interview studies. Mem Cogn. 1980;8(1):31–38.

26   Healy D, Williams J. Dysrhythmia, dysphoria, and depression: The interaction of learned helplessness and circadian dysrhythmia in the pathogenesis of depression. Psychol Bull. 1988;103(2):163.

27   Matlin MW, Matlin MWC. Cognitive psychology. 7th ed. International student ed. Hoboken, NJ: Wiley; 2009.

28   Baddeley A, Wilson B. Frontal amnesia and the dysexecutive syndrome. Brain Cogn. 1988;7(2):212–230.

29   Stuss DT, Levine B. Adult clinical neuropsychology: Lessons from studies of the frontal lobes. Annu Rev Psychol. 2002;53(1):401–433.

30   Rylander G. Personality changes after operations on the frontal lobes: A clinical study of 32 cases. Acta Psychiatr Neurol Scand. 1939;20:1–327.

31   Moulin C. Dysexecutive syndrome. In: Davey G, editor. The encyclopaedic dictionary of psychology. London: Hodder Arnold; 2006.

32   Alexopoulos GS. Depression executive dysfunction syndrome. In: Ingram RE, editor. The international encyclopedia of depression. New York; London: Springer Publishing/Company; 2009.

33   Alexopoulos GS. "The depression-executive dysfunction syndrome of late life": A specific target for D3 agonists? Am J Geriatr Psychiatry. 2001;9(1):22–29.

34   Alexopoulos GS. Depression in the elderly. Lancet. 2005;365(9475):1961–1970.

35   Alexopoulos GS, Kiosses DN, Heo M, Murphy CF, Shanmugham B, Gunning-Dixon F. Executive dysfunction and the course of geriatric depression. Biol Psychiatry. 2005;58(3):204–210.

36   Scott W, Penningroth SL. Self-regulation. In: Ingram RE, editor. The international encyclopedia of depression. New York; London: Springer; 2009.

37   Strauman TJ. Self-regulation and depression. Self Identity. 2002;1(2):151–157.

38   Dweck CS. Self-theories: Their role in motivation, personality, and development. Philadelphia; PA: Psychology Press; 2000.

39   Higgins ET. Beyond pleasure and pain. Am Psychol. 1997;52(12):1280–1300.

40   Locke EA, Latham GP. A theory of goal setting & task performance. Englewood Cliffs; London: Prentice-Hall, Inc; 1990.

41   Cervone D, Scott WD. Self-efficacy theory of behavioral change: Foundations, conceptual issues, and therapeutic implications. In: O'Donohue WT, Krasner L, editors. Theories of behavior therapy: Exploring behavior change. Washington, DC: American Psychological Association; 1995, pp. 349–389.

42   Hewitt PL, Flett GL. Dimensions of perfectionism in unipolar depression. J Abnorm Psychol. 1991;100(1):98–101.

43   Tillema J, Cervone D, Scott W. Dysphoric mood, perceived self-efficacy, and personal standards for performance: The effects of attributional cues on self-defeating patterns of cognition. Cognit Ther Res. 2001;25:535–549.

44   Emmons RA. Abstract versus concrete goals: Personal striving level, physical illness, and psychological well-being. J Pers Soc Psychol. 1992;62(2):292–300.

45   Emmons RA, King LA. Conflict among personal strivings: Immediate and long-term implications for psychological and physical well-being. J Pers Soc Psychol. 1988;54(6):1040–1048.

46   Dunn BD, Dalgleish T, Lawrence AD, Ogilvie AD. The accuracy of self-monitoring and its relationship to self-focused attention in dysphoria and clinical depression. J Abnorm Psychol. 2007;116(1):1–15.

47   Alloy LB, Abramson LY. Depressive realism: Four theoretical perspectives. In: Alloy LB, editor. Cognitive processes in depression. New York: Guilford Press; 1987, pp. 223–266.

48   Ingram RE. Depressive realism. In: Ingram RE, editor. The international encyclopedia of depression. New York; London: Springer Publishing Company; 2009.

49   Wells A, Matthews G. Attention and emotion: A clinical perspective. Hove; Hillsdale: Lawrence Erlbaum Associates; 1994.

50   Wells A. Metacognitive therapy for anxiety and depression. New York; London: Guilford; 2009.

51   Wells A. Metacognition. In: Ingram RE, editor. The international encyclopedia of depression. New York; London: Springer; 2009.

52   Gross JJ. The emerging field of emotion regulation: An integrative review. Rev Gen Psychol. 1998;2(3):271–299.

53   Ismail S, Christopher G, Dodd E, Wildschut T, Sedikides C, Jones RW, et al. Psychological and mnemonic benefits of nostalgia for people with dementia. J Alzheimer's Dis. 2018:1–18.

54   Gyurak A, Etkin A. A neurobiological model of implicit and explicit emotion regulation. In: Gross JJPD, editor. Handbook of emotion regulation. New York; London: Guilford; 2007, pp. 76–90.

55   Damasio AR. Descartes' error: Emotion, reason and the human brain. London: Vintage; 2006.

56   Gross JJ. Emotion regulation: Conceptual and empirical foundations. In: Gross JJ, editors. Handbook of emotion regulation. New York; London: The Guilford Press. 2014, pp. 3–20.

57   Gross JJ, Richards JM, John OP. Emotion regulation in everyday life. In: Snyder DK, Simpson J, Hughes, JN, editors. Emotion regulation in couples and families: Pathways to dysfunction and health. Washington, DC; London: American Psychological Association. 2006, pp.13–35.

58   Peña-Sarrionandia A, Mikolajczak M, Gross JJ. Integrating emotion regulation and emotional intelligence traditions: A meta-analysis. Front Psychol. 2015;6:160.

59   Martell CR, Addis ME, Jacobson NS. Depression in context: Strategies for guided action. New York; London: W.W. Norton; 2001, xxx, 223 pp.

60   Thorndike EL. Intelligence and its uses. *Harper's Magazine.* 1920;140:227–235.

61   Gardner H. Frames of mind: The theory of multiple intelligences. London: Heinemann, 1983/1984.

62 Salovey P, Mayer JD. Emotional intelligence. Imagination, cognition and personality. Imagin Cogn Pers. 1990;9(3):185–211.

63 Goleman D. Emotional intelligence: Why it can matter more than IQ. London: Bloomsbury; 1996, xiv, 352pp.

64 Mayer JD, Salovey P, Caruso D. Models of emotional intelligence. In: Sternberg RJ, editor. The handbook of intelligence. New York: Cambridge University Press; 2000, pp. 392–420.

65 Petrides KV, Furnham A. Trait emotional intelligence: Behavioural validation in two studies of emotion recognition and reactivity to mood induction. Eur J Pers. 2003;17(1):39–57.

66 Mikolajczak M, Nelis D, Hansenne M, Quoidbach J. If you can regulate sadness, you can probably regulate shame: Associations between trait emotional intelligence, emotion regulation and coping efficiency across discrete emotions. Pers Individ Differ. 2008;44(6):1356–1368.

67 Mikolajczak M, Luminet O, Menil C. Predicting resistance to stress: Incremental validity of trait emotional intelligence over alexithymia and optimism. Psicothema. 2006;18.

68 Urquijo I, Extremera N, Villa A. Emotional intelligence, life satisfaction, and psychological well-being in graduates: The mediating effect of perceived stress. Appl Res Qual Life. 2016;11(4):1241–1252.

69 Mikolajczak M, Menil C, Luminet O. Explaining the protective effect of trait emotional intelligence regarding occupational stress: Exploration of emotional labour processes. J Res Pers. 2007;41(5):1107–1117.

70 Keltner D, Kring AM. Emotion, social function, and psychopathology. Rev Gen Psychol. 1998;2(3):320.

71 Bruchon-Schweitzer M, editor Psychologie de la santé. Modèles, concepts et méthodes. Annales Médico Psychologiques; 2003;161:838–840.

72 Gross JJ, Levenson RW. Hiding feelings: The acute effects of inhibiting negative and positive emotion. J Abnorm Psychol. 1997;106(1):95.

73 Gross JJ, John OP. Individual differences in two emotion regulation processes: Implications for affect, relationships, and well-being. J Pers Soc Psychol. 2003;85(2):348.

74 Schutte NS, Malouff JM, Thorsteinsson EB, Bhullar N, Rooke SE. A meta-analytic investigation of the relationship between emotional intelligence and health. Pers Individ Differ. 2007;42(6):921–933.

75 Campbell-Sills L, Barlow DH. Incorporating emotion regulation into conceptualizations and treatments of anxiety and mood disorders. In: Gross JJ, editor. Handbook of emotion regulation. New York; London: The Guilford Press; 2007, pp. 542–559.

76 Mikolajczak M, Luminet O. Trait emotional intelligence and the cognitive appraisal of stressful events: An exploratory study. Pers Individ Differ. 2008;44(7):1445–1453.

77 Saklofske DH, Austin EJ, Galloway J, Davidson K. Individual difference correlates of health-related behaviours: Preliminary evidence for links between emotional intelligence and coping. Pers Individ Differ. 2007;42(3):491–502.

78 Christopher G, Thomas M. Social problem solving in chronic fatigue syndrome: Preliminary findings. Stress Heal. 2009;25(2):161–169.

79 LeDoux J. The emotional brain: The mysterious underpinnings of emotional life. London: Weidenfeld & Nicolson; 1998.

80 Blanchard-Fields F, Jahnke HC, Camp C. Age differences in problem-solving style: The role of emotional salience. Psychol Aging. 1995;10(2):173–180.

81 Marcus Aurelius EoR. Meditations. London: Penguin; 2004.

82   Sifneos PE. Short-term psychotherapy and emotional crisis. Cambridge, MA: Harvard University Press; 1972.

83   Taylor GJ. Alexithymia: Concept, measurement, and implications for treatment. Am J Psychiat. 1984;141(6):725–732.

84   Christopher G, McMurran M. Alexithymia, empathic concern, goal management, and social problem solving in adult male prisoners. Psychol Crime Law. 2009;15(8):697–709.

85   Salminen JK, Saarijärvi S, Äärelä E, Toikka T, Kauhanen J. Prevalence of alexithymia and its association with sociodemographic variables in the general population of Finland. J Psychosom Res. 1999;46(1):75–82.

86   Parker JD, Taylor GJ, Bagby RM. The alexithymia construct: Relationship with sociodemographic variables and intelligence. Compr Psychiatry. 1989;30(5):434–441.

87   Honkalampi K, Hintikka J, Tanskanen A, Lehtonen J, Viinamäki H. Depression is strongly associated with alexithymia in the general population. J Psychosom Res. 2000;48(1):99–104.

88   Rief W, Heuser J, Fichter MM. What does the Toronto Alexithymia Scale TAS-R measure? J Clin Psychol. 1996;52(4):423–429.

89   Parker JD, Bagby RM, Taylor GJ. Alexithymia and depression: Distinct or overlapping constructs? Compr Psychiat. 1991;32(5):387–394.

90   Grabe HJ, Frommer J, Ankerhold A, Ulrich C, Gröger R, Franke GH, et al. Alexithymia and outcome in psychotherapy. Psychother Psychosom. 2008;77(3):189–194.

91   Mayer JD, Salovey, P. Personality moderates the interaction of mood and cognition. In Fiedler K, Forgas J, editors. Affect, cognition and social behavior. Toronto: Hogrefe; 1988; pp. 87–99.

92   Forgas JP. Mood and judgment: The affect infusion model (AIM). Psychol Bull. 1995;117(1):39.

93   Bower GH, Monteiro KP, Gilligan SG. Emotional mood as a context for learning and recall. J Verbal Learn Verbal Behav. 1978;17(5):573–585.

94   Bower GH, Mayer JD. In search of mood-dependent retrieval. J Soc Behav Pers. 1989;4(2):121–156.

95   Ucros CG. Mood state-dependent memory: A meta-analysis. Cogn Emot. 1989;3(2):139–169.

96   Kihlstrom JF. On what does mood-dependent memory depend? J Soc Behav Pers. 1989;4(2):23.

97   Dozois DJ, Dobson KS. Information processing and cognitive organization in unipolar depression: Specificity and comorbidity issues. J Abnorm Psychol. 2001;110(2):236.

98   Ingram RE. Toward an information-processing analysis of depression. Cognit Ther Res. 1984;8(5):443–477.

99   Ramel W, Goldin PR, Eyler LT, Brown GG, Gotlib IH, McQuaid JR. Amygdala reactivity and mood-congruent memory in individuals at risk for depressive relapse. Biol Psychiatry. 2007;61(2):231–239.

100 Conway MA. Sensory—perceptual episodic memory and its context: Autobiographical memory. Philos Trans R Soc Lond B Biol Sci. 2001;356(1413):1375–1384.

101 Liu X, Li L, Xiao J, Yang J, Jiang X. Abnormalities of autobiographical memory of patients with depressive disorders: A meta-analysis. Psychol Psychother. 2013; 86(4):353–373.

102 Brittlebank A, Scott J, Mark J, Williams G, Ferrier I. Autobiographical memory in depression: State or trait marker? Br J Psychiat. 1993;162(1):118–121.

103 Debeer E, Raes F, Williams JMG, Hermans D. Context-dependent activation of reduced autobiographical memory specificity as an avoidant coping style. Emotion. 2011;11(6):1500.

104 Dalgleish T, Hill E, Golden A-MJ, Morant N, Dunn BD. The structure of past and future lives in depression. J Abnorm Psychol. 2011;120(1):1.

105 Williams JMG, Barnhofer T, Crane C, Herman D, Raes F, Watkins E, et al. Autobiographical memory specificity and emotional disorder. Psychol Bull. 2007;133(1):122.

106 Siegle G. Amygdala. In: Ingram RE, editor. The international encyclopedia of depression. New York; London: Springer Publishing Company; 2009.

107 Phillips ML, Ladouceur CD, Drevets WC. A neural model of voluntary and automatic emotion regulation: Implications for understanding the pathophysiology and neurodevelopment of bipolar disorder. Mol Psychiat. 2008;13(9):833.

108 Leppänen JM. Emotional information processing in mood disorders: A review of behavioral and neuroimaging findings. Curr Opin Psychiat. 2006;19(1):34–39.

Chapter 5

Depression, health, and well-being

Psychosocial functioning

A person's ability to relate to other people and function within a social environment is severely affected by depression. Many factors influence how severe these problems are, including how the individual is responding to treatment and how persistent the depression is, among other things (1). Psychosocial functioning can be assessed in terms of both a person's satisfaction with their job, their relationships, and their free time, and looking at indicators of someone's performance in each of these areas (2).

It is clear that depression causes much disruption to relationships in all their forms, be it at home or at work. When looking specifically at the work environment, depression proves hugely costly for the employer. The main culprit here is the number of days absent from work. This amounts to losses in the billions of pounds each year (1). This disruption to employment continues throughout the condition as most experience relapses following treatment (3). There are also significant disruptions to hobbies and pleasurable activities that persist even following remission (1).

Interpersonal relationships

An area of considerable disruption is that of personal relationships. Many problems are experienced in everyday interactions with others when a person is experiencing depression. This includes family, friends, and colleagues, among others. Feelings of loneliness are a real problem (4).

The effect is even more profound when looking at the impact on intimate relationships, with poor communication and feelings of guilt being standard (5). Problems do not resolve immediately following remission as one might expect. Indeed, problems can last many years (6).

In addition, it is clear that, as in many cases, it is not just the person diagnosed with the condition that is negatively affected. In many cases, the impacted partner or spouse may see the person with depression as a burden, as someone who is slowly draining away all vitality in the relationship (5). Indeed, those close to the

DOI:10.4324/9781315688879-5

person with depression also show higher-than-usual levels of problems with every-day living. The cause may, in fact, be depression as well.

Occupation

The cost of depression concerning occupation is usually considered in two ways: the employer's cost and the individual's. Taking the first approach, depression does account for a great deal of loss for employers. This is due to a combination of many factors, such as the length of time a person is absent from work and reductions in productivity.

Personal costs include poor concentration and fatigue, which, among other things, lead to poor performance at work. Because of this, it is not always clear whether the best course of action is to take time off work—referred to as absentee-ism—or whether it is preferable to continue working while experiencing the symp-toms of depression—presenteeism. A study looking at this specific issue generally found costs—reduced productivity, higher service use, higher levels of antidepres-sants—were usually higher for absenteeism among blue- and white-collar groups. Interestingly, although lower, costs associated with presenteeism were still signifi-cant. The two groups are likely to differ in terms of the severity of symptoms (7). There is also the added risk of future recurrence of depression (8).

There is also the issue of the legacy of being diagnosed with a mental health problem, specifically in terms of returning to work, either for the same employer or seeking employment elsewhere (9). Although the Equality Act 2010 designates any discrimination against people with mental health problems illegal, stigma still exists (10). Much is being done to challenge stereotypes around mental health issues, but there is a long way to go.

Recreation

Engaging in enjoyable activities outside of work time is something we all hold dear. Finding the time and headspace to do so can be a real challenge. This is especially so for someone with depression. An inability to derive pleasures from life is a fundamental characteristic of this condition, as we have seen. As has been the case throughout the history of psychology, there is an overriding emphasis on negative qualities. In the case of depression, it is negative mood states. There is a comparative lack of attention on indicating ways to help people with depression connect once more with aspects of their life from which they derive pleasures (11).

Long-term health problems

Depression does not occur in isolation. Instead, many also have long-term health conditions as well. In fact, depression is up to three times higher in those with chronic health problems (12), accounting for around 20 per cent of this group. Conditions such as musculoskeletal problems, heart disease, and cancer are chronic conditions that affect many. In some cases, a person may already experience depression, so the diagnosis of a chronic health condition is likely to make the depression worse. In other instances, depression may occur in response to a decline in physical health.

There is a great deal of evidence showing the impact of depression on health outcomes. Depression heightens the distress and discomfort experienced with a physical health problem. Depression is also associated with longer recovery times and less successful outcomes. It is also linked to a shorter life expectancy.

We also know that depression is a substantial risk factor for several complaints, for example, cardiovascular disease.

The degree of functional impairment is worse when depression coexists alongside a physical health complaint. In other words, the combined effect of the two is more significant than either depression or the health problem on its own (13).

Declining health at any age necessitates changes across the board. Our way of life has to change in several obvious but sometimes also subtle ways. These changes have a cumulative effect on how we see ourselves and how other people see us. As a result, there are often considerable changes in our work lives and our personal lives. Some of these changes might be temporary, others permanent. Due to the nature of the changes that have to be made, this leads to depression for many.

We know that significant, life-threatening conditions can lead to depression. For example, cancer and severe heart surgery, where extensive intervention or surgery is needed, have clear links with depression. However, a condition does not have to be life-threatening to lead to someone developing depression. Chronic health complaints are also a concern here.

Conversely, a person may experience pain without there being an identifiable cause. These are psychosomatic symptoms, which are driven by an underlying psychological issue rather than being organic in origin. As should always be the case in such instances, it is crucial to acknowledge that just because a physical cause of the problem cannot be located, that does not mean one does not exist. It might be the case that some organic cause is present, but it eludes current methods of investigation. However, this can lead to protracted and psychologically (and in some cases, physically) stressful consultations with various healthcare professionals before a final, and hopefully, accurate diagnosis is made.

This can be worrisome as months or years can go by before a definitive diagnosis is made. Part of the problem here is likely to be the individual's difficulty expressing how they are feeling emotionally and making links between their current state and events in their lives. The issue of alexithymia—an inability to identify and describe our own emotions—was discussed in detail in Chapter 4. The physical symptoms may be the only way of signalling that something is awry in their lives.

The most common form of physical manifestation of depression is pain in the joints and muscles. Heart palpitations may be experienced as well as angina-like symptoms. The person may express feelings of general malaise, numbness, and giddiness. These can be extremely worrying for someone at any age and may lead that person to fear an underlying medical condition that is potentially lethal.

Although it may very well be an inability to connect with one's own emotions that leads to the predominance of physical sensations, we should also consider that physical ailments do not carry the additional baggage that psychological symptoms do in terms of stigma. There are also cultural differences here. Reporting physical problems is a lot more acceptable for many. In this sense, the bias may be societal rather than personal (14).

Risk factors

Many medical conditions have been shown to increase the risk of depression, either directly or indirectly. One way this happens is where a medical condition impacts brain regions associated with the regulation of emotional responses (15), such as the orbital frontal cortex and the basal ganglia. Among these are various neurological conditions such as Parkinson's disease and multiple sclerosis. Also, cardiovascular disease and diabetes can affect neural systems, resulting in mood changes (16, 17).

Many of the symptoms associated with various medical conditions increase the risk of depression. Such symptoms include disruptions to sleep, pain, and also fatigue (18, 19). Changes in a person's ability to function in their daily lives can either worsen the symptoms of depression or lead to the onset of a depressive episode (20).

It is not just medical conditions themselves that have repercussions in terms of mood, but also the various treatments employed. In a previous chapter, we talked about the impact of therapies linked to immune function and how these affect mood. For example, cytokine treatments can lead to depression or aggravate symptoms in someone currently experiencing a depressive episode (21).

Of course, there is the flip side to this. Rather than medical conditions increasing the risk of depression, depression increases the likelihood of certain medical conditions manifesting in the first place. We have already seen that depression interferes with a range of bodily systems. These include, among others, the immune system and the neuroendocrine system.

Aside from interfering with the internal functioning of the body, depression impacts on a person's overt behaviour. People with depression are more likely to adopt negative health behaviours, such as smoking or excessive alcohol use. They are also less likely to exercise regularly (17, 22).

We know that depression dampens a person's interest in life, their motivation to perform activities. This translates into poor adherence to treatment plans. A person will be less inclined to take prescribed medication, attend medical appointments, and monitor how they are doing (23). Failure to do all this will result in poorer outcomes regarding any comorbid medical condition (15).

Moderating the risk

In addition to identifying what factors increase the risk of depression, it is equally important to consider how such risk can be attenuated. A prime example is that risk of depression in light of a medical diagnosis is higher for those who have experienced episodes of depression in the past. There is also some evidence, albeit inconclusive that various demographic characteristics may exert an effect, such as socio-economic status and living conditions (15).

We will now explore some of the leading health conditions affected by depression.

Musculoskeletal problems

Musculoskeletal disorders are a significant problem. They refer to a range of conditions where injury or pain is experienced in a person's joints, muscles, and bones. It affects around one in four of the population in the UK (24, 25). They cost the NHS around £5 billion (Department of Health (2011), Programme Budgeting Data 2009–10, June, (25)). Diagnoses include back pain, tendinitis, and carpal tunnel syndrome. Potential causes are numerous and include being in a job that demands repetitive movement (26), working in a stressful environment, or being stuck in one position for prolonged periods. Several factors are known to exacerbate a variety of musculoskeletal problems. One of the most commonly linked conditions is depression. Indeed, depression is common among those with a chronic illness in general (27). As might be expected, there is a bidirectional relationship here, with depression leading to musculoskeletal pain and musculoskeletal problems leading to depression. However, the mechanism underlying this is unclear (28, 29).

Diabetes

Different types of diabetes reflect either a lack of insulin production—type 1 diabetes—or a situation where insulin levels do not meet the body's requirements or, in some cases, the body fails to use up all of the insulin produced by the body—type 2 diabetes. Insulin is a hormone that instigates blood sugar uptake to muscle and fat cells after a meal has been ingested. Glucose from food is a much-needed source of energy for cells. When insulin is not produced in sufficient quantities, the glucose remains in the blood and is not utilized by cells.

Depression is higher in those with diabetes compared to the general population (30). However, the reasons for this are far from clear. As with other conditions, it could be the case that depression occurs due to a combination of worry about the impact of diabetes on a person's life and poor coping strategies. However, in the case of type 2 diabetes, depression often precedes it (31). This is not the case for type 1 diabetes, with depression occurring post-diagnosis. However, it is unclear if, in the case of type 1 diabetes, depression occurs as a result of the diagnosis.

It has been suggested that depression occurs due to the additional strain felt by someone who has received a diagnosis of a chronic medical condition (32). More specifically, problems with adapting to the illness (33).

As depression occurs before the onset of diabetic symptoms in many cases, it may be the case that the increased insulin resistance and reduced glucose uptake seen in depression increases the risk of developing type 2 diabetes (34). It is less evident in the case of type 1 diabetes. However, it appears to be similar to depression experienced in the general population (19).

Kidney disease

Chronic kidney disease describes a condition where damaged kidneys no longer function as they should. In such cases, they can no longer remove fluid and waste—urea—that build up in the body. It affects around 10 per cent of the population (35). Depression is widespread, with distress being highest for those who require dialysis treatment (36). Less is known about levels of depression for people in the early stages of kidney disease. A review of relevant studies indicated that around 25 per cent show signs of depression (37).

Lung disease

Chronic obstructive pulmonary disease (COPD) is one of the leading causes of death in many countries. It is a progressive disease that affects the lungs and the associated airways. The end result is a loss of lung function. Some explanations have been offered why there is a high prevalence of depression in COPD. One argument concerns genetic predisposition and behaviour during adolescence, where adolescents who are depressed are more likely to become addicted to nicotine (38). This addiction is maintained throughout life in many cases. There is some evidence to suggest that brain pathology associated with depression affects respiration (39).

Heart disease

Depression often follows heart disease, especially after someone has experienced a myocardial infarction (40). Diagnosis of depression in such cases is critical as depression is linked to poor medical outcomes and higher mortality rates (40, 41).

Depression frequently occurs following stroke (42). Again, it negatively affects recovery, such as being less able to perform everyday activities and showing poorer performance during rehabilitation (43).

There is a weighty and ever-expanding body of evidence to show that a range of psychosocial variables affects the outcome of someone who has been diagnosed with heart disease. It is common knowledge now that a range of lifestyle choices increase one's risk of experiencing a myocardial infarction or heart attack. The majority are entirely under personal control and so are deemed modifiable. These include smoking, exercise, diet, and so on (44). We also know that stress is a major contributing factor in many cases, whether in home life, work, or finances (45).

Depression is a significant factor also (46). Depression generally occurs after a person has received a diagnosis of coronary heart disease. Such a diagnosis often stirs up powerful emotions. In some cases, the combination of depression and anger experienced leads people to become isolated (47).

In terms of health outcomes, depression presages a considerable threat of death in some cases. Depression increases the relative risk of mortality from cardiovascular disease (48).

A point that forever needs stressing is keeping a close eye on what medications a person is taking. This is particularly pertinent as one ages, given the increased likelihood of comorbidity. Drugs, as we know, interact to produce some rather nasty side effects. Such side effects might be severe enough to induce states that resemble the onset of another condition. As a case in point, a person may have undergone a major, invasive operation to reverse or stabilize a life-threatening medical condition. Following an operation, such as heart surgery, a person is at risk of developing depression. This is only natural as they have almost stared death in the face. Their life has been turned upside-down due to changes in diet and habits to support the surgery to improve outcome. On discharge, the person might be prescribed strong painkillers to ease post-operative pain. The person might also experience extreme pain resulting from inflamed joints, again requiring analgesics to help with the pain. Strong analgesic medication can result in extreme confusion, mental blunting, and increased sleepiness. The effects on cognitive functioning can be so significant that others start to suspect that there might be a more insidious process at play, namely underlying dementia. Imagine, then, the situation, surviving major surgery and then beginning to manifest the symptoms of severe cognitive decline. This, indeed, might be the case. Equally, it might be that the person is receiving too high a dosage of painkillers. By merely reducing the dose or switching to a nonnarcotic form of analgesia, the worrying symptoms portending dementia disappear.

Cancer

Cancer refers to a group of diseases where the body's cells start to grow uncontrollably at different sites throughout the body. Around one-fifth of cancer patients experience depression. Successfully recognizing that someone with cancer also has depression improves their quality of life and their chances of survival (49). There are several possible explanations for the high rates of depression in this group. It may be the case, as with other conditions, that a diagnosis of cancer leads to someone developing depression. However, other mechanisms may be at work. For example, some cancers lead to the release of chemicals that are believed to cause the onset of depression. Some cancer treatments themselves seem to increase the likelihood of depression developing. However, successfully diagnosing depression is not the only thing to consider. Because depression is often treated by prescribing antidepressant medication, clinicians need also be aware that certain antidepressants actually exacerbate cancer symptoms and interfere with some of the treatment regimens.

Neurological disorders

Depression is prevalent among a range of neurological disorders. The term neurological disorders reflect a wide range of conditions with severe cognitive and/or motor impairment due to damage to the nervous system. These include Parkinson's disease, multiple sclerosis, and stroke. There is a complex relationship between dementia and depression, with early symptoms of cognitive decline mirroring those of depression (50). In such cases, it is incredibly challenging to separate out signs of depression from those associated with the underlying neurodegenerative condition. In many of these conditions, numerous factors are at play to increase a person's susceptibility to depression, including receiving the diagnosis itself, the pain and fatigue associated with it, the poor prognosis, and many other things that exacerbate the situation (51). In the case of dementia, there is even believed to be a common pathway rooted in the body's inflammatory response (52).

Alcohol and substance misuse

There are few among us who do not use strategies to help compensate for reductions in performance. Suppose we begin to experience our minds drifting or feel that our eyelids are becoming heavy. In that case, we generally get up from our desks, make the pained journey to the kitchen, and fix ourselves the (mental) life-giving preparation that is coffee. We all know that caffeine aids the under-performing mind. In a genuine sense, this is a form of self-medication. We all do it. It might not be coffee. Instead, a hot cup of tea is the desired potion in some cases. Others might indulge in a cigarette, making use of the cognitive-enhancing effects of nicotine. Some might go for a run, harnessing the positive influence of the endocannabinoids that course through our bodies during exercise.

Sometimes, however, this self-medication can lead the person to tread more dangerous waters. One would inevitably place cigarettes here on health grounds. However, what I am alluding to here is alcohol or drugs to help fight against depression. However, before moving on to this, we should look at nicotine in more detail. Some smoke to help alleviate their depression. This is in part borne out by higher rates of smoking in depression. Nicotine causes the release of the neurotransmitter dopamine, 3-hydroxytyramine. Dopamine leads to an increase in positive mood. Dopamine levels are reduced in those with depression, so smoking is one way to offset this decline. However, raising dopamine levels through smoking cigarettes makes it less likely that the body produces its own supply (53).

Many of us look forward to a well-deserved drink at the weekend. However, it is when drinking alcohol is no longer contained within strict personal boundaries that it becomes problematic. A drink during the week to unwind can quickly lead to a situation where a person is finding themselves pouring a glass every night. Some might find they reach for the bottle during work to steady their nerves before an important meeting. Very quickly, the dependence on the soothing effects of alcohol can get out of hand.

Most are aware of the unfortunate side effects of alcohol. I am not referring to the hangover, although that is bad enough; instead, I allude to the destructive impact of alcohol on mood. Although at first it makes a person feel more relaxed, one cannot get away from the fact that alcohol is a central nervous system depressant, reducing arousal levels. It slows mental and physical functioning. Continuous use will quickly lead to dependency.

In terms of other drugs, depression is common for those with substance use disorders (54). For most, depression occurs before the substance use disorder (55). Much in the same way as alcohol, the use of drugs will intensify the symptoms of depression over time. As with all drugs of this nature, the more one is exposed to it, the more one needs to obtain the desired effect due to building tolerance. As we saw in the chapter on diagnosis, where alcohol or substance misuse is suspected, it is vital to assess the individual for depression once the drug is out of their system to arrive at an accurate diagnosis.

Eating disorders

Depression is common in those diagnosed with either anorexia nervosa or bulimia nervosa (56). The word "anorexia" means a loss of appetite. Anorexia nervosa is a condition where someone believes they are overweight when, in fact, they are not. In many cases, this can lead to emaciation. In the case of bulimia nervosa—bulimia means gorging—a person oscillates between binge-eating and forced vomiting or use of laxatives. The co-occurrence of depression with an eating disorder increases the risk of suicide.

Sleep

Sleep is fundamentally important to us all. However, its status as a vital determiner of health and well-being has been eroded over the years. To survive on minimal sleep is something many aspire to. However, recent research has shown how genuinely damaging such behaviour can be. Adequate sleep each night is essential for our long-term health.

Sleep is something that we all do, but few do it well. Modern life, with all its trapping, impedes the sanctity of this much-needed downtime. One of the most important things to consider is sleep hygiene. We can all make improvements there. If it is not the much-revered yet much-reviled smartphone, it is the tablet or laptop that awash the walls of our temples of rest and our tired peepers with blue light. We grab these moments at the end of the day to read our e-books or watch boxsets. The activities themselves may, in fact, be effective ways of de-stressing. Still, the vehicles for our pleasure are far from ideal. The stimuli received from our electronic devices act against our need for sleep. This is because it has been suggested that blue light interferes with levels of melatonin. Levels of this hormone dictate the body's natural diurnal—day and night—rhythm. However, in the end, it may not be the devices themselves that are at fault; instead, it is how we choose to interact with them (57). Ways to improve sleep hygiene will be discussed later in this section.

Sleep performs several essential functions. It is not merely a time of rest. It helps our brains sift through what they have processed during the day and facilitates the strengthening and integration of memories, referred to as consolidation.

It has been suggested that adults need around 7–9 hours of sleep each night. Children need more prolonged periods of sleep to help with the massive influx of new knowledge and skills they acquire. To attain a healthy sleep pattern, our behaviour needs to be consistent (58).

Depression is characterized by marked sleep disturbances. We have been talking about improving sleep hygiene to help attain adequate sleep. Sleep quality is determined by how long it takes a person to fall asleep and how long it is maintained once asleep. People with depression find it difficult to fall asleep. This insomnia is due to the negative thoughts that are swirling around inside their heads. Once sleep is achieved, it tends to be less restful than someone who is not experiencing depression. There are more interruptions during the sleep stages. Deep sleep is notably lacking. On waking, people generally do not feel rested.

Antidepressants often interfere with sleep in varying ways. Although over time, sleep patterns may normalize, in the short term, sleep can either be disrupted due to the activating nature of some medication (e.g. fluoxetine), or over-sedation may occur (e.g. trazodone) (59).

However, there is much we can do to help ourselves sleep better aside from medication. These are things that we could all benefit from, not just those who experience depression. There is much benefit to be gained from maintaining regular times for retiring at night and getting up in the morning. If sleep escapes us, it is better to get out of bed and go into another room rather than catch increasingly frantic glances at the alarm clock.

In terms of the bedroom itself, it should be dark and maintained at a cool temperature. If possible, fresh air should permeate the room. If the surrounding environment is noisy, it might be wise to invest in earplugs. There is growing evidence that white noise can help those who find distraction a substantial barrier to a good night's sleep (60). White noise—although other flavours are available, such as pink and brown—acts as a buffer against background sounds. It presents the ears with a wall of unflinching noise that masks all the annoying little clicks, gurgles, squeaks, and so on that present themselves to a mind determined to be distracted rather than rest. A fan in the bedroom can have the same sort of effect. Anything that exudes a constant sound (61). Only the most persistent sound gets through this filter.

Ensuring one has the right state of mind for sleep is all-important. Some find gentle exercise conducive. Obviously, before sleep, not while trying to sleep. Others find engaging in relaxation or mindfulness exercises beneficial. The myth of a nightcap aiding sleep is just that. Although alcohol often allows one to sleep more quickly, the actual quality of sleep is poor.

We all have a tendency to sleep in at the weekend if possible. This is seen as being a reward for all the early starts during the working week. However, this might be doing us more harm than good. There is recent research to show that we are inducing a state comparable to jetlag. In fact, it is referred to as social jetlag. This is where there is a disconnect between the body's natural circadian rhythm and a socially imposed sleep pattern (62). Sleeping in does not undo the effects of chronic sleep debt incurred throughout the working week. It can also throw the body out-of-sync. To achieve the best sleep, it has been suggested that a person needs to stick to a routine regardless of whether it is a workday or not (63).

Caregivers

As might be expected, we have spent this chapter looking at the general health and well-being of the person who has been diagnosed with depression. However, as with many conditions, one must look too at the quality of life of other people in their life, specifically those who might have found themselves in the role of carer. Given the emotional roller coaster that is depression, it might not be surprising to know that the toll on loved ones is significant in many cases.

People who care for someone with a long-term condition often develop depression. Prevalence of depression varies significantly with the condition, with rates being exceptionally high in those who care for someone with dementia (64).

Having looked in some depth at the health of those with depression, the final section of this chapter will explore a couple of related issues. The first concerns the challenge of making an accurate diagnosis of depression amidst all the confounding symptoms of comorbid complaints. This will be followed by a section on the prescription of antidepressant medication when there is a comorbid health condition.

Making an accurate diagnosis

Making an accurate diagnosis can be challenging at the best of times. However, differentiating depression from a host of symptoms associated with ongoing medical complaints adds another dimension of difficulty (15). Many of the symptoms we associate with depression can be brought on by a variety of medical complaints. There are strategies to help achieve an accurate diagnosis, however. One method is to exclude symptoms due to a medical condition and then assess the case for depression based on those that remain. Alternatively, clinicians may decide to give equal weighting to all symptoms regardless of their possible origin and then evaluate each in terms of its severity. Suppose the seriousness of the potential symptom(s) of depression exceeds what might be expected based on the ongoing medical complaint. In that case, it is considered likely to go some way in supporting a diagnosis of depression. A time frame of symptom onset is built up to see if there are temporal clustering of symptoms indicative of depression. In other words, is there a point in time when a critical clustering of symptoms linked to depression occurs that is separated sufficiently in time from onset or changes in the status of an underlying medical condition?

Antidepressants in those with health complaints

As we shall see in Chapter 8, there are several drug interactions to contemplate when prescribing additional medication. Such effects can be exacerbated by several factors. One is the presence of a physical health complaint when a person has been diagnosed with depression. Antidepressant medication, especially selective serotonin reuptake inhibitors (SSRIs; see Chapter 5), may exacerbate some physical symptoms. There are also the issues associated with polypharmacy, where antidepressant medication might interact with existing medicines prescribed for other conditions.

Summary

We tend to think of depression as a condition of the mind. A complaint that is characterized by mental anguish, severely lowered mood, and isolation. These are indeed chief characteristics, but we also know from reading Chapter 1 that depression manifests as a range of varied physical symptoms. In this chapter, we have seen how this can act as a major confound when clinicians attempt to make a positive diagnosis of depression. They have to decide initially whether they are facing a physical health problem or a mental health one. We have also seen here that the fact that depression is associated with somatic complaints makes the issue of diagnosing a comorbid physical condition more difficult. Do the symptoms reflect various manifestations of depression, or is there another hidden physical condition alongside the depression? We know now that depression operates on several levels. It can increase the likelihood of someone developing a chronic health condition. It can certainly influence how well a person responds to treatment or surgery for a medical condition. We also know that being diagnosed with a medical complaint can itself lead to depression. It is a complex picture. Depression then is a major concern not just in terms of escalating mental torment, with the ever-present spectre of suicide in many cases, but in terms of physical health as well.

References

1 Dunn T, Jarrett RB. Psychosocial functioning. In: Ingram RE, editor. The international encyclopedia of depression. New York; London: Springer; 2009.
2 Hirschfeld RM, Montgomery SA, Keller MB, Kasper S, Schatzberg AF, Moller HJ, et al. Social functioning in depression: A review. J Clin Psychiatry. 2000;61(4):268–275.
3 Mintz J, Mintz LI, Arruda MJ, Hwang SS. Treatments of depression and the functional capacity to work. Arch Gen Psychiatry. 1992;49(10):761–768.
4 Ara EM, Talepasand S, Rezaei AM. A structural model of depression based on interpersonal relationships: The mediating role of coping strategies and loneliness. Arch Neuropsychiat. 2017;54(2):125.
5 Relate. Relationships and depression: Relate; 2019. Available from: www.relate.org.uk/relationship-help/help-relationships/mental-health/relationships-and-depression.
6 Bothwell S, Weissman MM. Social impairments four years after an acute depressive episode. Am J Orthopsychiatry. 1977;47(2):231.
7 Cocker F, Nicholson JM, Graves N, Oldenburg B, Palmer AJ, Martin A, et al. Depression in working adults: Comparing the costs and health outcomes of working when ill. PLoS One. 2014;9(9):e105430.

8   Mintz J, Mintz LI, Arruda MJ, Hwang SS. Treatments of depression and the functional capacity to work. Arch Gen Psychiatry. 1992;49(10):761–768.

9   Szeto AC, Dobson KS. Reducing the stigma of mental disorders at work: A review of current workplace anti-stigma intervention programs. Appl Prev Psychol. 2010; 14(1–4):41–56.

10 Stigma and discrimination: Mental Health Foundation; 2018. Available from: www. mentalhealth.org.uk/a-to-z/s/stigma-and-discrimination.

11 Dunn BD. Helping depressed clients reconnect to positive emotion experience: Current insights and future directions. Clin Psychol Psychother. 2012;19(4):326–340.

12 National Collaborating Centre for Mental Health (UK). Depression in Adults with a Chronic Physical Health Problem: Treatment and Management. Leicester (UK): British Psychological Society (UK); 2010.

13 National Institute for Health and Care Excellence. Depression in adults with a chronic physical health problem: Recognition and management; 2009. Available from: www. nice.org.uk/guidance/cg91.

14 Wasserman D. Depression. 2nd ed. Oxford: Oxford University Press; 2011.

15 Amanda Dew M, Cyranowski JM, Pilkonis PA. Medical conditions and depression. In: Ingram RE, editor. The international encyclopedia of depression. New York; London: Springer Publishing Company; 2009.

16 Dew MA, Switzer GE, Myaskovsky L, DiMartini AF, Tovt-Korshynska MI. Rating scales for mood disorders. In: Stein DJ, Kupfer DJ, Schatzberg AF, editors. The American Psychiatric Publishing textbook of mood disorders. Washington, DC: American Psychiatric Publishing; 2007, pp. 69–97.

17 Norwood R. Prevalence and impact of depression in chronic obstructive pulmonary disease patients. Curr Opin Pulm Med. 2006;12(2):113–117.

18 Buysse DJ. Insomnia, depression and aging. Assessing sleep and mood interactions in older adults. Geriatrics. 2004;59(2):47–51; quiz 2.

19 Talbot F, Nouwen A. A review of the relationship between depression and diabetes in adults: Is there a link? Diabetes Care. 2000;23(10):1556–1562.

20 Dew MA. Psychiatric disorder in the context of physical illness. In: Dohrenwend BP, editor. Adversity, stress, and psychopathology. Oxford: Oxford University Press; 1998, pp. 177–218.

21 Capuron L, Neurauter G, Musselman DL, Lawson DH, Nemeroff CB, Fuchs D, et al. Interferon-alpha-induced changes in tryptophan metabolism: Relationship to depression and paroxetine treatment. Biol Psychiatry. 2003;54(9):906–914.

22 Eaton WW, Fogel J, Armenian HK. The consequences of psychopathology in the Baltimore Epidemiologic Catchment Area follow-up. In: American Psychological Association, editor. Medical and psychiatric comorbidity over the course of life. Washington, DC; American Psychiatric Publishing; 2007, pp. 21–36.

23 DiMatteo MR, Lepper HS, Croghan TW. Depression is a risk factor for noncompliance with medical treatment: Meta-analysis of the effects of anxiety and depression on patient adherence. Arch Intern Med. 2000;160(14):2101–2107.

24 Stringer G. Musculoskeletal diseases. In: Hansard, editor. UK Parliament; 2011. Available from: https://hansard.parliament.uk/Commons/2011-07-04/debates/11070442000002/MusculoskeletalDiseases.

25 NHS England. Musculoskeletal conditions. NHS England; 2019. Available from: www.england.nhs.uk/ourwork/clinical-policy/ltc/our-work-on-long-term-conditions/musculoskeletal/.

26 International Labour Office. Committee of Experts on the Application of Conventions. ILO standards on occupational safety and health: Promoting a safe and healthy working environment. Geneva: International Labour Office; 2009.

27 Katon WJ. Epidemiology and treatment of depression in patients with chronic medical illness. Dialogues Clin Neurosci. 2011;13(1):7–23.

28 Lépine JP, Briley M. The epidemiology of pain in depression. Hum Psychopharmacol. 2004;19 Suppl 1:S3–S7.

29 Poleshuck EL, Bair MJ, Kroenke K, Damush TM, Tu W, Wu J, et al. Psychosocial stress and anxiety in musculoskeletal pain patients with and without depression. Gen Hosp Psychiatry. 2009;31(2):116–122.

30 Gavard JA, Lustman PJ, Clouse RE. Prevalence of depression in adults with diabetes. An epidemiological evaluation. Diabetes Care. 1993;16(8):1167–1178.

31 Lustman PJ, Griffith LS, Clouse RE. Depression in adults with diabetes. Results of 5-yr follow-up study. Diabetes Care. 1988;11(8):605–612.

32 Jacobson AM. Depression and diabetes. Diabetes Care. 1993;16(12):1621–1623.

33 Bernbaum M, Albert SG, Duckro PN. Psychosocial profiles in patients with visual impairment due to diabetic retinopathy. Diabetes Care. 1988;11(7):551–557.

34 Hother-Nielsen O, Beck-Nielsen H. Basal glucose metabolism in type 2 diabetes. A critical review. Diabet Metab. 1991;17(1 Pt 2):136–145.

35 Coresh J, Byrd-Holt D, Astor BC, Briggs JP, Eggers PW, Lacher DA, et al. Chronic kidney disease awareness, prevalence, and trends among U.S. adults, 1999 to 2000. J Am Soc Nephrol. 2005;16(1):180–188.

36 Tong A, Sainsbury P, Chadban S, Walker RG, Harris DC, Carter SM, et al. Patients' experiences and perspectives of living with CKD. Am J Kidney Dis. 2009;53(4):689–700.

37 Palmer S, Vecchio M, Craig JC, Tonelli M, Johnson DW, Nicolucci A, et al. Prevalence of depression in chronic kidney disease: Systematic review and meta-analysis of observational studies. Kidney Int. 2013;84(1):179–191.

38 Fergusson DM, Lynskey MT, Horwood LJ. Comorbidity between depressive disorders and nicotine dependence in a cohort of 16-year-olds. Arch Gen Psychiatry. 1996;53(11):1043–1047.

39 Campbell JJ, Coffey CE. Neuropsychiatric significance of subcortical hyperintensity. J Neuropsychiatry Clin Neurosci. 2001;13(2):261–288.

40 Frasure-Smith N, Lespérance F, Talajic M. Depression following myocardial infarction: Impact on 6-month survival. JAMA. 1993;270(15):1819–1825.

41 Roose SP, Dalack GW, Woodring S. Death, depression, and heart disease. J Clin Psychiatry. 1991;52(Suppl):34–39.

42 Robinson RG, Starkstein SE. Current research in affective disorders following stroke. J Neuropsychiatry Clin Neurosci. 1990;2(1):1–14.

43 Verhey FRJ, Honig A. Depression in the elderly. In: Maes M, Honig A, van Praag H, editors. Depression: Neurobiological psychopathological and therapeutic advances; Chichester: Wiley; 1997.

44 Yusuf S, Hawken S, Ôunpuu S, Dans T, Avezum A, Lanas F, et al. Effect of potentially modifiable risk factors associated with myocardial infarction in 52 countries (the INTERHEART study): Case-control study. Lancet. 2004;364(9438):937–952.

45 Rosengren A, Hawken S, Ôunpuu S, Sliwa K, Zubaid M, Almahmeed WA, et al. Association of psychosocial risk factors with risk of acute myocardial infarction in 11 119 cases and 13 648 controls from 52 countries (the INTERHEART study): Case-control study. Lancet. 2004;364(9438):953–962.

46 Smith TW, Ruiz JM. Psychosocial influences on the development and course of coronary heart disease: Current status and implications for research and practice. J Consult Clin Psychol. 2002;70(3):548.

47 Raynor DA, Pogue-Geile MF, Kamarck TW, McCaffery JM, Manuck SB. Covariation of psychosocial characteristics associated with cardiovascular disease: Genetic and environmental influences. Psychosom Med. 2002;64(2):191–203.

48 Ferketich AK, Schwartzbaum JA, Frid DJ, Moeschberger ML. Depression as an antecedent to heart disease among women and men in the NHANES I study. Arch Intern Med. 2000;160(9):1261–1268.

49 Pitman A, Suleman S, Hyde N, Hodgkiss A. Depression and anxiety in patients with cancer. BMJ. 2018;361:k1415.

50 Christopher G. The psychology of ageing: From mind to society. Basingstoke, Hampshire: Palgrave Macmillan; 2014.

51 Rickards H. Depression in neurological disorders: Parkinson's disease, multiple sclerosis, and stroke. J Neurol Neurosurg Psychiatry. 2005;76(Suppl 1):i48–i52.

52 Leonard BE. Inflammation, depression and dementia: Are they connected? Neurochem Res. 2007;32(10):1749–1756.

53 Mental Health Foundation. Smoking and mental health. Mental Health Foundation; 2019. Available from: www.mentalhealth.org.uk/a-to-z/s/smoking-and-mental-health.

54 Hasin D, Liu X, Nunes E, McCloud S, Samet S, Endicott J. Effects of major depression on remission and relapse of substance dependence. Arch Gen Psychiatry. 2002; 59(4):375–380.

55 Gilman SE, Abraham HD. A longitudinal study of the order of onset of alcohol dependence and major depression. Drug Alcohol Depend. 2001;63(3):277–286.

56 Bulik CM. Anxiety, depression and eating disorders. In: Fairburn CG, Brownell KD, editors. Eating disorders and obesity: A comprehensive handbook. New York; London: Guilford Press; 2002. pp. 193–198.

57 NHS Website. Do iPads and electric lights disturb sleep? NHS; 2013. Available from: www.nhs.uk/news/lifestyle-and-exercise/do-ipads-and-electric-lights-disturb-sleep/.

58 National Sleep Foundation. Why do we need sleep? National Sleep Foundation; 2019. Available from: www.sleepfoundation.org/articles/why-do-we-need-sleep.

59 Wichniak A, Wierzbicka A, Wałęcka M, Jernajczyk W. Effects of Antidepressants on Sleep. Curr Psychiatry Rep. 2017;19(9):63.

60 Stanchina ML, Abu-Hijleh M, Chaudhry BK, Carlisle CC, Millman RP. The influence of white noise on sleep in subjects exposed to ICU noise. Sleep Med. 2005;6(5):423–428.

61 National Sleep Foundation. What is White noise?. National Sleep Foundation; 2019. Available from: www.sleepfoundation.org/bedroom-environment/hear/what-white-noise.

62 The National Sleep Foundation. Is it ok to sleep in on Wee. The National Sleep Foundation. Available from: www.sleep.org/articles/ok-to-sleep-in-on-weekends/.

63 Geddes L. Late nights and lie-ins at the weekend are bad for your health. New Sci. 2017;06 June. Available from: https://www.newscientist.com/article/2133761-late-nights-and-lie-ins-at-the-weekend-are-bad-for-your-health/.

64 Gallagher D, Rose J, Rivera P, Lovett S, Thompson LW. Prevalence of depression in family caregivers. Gerontologist. 1989;29(4):449–456.

Chapter 6

Depression across the lifespan

Age of onset

Although controversial until the last 40 or so years, the concept that children can experience the key symptoms of depression is reasonably established (1). That said, prevalence is low until adolescence, where rates hit adult levels, especially girls (2). Although it might be argued that depression exists in younger age groups, there is undoubtedly debate whether child-onset and adult-onset depression are the same condition. Genetic evidence indicates that, of those who develop depression as children, there is a higher likelihood their relatives will also develop depression (3). Also, those who experience depression during childhood are more likely to experience depression in adulthood (4). However, when looking at the effectiveness of drug therapy, specifically tricyclics, whereas adults respond well, children fail to reap any benefit (5).

When attempting to consider the age at which people are most likely to develop depression, estimates vary. One study suggested that if one were to consider all those diagnosed with depression, roughly one half would have experienced onset around the age of 30, with a significant proportion of this group encountering symptoms at 18 (6). The main issue here is the accuracy of retrospective accounts. It is uncertain how well people can reflect back and recall when they started to experience depression. When looking at data from a longitudinal study, specifically the first 32 years of life, half of the women and around a third of the men in the sample had experienced at least one episode of depression (7).

Comorbidity with anxiety is linked to early onset of depression, as is oppositional disorder for girls, a condition linked to impulse control. Depression early on increases the chances of developing other mental health disorders at an early age, with generalized anxiety disorder and attention-deficit hyperactivity disorder being clear examples where this happens (8).

The way depression manifests in different age groups varies. There is a tendency for a predominance of behavioural symptoms in children and young adults. In contrast, older adults tend to report bodily sensations rather than lowered mood (9).

DOI:10.4324/9781315688879-6

Children and young adults

Psychopathology in children is higher among those raised by a parent with depression (10). The argument here is that the mother (the principal caregiver in many studies) is less responsive and less active and does not share the same quality of interactions with their child as non-depressed caregivers (11, 12). This leads to attachment issues and concomitant emotion dysregulation (13, 14). Other factors that increase the risk of a child developing depression is disharmony within the family unit, being the recipient of bullying behaviour, abuse, and familial history of mental health problems (15). It can also be tied to a specific event, such as a break-up in the family, a bereavement, or a medical condition.

Regarding the treatment guidelines published by NICE, children refer to ages 5–11, young people 12–18. This section is based on the guidance document produced by NICE (16). I strongly recommend you read this document in depth for further details.

Because depression can manifest in different ways in different people, when prompted to assess for depression in children or young people, their behaviour in other contexts needs to be considered. For example, an assessment of impairment in function should take into consideration school, relationships with their peers, and also how they are functioning within the family unit. Only by doing so will the clinician garner a clearer understanding of the underlying problem.

When considering care, there is the issue of consent. Family members or carers are provided with the appropriate information to help those under 16 make the necessary decisions.

There are several mechanisms to support the needs of those with mental health problems at an early age. There are trained staff at all levels such that they are ideally placed to detect signs of depression early on. These include schools and primary care. As is the case with adult mental health, the picture is often complex. Key risk factors for this age group include disharmony within the family setting, bullying at school, living in institutional care, and drug and/or alcohol use, among others (16). It might simply be the case that the depression results from a single undesirable event, such as a recent bereavement. Assessing the child or young person for risk of self-harm or the presence of suicidal ideation is very important.

If depression is diagnosed, a referral is made to Child and Adolescent Mental Health Services (CAMHS). CAMHS is a service offered to children and young people who experience emotional and behavioural difficulties. CAMHS work with other healthcare and social care professionals in various settings to help support the individual and ensure the necessary referrals are being made. There are multiple levels of care set out for this age group. Tier 1 refers to support within a primary care setting and includes GPs and social workers, among others. Tiers 2 through 4 involve CAMHS. Tier 2 requires input from clinical psychologists, educational psychologists, community nurses, and so on. At Tier 3, more specialist care is offered as cases considered here are more complex. For example, there is a role for occupational therapists, speech and language therapists, and a host of other services to address the persistent nature of the symptoms. Finally, Tier 4 offers inpatient care (tertiary care) and a range of day care units and outpatient services.

In cases of mild depression, antidepressants should not be the first option considered for this section of the population. Looking after the individual occurs within the primary care setting (Tier 1). Similarly, medication should not be the first considered option when diagnosed with moderate-to-severe depression (16). Instead, individual CBT, interpersonal therapy, family therapy, or psychodynamic therapy should be preferred. For these cases, individuals are managed within CAMHS Tier 2 or 3.

In some cases, medication in conjunction with talking therapy might be considered, but not the first option. Where medication is prescribed to children or young people, there needs to be strict monitoring to ensure there are no adverse events. Tier 3 or 4 is for individuals who are unresponsive to treatment or experiencing psychotic symptoms alongside the depression. Some of these cases may require inpatient care.

In terms of interventions for mild depression, group CBT, non-directive supportive therapy, or guided self-help would be offered for up to three months. If there is no perceivable response after this period, they would be referred to CAMHS (Tier 2 or 3). Where the depression is more severe, it is more appropriate to enrol the child or young person on a programme of individual CBT, interpersonal therapy, family therapy, or psychotherapy. Medication, specifically fluoxetine, might be considered if there is no response to the treatment. There is no objective evidence of effectiveness in using fluoxetine in children. However, there is supportive evidence for its efficacy in young people (16). If fluoxetine appears not to be working, sertraline or citalopram are alternatives. Other forms of antidepressants are not appropriate to be used for this age group. As is the case with adults, an atypical antipsychotic should be prescribed to augment the antidepressant. These are less likely to lead to the types of side effects associated with first-generation antipsychotics. However, there are still problems (17).

Where there is a considerable risk of self-harm or suicide, inpatient care is the best option. Hospital admission might also be considered in situations where intensive assessment or treatment is required and might not be available elsewhere. ECT might be considered if the depression is severe enough and is unresponsive to other forms of intervention. ECT will also be considered if the risk of suicide is extremely high. However, ECT is not recommended for children below the age of 12.

When considering treatment for children and young people, one should also consider the mental health of the parent or carer. It might be the case that there is an underlying psychiatric problem that needs addressing as well.

What can be done?

There is a growing initiative to incorporate prevention programmes in a range of settings, including schools. These programmes focus on instilling more adaptive ways of thinking about issues, emphasizing positive psychology. It might also be the case that targeting the parent(s) of children who have behavioural problems may help both parent and child (18).

Undergraduates

Before we turn our attention to older adults, let us first focus on young adults as they enter university. I am a senior lecturer, and I know how students are increasingly finding the transition into higher education a challenge, in terms of not only moving up an academic notch but also considering what faces them at the end of the degree.

It is evident that anxiety and depression plague seemingly increasing numbers of students during their time at university. There have been various attempts to provide context for this worrying trend, with most coming to the same conclusion that students feel under ever-mounting pressure both financially and academically (19). Levels of depression appear highest in the final year at university. This is likely linked to fears about entering an increasingly competitive job market. This is, again, an important transition point for students.

Increasing numbers of students with a variety of disabilities are attending university each year. The Higher Education Statistics Agency[1] reports a sharp rise in the number of undergraduate students declaring a disability from 194,985 in 2013–2014 to 250,170 in 2017–2018. HESA data also suggests approximately 50 per cent of these students reported having a neurodevelopmental disorder (NDD). These disorders are lifelong and severely affect daily living. NDDs are designated mental health conditions in the Diagnostic and Statistical Manual for Mental Disorders (DSM-5; 20). They include attention-deficit hyperactivity disorder (inattentiveness and impulsiveness), autism spectrum disorder (problems with social functioning), developmental coordination disorder (problems with motor skills), and dyslexia (difficulties with reading). These are far more complex than the very brief descriptions would lead you to believe. In fact, to some extent, this mirrors the public perception of these conditions. Some are more familiar than others, but, as with many conditions, people generally underestimate the level of impairment experienced by people with these diagnoses. Dyslexia is not just about needing longer to read something—the general misconception—but, instead, it affects all areas of a person's life. To further complicate the issue, NDDs often overlap with each other (21). Interestingly, where overlap occurred, deficits further compound difficulties faced.

In many cases, students arrive having been diagnosed at an earlier point in their lives. However, many do not receive a diagnosis until they enter higher education, and more still may not receive a diagnosis. Those with no formal diagnosis still report experiencing difficulties with their academic studies. However, without a diagnosis, these students will not have access to support services. They will not be offered the necessary adjustments awarded to other students in a similar situation.

Children with NDDs report higher levels of anxiety and depression compared to typically developing peers (22). In a study I conducted with a colleague, when considering developmental coordination disorder (DCD), these increased levels of anxiety and depression continue into adulthood (23).

Alongside levels of depression, NDDs are associated with problems with activities requiring planning and organization, which I have already referred to in previous chapters as executive functions. Such skills are vital to new students arriving at university who need to quickly adapt to a new environment where the scaffolding and support structures previously provided by parents and schools are reduced. Studies have identified an association between NDD and executive function (EF) skills (24). The transition to more independent learning relies on the student's ability to organize and work autonomously to overcome new challenges. Individuals with NDD may not have fully developed the EF skills needed to cope with this change. For this reason, many individuals with NDD seek support for the first time when they arrive at university (25). This potential tipping point may result in a previously seemingly competent student dropping out of university.

It was thought that NDDs are more prevalent in males than in females at approximately 3:1. However, in recent online surveys of adults with DCD and ADHD (23), twice as many females responded to the study than males. Of more importance is that in one of our previous studies, significantly more females reported not having a formal diagnosis of NDD but were having difficulties with their studies (26). Females with NDD are likely to be missed in the formal diagnostic pathway.

What can be done?

There are many ways universities are now trying to help their students throughout their degree. One of the main buzzwords is resilience, and in particular, resilience training. Resilience means different things to different people, but it is primarily associated either with an ability to adapt to stress positively (27) or it refers to a person's capacity to maintain functioning during a period of stress (28). People often talk about bouncing back following a stressful or traumatic event (29). A systematic review published in 2017 showed certain types of resilience training to be effective, especially those involving CBT or mindfulness meditation (30). There is no consistency in terms of the content and delivery of these training sessions, which makes comparison difficult, to say the least.

Now that we have looked at depression in children, adolescents, and young adults, we shall skip to later in life, the period of older adulthood, to see how depression impacts there and identify some of the main changes for management and treatment for this age group.

Older adults

Prevalence

Depression in older adults is a major problem that is mostly unreported or under-diagnosed in all too many cases (31). There are several explanations for this. One major one is that older adults tend not to report symptoms in a way that the GP immediately identifies them as indicators of depression, focusing instead on re-laying somatic symptoms. One would hope this reticence to talk about emotional problems will eventually diminish with each successive generation of older adults. In other cases, symptoms experienced are explained away by age itself; in other words, the feelings merely indicate a person's advanced years. The context within which depression occurs in older adults also makes it difficult for a clinician to make accurate diagnoses, such that depression may occur alongside other physi-cal or mental health conditions. This is something we looked at in some detail in Chapter 5. In many instances, the symptoms of depression and the symptoms of comorbid medical or psychological conditions overlap.

Overall, depression among older adults is underdiagnosed, as we have seen, and this is mainly the case with men. This is chiefly due to a focus away from reporting psychological symptoms.

Issues with diagnosis

Several medical conditions can result in depression. These include infections, cardiovascular disease, hypothyroidism, vitamin (B-12) deficiency, and neu-rological disorders. As with all age groups, drug or alcohol misuse can result in depression. Such behaviour also plays a hand in maintaining the lowered mood. Medication can also be a factor here, with drug interactions leading to unintended effects on a person's functioning.

The presence of psychotic symptoms is more likely in cases of depression that develop later in life, particularly delusions. Delusions may be around persecution, but they are often focused on the belief that the person is suffering from an incur-able medical condition. With such severe forms of depression, the risk of suicide is exceptionally high.

Prevalent symptoms

We have seen that many things act to influence how a person experiences depression. As a result, how their depression manifests and appears to others. Health-related problems are likely to be prominent the older we get, so it is common for physi-cal complaints to be the prevalent depressive symptomatology. In such cases, older adults with depression will show exhaustion, aches, and pains in various joints, head-aches, various complaints of the cardiovascular system, and others. In many cases, older adults with depression will rapidly lose weight. Combined, this makes early, accurate diagnosis extremely difficult. Because some of these potential symptoms of depression are subtle, the following question is often mooted: Are these benign manifestations of older age or are they early signs of a deepening depression?

Sleep problems become more apparent with increasing age. It is a myth that, as we age, we require less sleep. Prolonged sleep deprivation at any age is deleterious to physical and mental health. Sleep becomes gradually disturbed as we age, mainly due to the need to make increasing numbers of loo visits. Insomnia is a symptom of depression. There is also the tendency for people to sleep more and more during the day. Daytime sleepiness may itself be a sign that some underlying health problem is making someone feel like this. Aside from being a symptom of depression, excessive sleepiness during the day may suggest obstructive sleep apnoea. In this condition, the walls of the throat narrow and a person's breathing is interrupted multiple times throughout the night. Many of us find solace in afternoon naps. Still, there is evidence to show that sleeping too long during the day can adversely affect a person's health (32), although why this might be the case is not yet certain.

Environment

A person's environment plays a big part here. Rates of depression are a lot higher when an older adult is either in a hospital or staying in a nursing home when compared to living in their own house (31).

Distinct profile

Evidence suggests that depression that develops later in life is relatively distinct from depression when a person is younger. Based purely on the fact that people who develop depression early in life live longer with the condition, the degree of cognitive and structural change is more considerable. The hippocampus shrinks over time in those with depression, which is mainly due to prolonged, elevated cortisol levels, a condition called hypercortisolemia. Some of the cognitive deficits associated with depression, such as those linked to verbal memory, are potentially explained by these abnormalities in cortisol levels. There are health implications associated with lifelong depression, including, among other things, an increased risk of heart disease (31).

Because depression does not occur until later in life, it is clear that there is less of a familial link to explain late-onset depression. Instead, likely explanations for depression in this age group include neurological or cerebrovascular changes. Cognitive impairment is also higher in this group. Structurally, the brains of those with late-onset depression evidence enlarged ventricles—cavities in the brain filled with cerebrovascular fluid—and white matter hyperintensities—lesions in the brain. Late-onset depression is also more impervious to treatment and follows a more rapid trajectory of decline (31).

There are high rates of depression in those also diagnosed with dementia. In some cases, a rise in depression precedes the decline in cognitive functioning associated with dementia.

Neurotransmitters

Importantly, levels of neurotransmitters such as serotonin and noradrenaline, intimately entwined in cognition and emotion, are significantly reduced in older adults.

On the other hand, monoamine oxidase, an enzyme that metabolizes serotonin and noradrenaline and decreases their availability, increases with age. The resultant effect nonetheless is an overall reduction in levels of these critical monoamines.

Antidepressants for older adults

Although it is the focus of Chapter 8 to examine various drug treatment options for depression, including that of antidepressant medication, it is imperative here in this chapter to consider some of the age-related factors that need to be considered when prescribing such medicines for older adults. In Chapter 5, we also looked at the impact of health conditions on the use of antidepressants.

Age should be taken into consideration when deciding on the dose to be prescribed. This is because there are age-related changes in pharmacokinetics and pharmacodynamics (33). Also, physical health conditions and other medications will affect how the antidepressant works (34). Add the likelihood of sensory impairment and various other factors into the mix, the picture becomes increasingly complicated. Because of this, in all cases, the individual should undergo careful monitoring to ensure they are not experiencing any adverse effects.

Psychosocial factors

Other important factors linked to depression in older adults include a lack of social support, feeling isolated and lonely, and lower education levels. It is perhaps inevitable to associate ageing with the loss of friends and family. Bereavement is clearly linked to depression. In many cases, the natural course of loss means that, with sufficient time, a person once more regains a sense of balance, a new outlook, albeit one tempered by the grief experienced. However, for some, there is no natural resolution. In such cases, depression continues long after the event.

Care providers

Depression among caregivers is high. This is perhaps not surprising. It is exceptionally high in those who care for someone with dementia. In many cases, the presence of depression presages a decline in a person's general health as well (31).

Suicide

Someone who experiences severe depression clearly presents a higher suicide risk. Previous attempts at suicide boost this risk even higher. For older adults, a decline in health or the experience of a significant loss most commonly triggers suicidal thoughts. The presence of suicidal ideation renders depression even more difficult to treat (35).

Comorbid medical conditions

Quite understandably, depression often occurs in those who have comorbid medical conditions. Depression is often the reaction to unsettling news, especially in instances linked intrinsically to a person's sense of self. Such situations may best be described as ego-threatening. In terms of the long-term consequences of depression and the disruptions of mood and functioning, prognoses of medical conditions are also affected. As a case in point, patients with depression who experience a myocardial infarction have a higher mortality rate (31). Depression causes numerous complications that contribute to this statistic, such as cortisol hyperactivity and reductions in the levels of noradrenaline and dopamine. There is also a lower level of compliance in this group. If a person is depressed, they will be less likely to adhere to instructions to increase their daily exercise level, eat more healthily, and so on.

Recurrent depression

Experiencing depression at any point in one's life makes it increasingly likely that it will not be an isolated incident. More often than not, such episodes will recur with varying frequency throughout a person's life. Rates of this happening increase with age, and the actual duration of the depressive episode also increases. As we have already seen, comorbidities make it more likely that depression will reappear (36).

It is important to note that several factors improve outcomes, including experience of and recovery from depression in the past, being female, and being extroverted (31).

Deciding upon appropriate treatment

Just as it is crucial to assess a range of things before arriving at a diagnosis, the same is true when determining the most appropriate treatment. Foremost is an assessment of the presenting symptoms, including their severity. In particular, the clinician is required to accurately assess whether the patient poses a suicide risk. Coexisting medical complaints should also be considered. In many cases, medication will be prescribed. That being the case, it is critical to list all medications the patient is taking, both prescribed and over-the-counter. For older adults, this is especially important because many will be taking a range of drugs, a situation referred to as polypharmacy (33). Also, a person's level of functioning should be evaluated, both physical and mental.

Use of antidepressant medication

A large majority of patients prescribed an antidepressant respond well. This does not seem to be affected by age. Antidepressant medication has been around for a long time now. Since the initial breakthroughs of the 1950s, there has been a profusion of drugs available to treat depression in its many forms, each focused on different neurotransmitter systems to produce the desired effect. Any drug therapy aims to have a targeted impact with minimal side effects. In the treatment of conditions such as depression, the success of this can vary considerably from one patient to the next.

The primary antidepressants prescribed to older adults include selective serotonin reuptake inhibitors (SSRIs), tricyclic antidepressants, and monoamine oxidase inhibitors (MAOIs).

With age, how our bodies deal with drugs changes. Because of this, a standard adult dose may result in higher drug concentrations in older adults than would be expected in adults. This is because of variation in the pharmacokinetic differences between individuals (37). In other words, there are age-related differences in terms of the time taken for a medication to enter a person's bloodstream (absorption), its dispersal (distribution), the length of time that it is active (metabolism), and how efficiently it is removed from the body after use (excretion). The density of available receptors changes with age, affecting how much of a drug is needed for it to be effective (pharmacodynamics).

Careful monitoring of prescriptions in older adults is essential for many reasons. A chief reason is that we do not know how to predict how the body will respond to the various medications in this age group. This is because drug trials tend to exclude anyone with comorbid complaints. In this sense, clinical trials focus on relatively pure cases of particular diseases or disorders and evaluate the efficacy of drugs in a relatively isolated way. This may represent a few lucky individuals, but in most cases, conditions rarely occur on their own. Most will have one or more comorbid medical or psychological conditions. This will inevitably mean they have prescribed medication for this complaint as well. Therefore, relatively pure drug trials can tell us little about how a drug will work in this tainted environment (31).

Adverse effects

As we have seen, several factors interfere with the predicted course of a drug in older adults. Some of these factors are associated with age-related physiological changes; others result from concomitant health and mental health issues. The resultant effect here is that older adults are even more prone to experiencing a range of adverse effects from taking medications.

Given there is an increased risk of high doses of drugs accumulating in the body, which raises concerns about toxicity, clinicians face a real challenge to ensure that this is accounted for while at the same time ensuring the person is receiving sufficient doses for the drug to have the desired effect. Caution can lead to under-medicating patients. Standard procedures are in place to help achieve this delicate balance. A tried-and-tested technique is to commence individuals on relatively low doses and gradually increase the amount until the desired level is attained. Because of this, it often takes several weeks to reach a clinically relevant dose. During this period, indications that the person is not suited to the current medication choice may manifest. In such cases, the clinician will then switch to another form or class of drug (38).

As mentioned previously, the pharmaceutical industry aims to provide clinically effective drugs that are targeted and have minimal side effects. Early psychiatric drugs were rather brutal in their approach. They caused problems that were, in many cases, comparable to, if not worse than, the original complaint. In the case of antidepressants, there is a need to be mindful of the real risk that someone will attempt to overdose on them. Early tricyclic and monoamine oxidase inhibitor (MAOI) antidepressants were lethal in high doses.

More recent classes have a much safer toxicity profile, although by no means entirely safe in high doses. In this sense, selective serotonin reuptake inhibitors (SSRIs) are usually the first port of call to treat depression in older adults. Given the age group, drugs should also be selected based on which neurotransmitter systems they target. Some forms of antidepressants reduce levels of acetylcholine. Acetylcholine is heavily implicated in a range of cognitive operations, as well as levels of alertness (39). Because of this, lowered levels of acetylcholine would produce deficits that would negatively impact a person's quality of life. It might also create a situation where these deficits might lead to concern that something more insidious is at play. Drugs such as citalopram and sertraline have less of an impact on levels of acetylcholine and lead to fewer complications with other medications.

Even though toxicity is no longer such a significant issue at recommended doses, antidepressants are still associated with a range of uncomfortable side effects. For many, nausea is a real issue. Sleep is also altered such that either people experience insomnia or they feel drowsy. Some drugs cause the person to feel agitated.

Tricyclic antidepressant tends not to be used except in cases of depression that is treatment-resistant, referred to as refractory depression. This class of medication is contraindicated in those with cardiovascular disease and/or cognitive impairment because they can cause an increase or irregularity in heart rate, confusion, and disorientation. The upshot of this is that patients tend to stop taking their medication (40).

The main concern with monoamine oxidase inhibitors (MAOIs) is monoamine oxidase inhibitors' interactions with different foodstuffs, specifically tyramine, a catecholamine-releasing agent that helps regulate blood pressure. By nature, MAOIs block the enzyme monoamine oxidase, usually breaking down any excess tyramine in the system. If a person's diet is not controlled, patients experience severe spikes in blood pressure that require immediate intervention. This, therefore, makes this class of drug potentially problematic when used with older adults.

Before moving on, there is a separate but related issue here. We know that physical illness is prominent among older adults. We also know that depression may occur due to specific combinations of medications or from their eventual withdrawal (41). Polypharmacy is increasingly common the older we become. It has been referred to several times in this chapter. Because of this, prescribing clinicians must be aware of the range of medications the person is taking. Sometimes it is the responsibility of the spouse or relatives to ensure the doctor has an accurate overview of the prescribed drugs and a comprehensive list of all the over-the-counter remedies a person is taking. This will help minimize potential drug interactions when a new combination of medications is prescribed.

Very much linked to this is the need to be vigilant of where medicines are kept. Most people, on achieving a certain age, find themselves in need of a medicine cupboard. Given the variety of prescriptions and combinations over the years, it is likely that the store of medications will contain items that are no longer prescribed. Once a drug is no longer on the current prescription list, it is wise to dispose of it appropriately. This will reduce the likelihood that the person will take a medicine no longer required and no longer accounted for in terms of potential drug interactions (41).

Maintenance therapy

In a previous section, we discussed how older adults are particularly prone to future episodes of depression. Because this increases with age, one way to minimize this from happening is to maintain prescriptions for antidepressant medication indefinitely (42). It is unclear whether antidepressants help prevent recurrent depression or whether drugs need to be combined with a psychological intervention (31).

Barriers to treatment

Depression in older adults tends to go unrecognized in many cases (43). The type of symptom reported tends to concern a lack of energy and bodily sensations. It is generally assumed that these are merely indicative of the normal ageing process. Any connection with a potential diagnosis is left unconsidered in many cases (44). Linked to this is the finding that many older adults who experience depression do not receive the appropriate treatment (45). This has significant cost implications, not only for the individual concerned but also for society in general. The care and management of depression demand a lot of resources from healthcare services. There is also an increased risk of hospitalization and a higher likelihood of serious injury or suicide (46, 47).

Summary

Whereas most of this book focuses on depression in adulthood, this chapter looks at the two extremes of the age spectrum; children and older adults. We have seen that depression in both instances tends to manifest quite differently. There are real ethical issues around prescribing medication to children, such as those involved with informed consent. There is a growing move towards devising and implementing programmes to prevent or at least reduce depression in this vulnerable age group. This is most obviously evidenced through the various resilience programmes in operation up and down the land. When looking at older adults, one of the major concerns was with diagnosis. Making an accurate diagnosis of depression in older adults is hugely challenging. Here too, there are issues with the prescribing of antidepressant medication. Some of the main concerns here reflect potential interactions with other prescribed and non-prescribed or over-the-counter medicines. This is particularly problematic when one considers comorbid conditions that are also being treated (see Chapter 5 for an in-depth discussion). Some of the material involving treatment discussed in this section will be developed further in Chapter 8, focusing on biological interventions.

Note

1 www.HESA.ac.uk

References

1 Costello E. Age of onset of depression. In: Ingram RE, editor. The international encyclopedia of depression. New York; London: Springer; 2009.
2 Angold A, Worthman CM, Costello E. Puberty and depression. In: Hayward C, editor. Gender differences at puberty. Cambridge: Cambridge University Press; 2003, pp. 137–164.
3 Warner V, Weissman MM, Mufson L, Wickramaratne PJ. Grandparents, parents, and grandchildren at high risk for depression: A three-generation study. J Am Acad Child Adolesc Psychiatry. 1999;38(3):289–296.
4 Reinherz HZ, Paradis AD, Giaconia RM, Stashwick CK, Fitzmaurice G. Childhood and adolescent predictors of major depression in the transition to adulthood. Am J Psychiatry. 2003;160(12):2141–2147.
5 Geller B, Reising D, Leonard HL, Riddle MA, Walsh BT. Critical review of tricyclic antidepressant use in children and adolescents. J Am Acad Child Adolesc Psychiatry. 1999;38(5):513–516.
6 Kessler RC, Berglund P, Demler O, Jin R, Merikangas KR, Walters EE. Lifetime prevalence and age-of-onset distributions of DSM-IV disorders in the National Comorbidity Survey Replication. Arch Gen Psychiatry. 2005;62(6):593–602.
7 Moffitt TE, Harrington H, Caspi A, Kim-Cohen J, Goldberg D, Gregory AM, et al. Depression and generalized anxiety disorder: Cumulative and sequential comorbidity in a birth cohort followed prospectively to age 32 years. Arch Gen Psychiatry. 2007;64(6):651–660.
8 Costello E, Angold A, Sweeney ME. Comorbidity with depression in children and adolescents. In: Tohen M, editor. Comorbidity in affective disorders. New York: Marcel Dekker; 1999.
9 Serby M, Yu M. Overview: Depression in the elderly. Mount Sinai J Med. 2003;70(1):38–44.
10 Gelfand DM, Teti DM. The effects of maternal depression on children. Clin Psychol Rev. 1990;10(3):329–353.
11 Bettes BA. Maternal depression and motherese: Temporal and intonational features. Child Dev. 1988;59(4):1089–1096.
12 Cole DA, Rehm LP. Family interaction patterns and childhood depression. J Abnorm Child Psychol. 1986;14(2):297–314.

13   Cohn JF, Tronick EZ. Three-month-old infants' reaction to simulated maternal depression. Child Dev. 1983;54(1):185–193.

14   Zahn-Waxler C, Cummings EM, Iannotti RJ, Radke-Yarrow M. Young offspring of depressed parents: A population at risk for affective problems. In: Cicchetti D, Schneider-Rosen K, editors. Childhood depression. San Francisco: Jossey-Bass; 1984, pp. 81–106.

15   NHS. Depression in children and teenagers. NHS; 2017. Available from: www.nhs.uk/conditions/stress-anxiety-depression/children-depressed-signs/.

16   National Collaborating Centre for Mental Health. Depression in children and young people: identification and management in primary, community and secondary care. Leicester: British Psychological Society. National Clinical Practice Guideline. 2005;28.

17   Mackin P, Thomas SH. Atypical antipsychotic drugs. BMJ. 2011;342: d1126.

18   World Health Organization. Depression: Fact sheet 2017. Available from: www.who.int/mediacentre/factsheets/fs369/en/.

19   Bewick BM, Mulhern B, Barkham M, Trusler K, Hill AJ, Stiles WB. Changes in undergraduate student alcohol consumption as they progress through university. BMC Public Health. 2008;8:163.

20   American Psychiatric Association. Diagnostic and statistical manual of mental disorders: DSM-5. 5th ed. Arlington, VA: American Psychiatric Association; 2013.

21   Martin NC, Piek J, Baynam G, Levy F, Hay D. An examination of the relationship between movement problems and four common developmental disorders. Hum Mov Sci. 2010;29(5):799–808.

22   Campbell W, Missiuna C, Vaillancourt T. Peer victimization and depression in children with and without motor coordination difficulties. Psychol Schools. 2012;49(4):328–341.

23   Thomas M, Christopher G. Fatigue in developmental coordination disorder: An exploratory study in adults. Fatigue. 2018;6(1):41–51.

24   Miller M, Hinshaw SP. Does childhood executive function predict adolescent functional outcomes in girls with ADHD? J abnormal child psychol. 2010;38:315–326.

25   Parker DR, Boutelle K. Executive function coaching for college students with learning disabilities and ADHD: A new approach for fostering self-determination. Learn Disabil Res Prac. 2009;24(4):204–215.

26   Thomas M, Williams N, Kirby A. Supporting students with specific learning difficulties in higher education: A preliminary comparative study of executive function skills. J Incl Pract Fur High Educ. 2015;6(1):36–47.

27   Luthar SS, Cicchetti D, Becker B. The construct of resilience: A critical evaluation and guidelines for future work. Child Dev. 2000;71(3):543–562.

28   Bonanno GA. Loss, trauma, and human resilience: Have we underestimated the human capacity to thrive after extremely aversive events? Am Psychol. 2004;59(1):20–28.

29   American Psychological Association. The road to resilience. Am Psychol Assoc.; 2019. Available from: www.apa.org/helpcenter/road-resilience.

30   Joyce S, Shand F, Tighe J, Laurent SJ, Bryant RA, Harvey SB. Road to resilience: A systematic review and meta-analysis of resilience training programmes and interventions. BMJ Open. 2018;8(6): e017858.

31   Scalco MZ, Pollock B. Geriatric depression. In: Ingram RE, editor. The international encyclopedia of depression. New York; London: Springer; 2009.

32   Zhong G, Wang Y, Tao T, Ying J, Zhao Y. Daytime napping and mortality from all causes, cardiovascular disease, and cancer: A meta-analysis of prospective cohort studies. Sleep Med. 2015;16(7):811–819.

33 Christopher G. The psychology of ageing: From mind to society. Basingstoke: Palgrave Macmillan; 2014.

34 National Institute for Health and Care Excellence. Depression in adults: Recognition and management. NICE guidelines [CG90]. 2009. https://www.nice.org.uk/guidance/cg90

35 Szanto K, Mulsant BH, Houck PR, Dew MA, Dombrovski A, Pollock BG, et al. Emergence, persistence, and resolution of suicidal ideation during treatment of depression in old age. J Affect Disord. 2007;98(1–2):153–161.

36 Rabheru K. Special issues in the management of depression in older patients. Can J Psychiatry. 2004;49(3 Suppl 1):41S–50S.

37 Boyce N, Walker Z, Rodda J. The old age psychiatry handbook: A practical guide. Chichester: John Wiley & Sons Ltd; 2008.

38 Mulsant BH, Houck PR, Gildengers AG, Andreescu C, Dew MA, Pollock BG, et al. What is the optimal duration of a short-term antidepressant trial when treating geriatric depression? J Clin Psychopharmacol. 2006;26(2):113–120.

39 Christopher G, Sutherland D, Smith A. Effects of caffeine in non-withdrawn volunteers. Hum Psychopharmacol. 2005;20(1):47–53.

40 Mottram P, Wilson K, Strobl J. Antidepressants for depressed elderly. Cochrane Database Syst Rev. 2006;(1): CD003491.

41 Wasserman D. Depression. 2nd ed. Oxford: Oxford University Press; 2011.

42 Reynolds CF, III, Dew MA, Pollock BG, Mulsant BH, Frank E, Miller MD, et al. Maintenance treatment of major depression in old age. N Engl J Med. 2006;354(11):1130–1138.

43 Mulsant BH, Ganguli M. Epidemiology and diagnosis of depression in late life. J Clin Psychiatry. 1999;60:9–15.

44 Karel MJ, Hinrichsen G. Treatment of depression in late life: Psychotherapeutic interventions. Clin Psychol Rev. 2000;20(6):707–729.

45 Hirschfeld RM, Keller MB, Panico S, Arons BS, Barlow D, Davidoff F, et al. The National Depressive and Manic-Depressive Association consensus statement on the undertreatment of depression. JAMA. 1997;277(4):333–340.

46 Ganguli M, Dodge HH, Mulsant BH. Rates and predictors of mortality in an aging, rural, community-based cohort: The role of depression. Arch Gen Psychiatry. 2002; 59(11):1046–1052.

47 Unützer J, Patrick DL, Diehr P, Simon G, Grembowski D, Katon W. Quality adjusted life years in older adults with depressive symptoms and chronic medical disorders. Int Psychogeriatr. 2000;12(1):15–33.

Chapter 7

Treatment and management
Psychological

Rising tide

Although there are many recognized interventions for depression, it is cause for concern that more than half of those in need fail to receive appropriate treatment. This figure is significantly lower in many countries (1). There are several explanations for this. These include insufficient funds and/or resources, a paucity of trained healthcare staff, and the ever-present threat of stigma. Even when people are identified as possibly experiencing depression, the assessment method may be flawed. The issue of assessment is described in more detail in Chapter 2. In many cases, this means people fall through the net and, as a result, do not receive the support that could be offered to them. Equally concerning is that many are misdiagnosed with depression and receive antidepressant medication when it is not required.

With concern over depression not being detected in many cases early on, initiatives have been set in action in the UK. Within the last decade, access to low-intensity psychosocial interventions has been improved by introducing graduate mental health workers (2). The introduction of the stepped care model described later in this chapter is incorporated in the Department of Health's Improving Access to Psychological Therapies (IAPT) programme (3) IAPT services offer evidence-based interventions for people diagnosed with anxiety and depression. There is a particular focus on those with long-term health conditions. This is facilitated by links between mental health and physical health services in the NHS (4).

Before we discuss various forms of intervention, we should first consider how success is measured. Clinicians talk about response and remission. Both are significant indices of treatment efficacy. Response refers to any abatement in symptoms that are seen to be clinically significant. For example, a 50 per cent drop in reported symptoms following treatment might be the benchmark set (5). On the other hand, remission describes the almost total absence of symptoms. Anything less than remission means that the individual still experiences a poor quality of life and is at risk of worsening symptoms.

When considering treatment and its relative success, it is not merely about reducing the number of depressive symptoms from an individual's perspective. Still,

DOI:10.4324/9781315688879-7

instead, success should only be heralded when the person experiences a return to normal functioning and an overall positive outlook on life is reinstated (6).

At various points here in this chapter and at other locations throughout this book, comments may be made concerning the efficacy of specific treatment approaches. A great deal of the material here is based on *The NICE guideline on treating and managing depression in adults* (7). However, as this publication clarifies, *absence of evidence is not evidence of absence*. In other words, although there is at the current time insufficient evidence to make conclusions about the success of a particular treatment, one cannot conclude that this treatment is ineffective. This would be an example of a false dichotomy. This is because there is a lack of evidence to make a concrete statement of the overall effect. It may very well be the case that it is without consequence. Still, the quality of the evidence at the moment does not allow us to make such conclusions with any confidence.

Shortly, we shall look at the various forms of intervention in detail. At this point, however, we should note that most support for these comes from trials that have recruited individuals with acute cases of mild-to-moderate depression. Unfortunately, it is still the case that, in certain instances, some do not respond well to either the drug treatment or psychological therapy offered (7). Even in the cases where there is an improvement, relapse at some future point is often the reality (8). Several factors increase the risk of relapse: a prior history of depression being the main one. In Chapter 8, we shall look at some strategies to help prevent or reduce the likelihood of relapse following recovery.

Evidence-based practice

Evidence-based practice is at the heart of clinical care. In other words, decisions are made on the best available evidence. Quite what constitutes an appropriate evidence base is contested (9).

Several processes need to be completed before an intervention is fully adopted into an offered care programme. The initial stage concerns identifying the specific theoretical basis for the intervention. This grows out of potential explanations for the behaviour under study. In other words, is the likely explanation for the observed behaviour related to a thought disorder or a chemical imbalance? The treatment protocol is then refined by accumulating additional evidence and clinical observation. This would then be followed by an uncontrolled open trial to confirm any potential success as an intervention. This is sometimes referred to as an uncontrolled open-label trial. These are trials where neither the research nor the participant is blinded to the treatment. All participants receive the same intervention. Once there is an indication that the proposed treatment might be effective, a standard randomized controlled trial (RCT) is conducted. Although not free from flaws, RCTs are by and large deemed the gold standard for demonstrating efficacy in clinical work. In an RCT, participants are randomly allocated to one of the treatment arms. In this sense, there is no bias in selection. The control in such trials is usually the current standard treatment for the condition under study, referred to as a positive-control study or equivalency trial (10). Sometimes a placebo is incorporated into the design, which would be a placebo-controlled randomized trial.

Other controls include attention control, treatment as usual (TAU), waiting list, and no treatment. Attention control is used when testing a behavioural intervention to control for non-specific effects, much like a placebo pill would be used to try a new drug. In other words, the amount of attention a patient receives, the number of contact points or visits made, and other elements of support that are not part of the active arm are balanced across the trial (11). TAU is sometimes referred to as routine care. This is where the active intervention standard for the condition being studied is compared to the new treatment. Although this is a common misconception, it is not the same as a placebo control group. Waiting list control is where a group receives no intervention until the end of the trial. This allows the comparison of the active treatment against an untreated control. A waiting list control is preferred over a "no treatment" control because there are ethical issues around denying patients access to treatment. RCT findings will enable the researchers to see if the proposed new intervention is either better than no treatment (as in the placebo or attentional control trials) or better than the existing treatment regimen (TAU).

Once there is ample evidence to suggest that a treatment is achieving the predicted effect, the next stage of enquiry is whether it remains an effective intervention once rolled out into the real world. There are myriad differences between the nicely controlled environment of the clinical trial and real-life settings, not least the variability in the training and competence of those responsible for delivering the therapy. Also, there is limited control over whether or not patients adhere to the indicated regimen. Given sufficient time, a reasonable body of evidence accumulates. This enables meta-analyses and systematic reviews to be conducted, further elucidating the impact of the targeted therapy on the chosen condition. Findings from these studies feedback into the further development of the intervention (7).

It is of interest to note that there is a more extensive evidence base for the various pharmacological interventions than for other forms of therapy as drug companies are better able to meet the costs, in terms of both time and money, to complete the necessary phases of the development process. The process takes a lot longer for most psychological therapies. As a case in point, for CBT, probably the most established psychological treatment, the original work was conducted in the 1960s. Still, it was not until the 2000s that studies were being undertaken looking at the cost-effectiveness of this approach. For a detailed account of the evidence base for the various therapies for depression, it is worth reading Anderson and colleagues (7).

Having set the scene, it is now time to explore in some detail the various interventions that are on offer for people with depression. We shall begin with self-directed approaches before progressing onto more therapist-driven techniques.

On a personal note, I have really enjoyed writing this section. The reason is that I very nearly went down the clinical psychology route. I had a place on a course. However, at the same time, I was successful in my application to the Economic and Social Research Council (ESRC) for PhD funding. This led me to develop the research I had carried out as an undergraduate on memory impairments in depression.

We often look back at past decisions and contemplate how our lives would have been different. Although there is a tinge of regret, I know I made the right decision. I would not have swapped the world of academic research for anything. Most importantly, my research is clinical to enjoy the best of both worlds. I am also acutely aware that I would have made a terrible therapist.

Self-help

Depending on the severity of the depression, there are several self-help strategies people can take to help with depression. So, before exploring some of the more intensive interventions, we shall look briefly at simple changes in lifestyle and the impact this may have on a person's mood.

We are in an age where self-help materials are readily available. Not only are there almost countless books published on the topic, most of which are available electronically, thereby increasing their accessibility, but there also are an increasing number of smartphone apps that people can engage with at any time of day, anywhere in the world. Before turning our attention to apps (see Chapter 9), I shall look at stress management strategies.

There are various stress management strategies. These include relaxation techniques, mindfulness, meditation, and yoga. Familiar to most of these is a focus on self-awareness. Many of these techniques help reduce both physiological and psychological arousal, thereby exerting a calming effect on the body and mind.

Maintaining a proper diet is very important: not only eating healthy food but also ensuring healthy eating habits; in other words, keeping to a regular routine. Diet should be balanced because it contains sufficient quantities of proteins and vitamins, among other things.

Tryptophan is a crucial element of a balanced diet and is present in mozzarella cheese, soy products, and egg whites (12). Tryptophan is an amino acid. Amino acids are essential for the production of proteins. Indeed, some depressive symptoms may be the result of deficiencies in a number of these essential amino acids, as well as vitamins and minerals (13). Tryptophan is involved in regulating mood, mainly since it is a vital ingredient for making the neurotransmitter serotonin.

It is often the case that, during a depressive episode, people experience an intense desire for sweet things. Carbohydrates contained in chocolate and other tempting delights provide the body with energy. They also help the process whereby tryptophan is absorbed. However, it is essential to offset the intake of carbohydrates with regular exercise (13).

We know there is plenty of evidence to show the positive effects of exercise for both body and mind. I shall examine physical activity in more detail near the end of this chapter. Suffice to say, increasing blood flow throughout the body is a good thing. It makes us more alert both physically and mentally. It also alleviates some of the tension we build up throughout the day.

On top of that, it acts as a distraction. Exercise also leads to an increase in the production of endorphins. Endorphins are natural substances involved in mood regulation and the pain response. Most people cannot help but feel the warm glow of achievement with a hint of smugness at the end of a bout of exercise.

Guided self-help

There are many guided self-help options available for those experiencing mild-to-moderate depression. Guided self-help is a relatively cheap intervention, with minimal input from a trained professional. There is, however, more to it than merely reading. The clinicians facilitate the process, an approach that, as we will see later in this chapter, computerized interventions attempt to mirror. They introduce the aims concerning the material provided and then monitor the individual throughout the process. After a prescribed time, the success of the process is evaluated. It is beneficial if family members are involved throughout. It often proves helpful in gaining a better understanding of the condition.

Social support

Social support aims to give a person the sense that they are valued and respected and may come in many forms, such as a sense that help is there if needed (perceived support) or a regularly meeting group where exchanges of support are made (social network) (14). Social isolation is a major contributing factor to depression and negatively impacts the outcome. Befriending schemes appear to have some benefits (15). Peer support is provided by various organizations, including *Depression Alliance* and *Mind*. Such schemes are generally adjuncts to drug therapy or psychological interventions (7).

There is good evidence showing that interventions that target psychosocial functioning, such as talking therapies or medication, have positive effects (16). Although there is evidence of improvement, it is not always clear that such developments bring individuals with depression back to a level of functioning experienced by people in the healthy control groups (17). It is also unclear whether improvements in psychosocial functioning alleviate the depression or if the lifting of depression accounts for the progress in psychosocial functioning (18). As is the case in most of this research, there is no way to pinpoint the direction of change.

Crisis resolution

For many managing a condition while still living in one's own home is essential and is the preferred option if deemed appropriate. Crisis resolution and home treatment teams (CRHTTs) provide this form of care. This avoids the need for in-patient care in all but the most severe cases (7).

At present, there is not enough evidence to indicate how successful this approach is in treating depression, especially in terms of suicide prevention. However, given that these services operate out of hours, they do likely provide a reasonable level of support for those in greater need.

Counselling

The roots of counselling are based on the work of Rogers (19). The ethos of the Rogerian approach is that, given the right setting, a person can be responsible for resolving their own issues and grow as an individual through that process. Rogers argues that for this to occur, the person needs to experience positive regard, genuineness, and empathy. These are referred to as the core conditions of this approach. In other words, the Rogerian approach emphasizes compassion and unconditional acceptance of our fellow human beings, being open, and the importance of being listened to and better understood. This approach is classified as humanistic therapy because the focus is on the therapeutic relationship (20), and it is the core conditions that facilitate change. Adaptations of Rogers' work include Egan's (21, 22) model centring on clarifying the problem (exploration), finding out what the person wants (personalising), and working through issues (action).

For several reasons, when one looks at what is offered under the umbrella of counselling, there is a great deal of variation (23).

Psychodynamic psychotherapy

Freud's *Mourning and Melancholia*, of 1917 (24), has been heralded as the precursor of modern psychological therapies to treat depression. As with most treatments, there are many different forms of psychodynamic psychotherapy. Psychoanalysis refers to intensive—by that, I mean several times a week—psychotherapy that can extend over many years. From this, developed psychoanalytic theory. Psychodynamic therapy is also psychoanalytic in that the underlying assumptions are primarily steeped in psychoanalytic theory. Still, the format of the sessions differs markedly from those just described. The duration of therapy is comparatively brief, with the number of sessions being similar to those of cognitive behavioural therapy (CBT) and held weekly (25). There are around six to ten sessions spaced out over up to 12 weeks (26).

The therapy focuses on identifying conflicts in a person's life, both within and external to critical relationships. Whereas some treatments focus specifically on the present, psychodynamic psychotherapy encourages the client to explore the past as a key to understanding the conscious and, often, unconscious conflicts at the root of their problems. The client is encouraged to work through these issues with the therapist, emphasizing transference and interpretation.

Transference is where powerful feelings associated with childhood are projected onto current relationships, including the therapist. Transference enables someone to re-experience feelings that may have been previously inaccessible, allowing the therapist to identify and analyse conflicts. It also shows that the client is repeating specific patterns of behaviour.

Whereas transference is seen as a positive process, counter-transference is seen as an impediment. This is where the therapist's unresolved conflicts are projected onto the client. However, it can be harnessed for the good of the therapeutic encounter. By better understanding their personal reaction to the client, the therapist can better understand how other people, those outside the therapy session, react to the client.

Interpretation is where the therapist makes statements that go beyond what the client has said to coax out new considerations of events. In doing so, the client can begin to appreciate the cause of some of the difficulties they are experiencing and gain more control over their lives.

Rational emotive behavioural therapy

Rational emotive behavioural therapy developed from the work of Ellis in the 1950s (27). In a similar way to some of the later approaches, specifically CBT, the focus is on how thinking styles directly impact how a person feels and behaves. The therapy deals with challenging these maladaptive patterns of thinking. The assumption here is that people experience problems when they hold inflexible and exaggerated beliefs about themselves, those around them, and their situation. By identifying irrational beliefs, a person can begin the process of altering them to become realistic and adaptive.

Cognitive behavioural therapy

One of the major criticisms levelled at psychoanalysis is that it lacks an evidence base to back up claims of success. The tradition of behavioural and cognitive approaches to treating depression addressed this.

Cognitive behavioural therapy (CBT) for depression grew out of the work of Beck in the 1950s. The formalization of the approach occurred with the publication of his book, *Cognitive Therapy of Depression*, in 1979 (28), with expansion to the model occurring at various points (for example, Ref. (29)). We examined the cognitive models of depression in detail in Chapter 3. CBT, as an intervention, focuses on the thinking styles of those with depression. In Beck's model, negative cognitive schemas are responsible for the maladaptive thinking styles associated with depression. Within the framework of CBT, the person with depression learns to identify instances of this maladaptive thinking. As a result, it challenges them in much the same way as testing a hypothesis in science. In other words, they test the validity of the thought or belief against reality, and then weigh up the evidence for and against the assumption. CBT is action-oriented, requiring the individual to carry out much work between individual therapy sessions.

In terms of delivery, CBT is time-limited and highly structured. In many cases, CBT is delivered over three to four months, usually of 16–20 sessions. For the first couple of weeks, a person attends two sessions each week. Following that, sessions are spread evenly over the intervening period. This is dependent mainly on the severity of the depression being treated (28). In conjunction with the therapist, the individual with depression identifies how their thoughts and underlying beliefs impact their own feelings and how this style of thinking leads to problem situations. Strategies to help combat this are then practised to change the default way of thinking, initiating a move away from maladaptive thinking style to more adaptive patterns.

Cognitive reactivity following CBT

In Chapter 3, we looked at the concept of cognitive reactivity. This refers to established patterns of negative thinking that are reactivated by relatively minor events. When comparing treatment with medication to CBT, the CBT group scored lower on reactivity scores during remission (30). This indicates that CBT alters the underlying cognitive processes previously associated with the development and maintenance of depression (31). Indeed, higher cognitive reactivity levels during remission are linked to an increased likelihood of subsequent relapse.

Group cognitive behavioural therapy

In some instances, group CBT might be offered. Groups consist of six to ten individuals, along with two who lead the sessions. This incorporates an element of psychoeducation around teaching techniques to help deal with a range of situations, including relaxation training and social skills workshops.

Mindfulness-based cognitive therapy

Mindfulness-based cognitive therapy (MBCT) was developed by Segal to help with the problem of relapse following a period of recovery (32). The format is based on a combination of mindfulness-based stress reduction and CBT (28, 33). Sessions generally run for eight weeks, with follow-up sessions once the weekly sessions have ended. MBCT is run with groups of up to 15 individuals. In terms of how it works, the emphasis is given to training the individual to become more aware of their bodies and the thoughts associated with depressive episodes. Once a person is mindful of ingrained modes of reacting to situations, this approach enables the individual to identify negative thoughts without responding emotionally to them, a process called decentring. The person learns, for example, that a thought does not equate to reality, to something that has happened, or indeed will occur at some future point. The concept of self-compassion is vital here. It encourages a person to self-soothe and provides self-encouragement. A person's awareness of the feelings and sensations deriving from their own body is utilized to transmute their experience of a situation. The aim is not to avoid or remove feelings of sadness but rather to change one's relationship with these emotions. The end result is moving away from responding automatically to situations with a negative mindset to embracing alternative and more positive outcomes. By becoming aware of some of the early warning signs of a depressive episode, MBCT instils within the individual strategies to help reduce the likelihood of future relapses, such as being on the lookout for reacting in a habitual negative way to a situation that presents itself (34).

Interpersonal therapy

Interpersonal therapy (IPT) is an example of integrative therapy such that it combines elements from different therapeutic models. Counselling can also be considered under this umbrella term in that they often combine elements from person-centred, psychodynamic, and cognitive and behavioural perspectives (35). The focus of IPT is a brief, focused intervention. It targets the interactions that occur within the current relationship. Depression can dramatically affect relationships with other people. It is these relationships and the roles people adopt that IPT hones in on. One area of particular interest is exploring the problems arising from a person's attempt to deal with difficult situations that emerge during an episode of depression. By improving their daily interactions with their partner, both the depression and any relationships issues should resolve through a series of social adjustments. This form of therapy is particularly suited when there is a clearly identifiable area of difficulty, usually in one of four areas: (1) a change in social role (e.g. divorce), (2) grief (e.g. death of a loved one), (3) conflict resolution (e.g. relationship problems), (4) absence of relationships (e.g. lack of significant others) (36). In fact, the therapist purposely only concentrates on one or two problem areas throughout treatment. People find it challenging to make the necessary adjustments in such situations, so support is needed to help someone find new opportunities.

Behavioural activation

As its name would imply, behavioural activation has grown out of the behaviourist tradition of therapy. It is associated with Lewinsohn (37), although, more recently, it has undergone several developments (38, 39). It is again time-limited and structured in its approach. It is based on operant conditioning, sometimes referred to as instrumental conditioning. However, it is more accurate to see instrumental conditioning as a specific form of operant conditioning. In other words, performing the desired behaviour is essential for reinforcement, or rather instrumental in producing this reinforcement.

In terms of a theory of depression, the argument is that behaviours associated with depression are learned because they tend to co-occur. In other words, they are contiguous. Therefore, depression is maintained through negative reinforcement and a lack of positive reinforcement. Negative reinforcement occurs as the result of avoidant or escape behaviour; the behaviour prevents the occurrence of an aversive event or terminates it. Because the feared event is evaded, similar behaviour is more likely in the future. Hence, it is negatively reinforced in depression. Positive reinforcement refers to a source of enjoyment after producing a specific behaviour or action. If this happens, a person is more likely to repeat that behaviour. In the case of depression, there is a lack of such positive reinforcement.

Oftentimes, the strategy mostly adopted is avoidance to reduce the likelihood of adverse outcomes. Behavioural activation comes into play when the individual is supported to nurture more task-focused behaviour where the prospect of a reward is higher. At the same time, they are encouraged to let go of patterns of behaviour linked to negative reinforcement.

At the start of the therapy, there is an exploration of the links between certain behaviours and their role in causing problems in the person's life. As we have seen, this is a behaviourist intervention. So the main activities include attempts to reduce avoidance behaviours, exposure to progressively more fear-inducing situations (graded exposure), increased engagement in rewarding behaviour (activity scheduling), and encouragement of positive reinforcement leading to more adaptive behaviour.

Third wave therapies

One of the most prominent third wave therapies is acceptance and commitment therapy, or ACT, although others include compassionate mind training, functional analytic psychotherapy, behavioural activation, metacognitive therapy, mindfulness-based cognitive therapy, and dialectical behaviour therapy. I have already talked about a couple of these—behavioural activation and mindfulness-based cognitive therapy—so I shall not repeat myself here. Interest in such approaches grew out of a reappraisal of the role and efficacy of cognitive and behavioural components in therapy. Evidence indicates that purely behavioural treatment for depression is just as effective as the standard CBT model (40, 41). This "third wave" of CBT focuses less on challenging underlying thoughts (42) and more on the emotional response to these thoughts. The emphasis is on the function of cognitions, such as attempts to avoid or suppress specific thoughts (43).

Acceptance and commitment therapy

The aim of acceptance and commitment therapy is to change how someone relates to their symptoms. Rather than trying to avoid depressive thoughts and feelings, people are instead encouraged to accept them as unpleasant but transitory (44, 45). This is achieved by embracing the six core components of this approach. The first element is to take experienced emotions or dredged up memories at face value, a process referred to as cognitive defusion. There is a tendency to over-identify with such items. Instead, the aim is to avoid falling into the trap of immediately taking action against the thought. This leads to acceptance, which encourages people to let thoughts and images come and go. Being aware of the present is vital, not what has happened in the past or contemplating fear about future events. ACT also encourages one to develop a state of transcendence where a person acts as an observer of their own behaviour. Having a sense of one's personal values is necessary because they are needed for the person to set goals and commit to an action plan (46).

Compassionate mind training

Compassionate mind training (CMT), or compassion-focused therapy, encourages people to be cognizant of their own needs and focus their energy on caring for their own well-being (47).

Functional analytic psychotherapy

Functional analytic psychotherapy is steeped in the traditions of behaviour therapy. We act as we do because of how past behaviours have been reinforced, referred to as contingencies. To change these actions, the therapeutic process must tap into the power of supporting specific activities to alter the consequences (48). It relies on the quality of the therapeutic relationship. Problem behaviours manifest during the session—referred to as clinically relevant behaviour—and, by reinforcing behavioural improvements, the therapist can facilitate change. Suppose the client–therapist relationship is of poor quality. In that case, the client is unlikely to exhibit behaviour that causes them problems once out of the therapy situation.

Metacognitive therapy

Metacognitive therapy (MCT) is based on the premise that depression persists because of rumination and self-focused attention (49). MCT includes an attention training (ATT) component, which aims to give a person control once again over what they focus on. I shall come back to attention training shortly.

Dialectical behaviour therapy

Dialectical behaviour therapy (DBT) emphasizes the need to accept parts of a person's life that cannot be altered (radical acceptance), non-judgemental awareness (mindfulness), attentional control, greater tolerance of distress, acting against urges (opposite action), and improved social skills (50).

The weight of evidence from a Cochrane Review published in 2013 indicates that the evidence base for the effectiveness of third wave CBT approaches is inconsistent. So the authors were unable to come to any firm conclusions (35). Long-term follow-up studies are in particular needed to assess if success is maintained.

Behavioural couples therapy

This is offered to individuals when a relationship is suspected of contributing to the condition. This form of therapy might also be considered if the partner's involvement will likely have a beneficial effect on the overall outcome. Behavioural couples therapy generally lasts between 15 and 20 sessions over around six months (26).

In many cases, this form of therapy will be offered where there appears to be some behaviour in the partner that elicits the depressive episode. Alternatively, rather than provoking the depression, a partner's behaviour might be seen to result in the depression being maintained over time or increase the likelihood of future relapse (51). Although men and women differ regarding particular susceptibilities to depression, an inability to deal effectively with conflict and problems with intimacy are common in both sexes (52).

As with other approaches, there are different variations. With systemic couples therapy, the therapist focuses on helping the couple alter their perspective on the problem at hand and aiding them in developing alternative ways of identifying and connecting with one another (53). The desired outcome of this therapy is that couples nurture a more caring relationship, one that is less marred by conflict.

Person-centred care

Therapy aims to ensure that the treatment package offered is sensitive to the individual's needs and preferences (26). It is the norm today that patients are involved wherever possible at all steps in the decision-making process involving their care. The only exceptions are where they do not have capacity to make such decisions. In this sense, there must be good communication between clinicians and patients. It is also essential that advice given and treatments offered are sensitive to the cultural values of the individuals concerned. Indeed, appropriate translations and culturally sensitive support should be available. Such options should also be available regardless of disabilities.

Attention training

In Chapter 5, an account was given of the basic cognitive processes underlying tasks and activities we all carry out in our everyday lives. An influential figure in attention literature is Posner (54).

Posner's theory argues there are three distinct processing networks, networks that are distinct in terms of both the operations they perform and where they are situated in the brain. The three functions reflect a capacity for vigilance (alerting), an ability to focus only on goal-specific information (orienting), and also an ability to give priority to one activity over another when competition for attention occurs (conflict monitoring).

An elegant way to quantify each of these performance characteristics is to use Attention Network Test (ANT) (54). This task manipulates key performance indices so that the individual processes can be assessed. Alerting is calculated by comparing performance on conditions where a neutral cue was presented instead of no cue. In other words, the presence of a cue triggers an increase in arousal so that the individual is prepared for action. Orienting is inferred by comparing performance when a spatial cue was presented to when a neutral one was shown. A spatial cue provides information concerning where a potential target might appear. In contrast, a neutral one does not provide any such information. Conflict monitoring is assessed when comparing the presence of congruent and incongruent targets. The presence of incongruent stimuli slows down processing time because they provide information conflicting with the intended response. This test has been used to examine the impact of meditation training on attention among those with depression (55).

Attention may be described as being either concentrative or receptive, both of which can be altered through the practice of meditation (56). An example where meditative practices emphasize concentrative attention is where the individual is instructed to focus on their in-breaths and out-breaths. Should their attention wander, they should gently return attention to their breathing. An alternative is where the meditation focuses on receptive attention. In such instances, instructions encourage the individual to be aware of what is occurring around them while remaining unreactive. To bring an analogy to the literature on attention, both concentrative and receptive attention differ on two dimensions, reflecting both the range of attentional focus and its intensity (55, 57). Using the aforementioned examples, it is clear then that concentrative attention is concerned with an intense and narrowed focus of attention to a specific sensation, often referred to as single-pointed practices. Receptive attention is in contrast to this. The focus of attention is relaxed, in both intensity and breadth of focus.

There is evidence to show that meditation training improves performance on the various components of the ANT. One study compared individuals on an eight-week mindfulness-based stress reduction (MBSR) course and those on a one-month meditation retreat to a control group where there was no intervention (58). Those attending the retreat were experienced at meditation. Findings showed that individuals who had prior experience with meditation, more specifically, concentrative meditation, showed the most significant improvements in conflict monitoring. On top of that, individuals in the MBSR who were not previously experienced in meditation improved on the orienting aspect of the ANT. This demonstrated that meditation can improve key components of attentional allocation. Also, the experienced meditators improved in their alerting response, making them more vigilant and ready for action.

These types of effects are important because depression is associated with a tendency to ruminate (59). Mindfulness techniques provide a means by which a person can successfully refocus their attention away from depressogenic thought processes to more adaptive activity (60).

Problem-solving therapy

Problem-solving therapy is a form of cognitive behavioural therapy that focuses specifically on deficits in social problem-solving skills. Poor social problem-solving has been linked to several psychological disorders. Social problem-solving forms the basis of what we all do every day of our lives. It refers to how successfully we can deal with stressful events, be they acute or chronic. More specifically, effective social problem-solving allows an individual to reflect on and change the nature of problem situations while at the same time regulating their level of distress provoked by the nature of the problem. Due to the complexity and variety of everyday social problems, there can never be a single effective solution that works all of the time. Each problem encountered has to be addressed individually. In addition, the types of problems we deal with day to day are not abstract puzzles set in a sterile laboratory environment. Instead, they are enmeshed in a web of emotions and incomplete information, all of which create suboptimal conditions to deal effectively and efficiently with the problem.

From a theoretical point of view, social problem-solving is driven by two aspects, one concerning a general problem-solving orientation, the other referring to specific problem-solving styles (61). Orientation reflects a person's general beliefs and attitudes towards problems and their ability to deal with them when required. There are two main dimensions to orientation, one positive, one negative. Someone who has a positive problem orientation shows a predilection to view problems as a challenge, something to tackle with enthusiasm and confidence. On the other hand, someone whose predominant outlook is that problems are a source of threat, feel ill-equipped to deal with them, and experience emotional turmoil would be described as holding a negative problem orientation. The two orientations can be best described as fuelling motivation to deal with problems, be it in a way that is adaptive or conversely in a highly disruptive manner.

Having looked at general orientations to problems, another important aspect of this approach is its descriptions of individual problem-solving styles. An adaptive approach to dealing with issues is described as a rational problem-solving style. The basis of this style is one in which individuals accurately define the problem and then generate potential solutions. The most appropriate option is chosen on the basis of reflection about which would seem most likely to succeed given the current parameters. The final stage is one of implementation and evaluation, which enables the individual to assess the success of their behaviour.

The remaining two styles are maladaptive. The first is described as an impulsivity/carelessness style. It refers to someone who acts rashly when faced with a problem. The other reflects an avoidance style where individuals tend to shy away from the situation and rely heavily on the help of others. The last two styles are deemed dysfunctional as they generally worsen the problems rather than any alleviation.

When looking at a social problem-solving intervention for depression, the various orientations and styles are seen as potential risk factors that might lead someone to develop depression given the appropriate circumstances (62). Seeing problems as a challenge and adopting rational ways to deal with such situations will help buffer someone against developing depression. If, however, problems are seen as a threat to self, and one's response is either impulsive reaction and/or avoidance, the risk of developing depression is higher (63).

Problem-solving therapy is not just concerned with developing more effective problem-solving skills; it is also focused on the individual's emotional response. How we each respond to problem situations in terms of emotion plays a considerable role in how we can deal with these situations. I return to emotional reactivity and regulation time and again in this book. This therapeutic approach also attempts to personalize the treatment by focusing on a person's individual strengths and weaknesses. Therefore, it is an all-encompassing approach that operates on intrapersonal, interpersonal, and existential levels.

Problem orientation

Part of problem-solving training is to engender a positive problem orientation. The therapist must address barriers the client has, such as prominent negative emotions, a tendency to worry and ruminate, and a lack of belief in their ability to deal with problem situations. Nezu and colleagues (63) emphasize visualization in their approach as a way for individuals to imagine what it would be like to have successfully dealt with a problem and then experience the positive outcomes of such actions. In this sense, the therapist can help clients develop a belief in their ability to successfully meet various challenges that they may face at some future point, a concept referred to as self-efficacy.

Some of the strategies used to tackle worry and rumination are adapted from cognitive therapy. One such approach is to consider that what a person thinks and believes determines how they act in different situations and decides how they feel emotionally. The therapist can help the client identify instances where negative thoughts and self-doubt lead to depressive feelings. It is then a matter of substituting these with more adaptive beliefs and assumptions. An alternative method to address negative thinking is for the therapist to act out particular beliefs and for the client to then challenge them by providing alternative interpretations.

There is a strong stop-and-think aspect to this approach (63). The aim is to view negative feelings as an alarm bell indicating that a problem exists that needs addressing rather than focusing on the feelings themselves. In other words, the aim is to correctly identify what is causing the emotional reaction and determine the true nature of the problem.

Problem-solving styles

This then leads to encouraging a more rational problem-solving style (63). As already described earlier, the first thing that needs to be tackled when faced with a problem is to accurately define exactly what the problem is. Essential elements of this process include a need to amass sufficient information about the situation, making sure to rid the mind of any false assumptions that might hinder the process later on, and attempts to recognize things that might hamper the process.

Following on from an accurate representation of the problem, a good problem-solver will generate several potential solutions to the issue at hand. In many cases, it is good to be creative, thereby preventing the mind from focusing on too narrow a range of potential options. In the longer term, this helps the person with depression to be aware that there are many alternative solutions to each of the problems they face rather than single, often extreme, solutions.

The next natural step in the process is to evaluate the potential alternative solutions generated to select the one which would seem to best fit the needs of the current situation. In other words, the person will need to assess if the potential solution will meet all the criteria of the problem at hand, if they have sufficient resources to successfully carry out the activity, and the likely consequences in both the short and long terms.

The final stage in this process requires the person to accurately monitor the chosen action's implementation and evaluate the degree of success of their endeavour. This will lead either to a reassessment period if the desired outcome has not occurred or to self-reinforcement if the solution proved a success (63).

Continuous practice of the skills is essential for the long-term effectiveness of this intervention. This allows the therapist to work on an individual's strengths and weaknesses in more detail and helps to make the application of the newly developed skills to novel problems more natural. In addition, practice is an excellent way to reduce relapse in the future (63). However, these skills do not only come in useful once one is faced with a stressful situation but they can also be employed to help predict future potentially stressful situations, thereby working by preventing events that might be potentially harmful.

There is evidence from randomized controlled trials to show that problem-solving therapy is an effective approach for treating depression (64). On top of this, when looking at different components of the treatment in isolation, it was found that the full problem-solving training showed the most significant positive effect when compared to a waiting-list control. Less of an impact was seen for training without the problem orientation component. However, this group showed significantly higher improvements than the controls (65).

Problem-solving therapy for older adults

We know that there are varying degrees of change in cognitive functioning as we age (66). It is also clear that depression itself is associated with cognitive impairment that covers various domains of operation (67, 68). Combined, these significantly erode away at a person's general well-being, manifesting as a severe and all-pervading disability (69). This is best demonstrated by evidence of significant difficulties with instrumental activities of daily living (IADLs) (70).

In the literature, the type of functional impairment experienced by older adults with depression is often referred to as depression-executive dysfunction syndrome. This is something that was covered in Chapter 4. In brief, it refers to significant impairment due to dysfunction in the frontostriatal regions of the brain. In cases where there is considerable executive impairment, the person experiences higher levels of psychomotor retardation, apathy, and poor insight into their difficulties (71).

For those with depression with a significant impairment in executive function, making plans is extremely difficult. Even when an activity is started, they find it increasingly difficult to complete it. Taken in the context of other symptoms of depression, such difficulties exacerbate feelings of hopelessness and an increasing acceptance that this is their lot.

As one would imagine, significant cognitive impairment can often limit the effectiveness of any intervention. In fact, it has even been shown to impede response to antidepressant medication (72). It is also associated with higher rates of relapse (73). Specifically, disruption within the neural substrate associated with executive function is most related to such effects (74). Because of this, there is good evidence that psychological therapies which help individuals develop constructive ways of coping with their situation can be highly effective. One such approach is problem-solving therapy.

Problem-solving therapy was essentially a response to the observation that people with depression tend to adopt maladaptive ways of dealing with their issues (75). The premise behind this form of therapy is that instructing a person with better strategies for identifying problems, generating solutions, and monitoring outcomes will ultimately improve their ability to deal more effectively with a range of situations. In this sense, problem-solving approaches aim to break the ever-widening spiral of dysfunction that results from this inability to handle the types of issues we all experience in our daily lives. Indeed, being able to more effectively address issues as they arise can only reinforce a growing sense that people can control the outcome of situations, and by extension, control over their lives (74).

In addition to the evidence showing the effectiveness of problem-solving therapy to treat depression in general (76), there is evidence that it is effective for those with significant executive dysfunction (77). There is also evidence that this form of intervention is valid for those whose depression is also worsened by significant executive dysfunction (74). Alexopoulos and colleagues (74) identify important ways to modify the existing problem-solving therapy to better fit the needs of those with significant executive dysfunction. They stress that it is essential that the therapist provides the person with depression with higher levels of structure and support, especially during the initial stages of the intervention. They also indicate that there must be a strong emphasis on accounting for the specific behavioural difficulties experienced by this group. In other words, there should be special dispensation for problems initiating, monitoring, and following through on actions, as well as problems with emotion regulation.

The issue with emotion regulation is particularly pertinent here. Older adults who are depressed and show marked impairment in executive function can be easily overwhelmed by distress when instructed to focus on a problem situation with a powerful emotional component. Because of this, as a temporary deviation from standard problem-solving therapy, for the patient group we are describing here, the therapist initially focuses the individual on developing essential problem-solving skills in the resolution of the issues without a concomitant emotional component.

An integral aspect of problem-solving therapy is the generation of alternative solutions to problems. This is highly demanding of cognitive resources and can pose a particular challenge for those with executive deficits. Because of this, additional prompts are needed to ensure people consider potential alternatives to try to deal with the problem.

We have also seen that initiating actions is a problem here. This is most salient during the implementation stage of the therapy, where individuals have selected a potential solution and are then required to implement it. Again, this is addressed by increased prompting by therapists. For example, therapists repeatedly call the person's attention back to the original plan of action and ask them to reflect on how well they are doing. Is the problem situation resolving? Encouraging involvement from caregivers is also helpful here. If caregivers are also trained in problem-solving methods, they will be able to more effectively support their spouse/family member.

Computer programmes and the internet

There are numerous treatment options for those with persistent subthreshold depressive symptoms, as well as those experiencing mild-to-moderate depression. These include computerized cognitive behavioural therapy (CCBT) packages.

There is an increasing demand for remote care across the board, encompassing mental and physical health. This is in part driven by a desire to meet the rising demand for such services while at the same time keeping within a tight, and it seems ever-tightening, budget. Some psychological interventions lend themselves more effectively from being delivered online than others. CBT appears to be one of these.

CCBT starts with an explanation of the standard CBT model of therapy. Between each session, the person is set several tasks which must be completed. Part of this process is monitoring behaviour and thoughts, exploring outcomes, and challenging assumptions. Support is provided by a therapist. Although therapist input is limited here, it is crucial for monitoring the progress of the individual. CCBT is a time-limited course of 9–12-week duration.

Issues with psychological therapies and counselling

Although outcomes are often positive, the types of feelings evoked and memories activated can make people feel worse at first. Some experience more detrimental lasting effects where their entire outlook is changed, thereby changing how they view their family and friends. In some cases, this can result in permanent disruption.

There is also the issue with availability. Demand outstrips supply considerably. As a result, waiting times to see a therapist can be protracted. Increasing public awareness of mental health problems only strains an overstretched service (78).

Sleep hygiene

It is generally acknowledged now how important sleep is for general physical and mental health. This has already been discussed in Chapter 5. We have seen that instructing people to establish adequate sleep hygiene is vital. It is important here in terms of depression also. Sleep hygiene is achieved through simple steps. The first is making sure regular sleep patterns are established and maintained. In other words, sticking with set times to retire to bed and wake in the morning. One should be careful what one eats or drinks before bed. Caffeine and nicotine intake should be carefully monitored close to the time set for sleep. The bedroom should be an appropriate environment for sleep, free from distractions that turn one's mind away from rest to mental activity. Something that helps prompt a healthy night's sleep is regular physical exercise.

Reminiscence therapy

Reminiscence therapy seems rife at the moment. Probably primarily associated with dementia, reminiscence therapy is also used to treat depression. The premise of this approach is to make use of various prompts to memory, aiming to encourage the person to talk in-depth about their previous experiences. Prompts include photographs, music, among other things (79).

Reminiscence therapy grew out of the concept of life review, an approach adopted in the 1960s by Butler (80). The rationale here was that, as we age and death appears to loom, we all desire to give perspective to our lives, to all that we have experienced. This belief is consistent with the work of Erikson (81). For him, later life is characterized by acknowledging that one's own death is inevitable. It is at this time people reflect on their life. People who feel that they have led a meaningful life are better able to accept that death is a reality because they have a sense of contentment, of being whole. Suppose on examination, their life is seen as one disappointment after another. In that case, death is looked on with a growing sense of despondency. This is what Erikson referred to as wisdom. His wife and long-term collaborator added an additional stage, the ninth stage, to encompass the extended life (82). At this stage, the individual again faces the crises of the previous eight steps.

Various topics can be explored within reminiscence therapy. These include relationships with others, accomplishments and failures, and multiple adaptations throughout a person's life in response to changing circumstances. The aim here is to boost someone's mood and help communication, among other things.

The literature has shown reminiscence therapy to be useful for depression in older adults. A review of reminiscence therapy by Hsieh and Wang (83) showed that, although there was a reduction in depression following an intervention among older adults outside of primary care, when looking at those in care, depression alongside anxiety and loneliness are significant problems still. The review by Elias, Neville, and Scott (84) showed group reminiscence therapy to effectively reduce depression, but less so for anxiety and loneliness. Bohlmeijer, Westerhof, and Jong (85) also showed that reminiscence therapy improved a person's sense of meaning in life.

Evidence from reminiscence therapy is generally positive, although there are limitations associated with individual studies. However, its use comes with a note for caution. When assessing treatments, there is always the need to consider adverse effects. With reminiscence therapy, there is a need to proceed with care. Although, at first glance, it would seem an innocuous form of intervention, one needs to consider that not all memories will be pleasant (86). We have found this in our work on nostalgia in treating dementia (87).

Physical exercise

Physical activity programmes are an essential component of treatment for depression. Activity programmes are often group-based, with multiple sessions each week of up to an hour in length, extending for around three months.

Exercise is an effective intervention for many conditions, improving both physical health and mental health. In the case of depression, exercise not only helps to ease some of the symptoms, but it can also work by protecting someone against developing depression in the first place, or at the very least helping to prevent it from occurring again (88).

Longitudinal studies have produced some encouraging findings. One such study showed that those who were most physically active were less likely to be diagnosed with depression years down the line (89). In fact, there was a clear relationship between the duration of daily exercise and a reduction in the risk of depression. However, for many studies, the causality of effect is difficult to determine (90).

When looking at exercise within the framework of a randomized controlled trial, there is strong evidence to show that self-reported symptoms of depression reduce as a result of the intervention (91). Indeed, the authors of this study likened the positive effects of physical exercise to that of cognitive behavioural therapy.

In most cases, exercise is used in conjunction with an existing accepted form of intervention and, in this sense, is referred to as an adjunct to a particular therapy (92). However, studies have been conducted to examine the impact of exercise as a stand-alone therapy. One study compared different intensities of exercise and varied the frequency of sessions and showed that higher intensity exercise was central to reducing self-ratings of depression independent of the number of sessions carried out per week (92).

Even when exercise is explicitly compared to drug therapy, the results are encouraging. Blumenthal and colleagues (93) showed no difference between an exercise group and one receiving medication. This finding was mirrored when looking at those in remission following the intervention, with no difference between the exercise and medication groups.

Once initiated, exercise also seems to lessen the likelihood of future episodes of depression. Following instructions to continue the regular exercise on completion of the trial, one study produced findings that indicated the exercise group was linked to lower rates of relapse when compared to the group receiving medication (94). This and similar findings support the notion that physical exercise is not only good as an intervention in the short term but also there appear to be long-term benefits for the individual if the activity is maintained (95).

However, these findings are not necessarily as clear-cut as once thought due to several flaws in methodology (91).

Regarding how to prescribe exercise, one must consider different things, including the form the activity takes, the intensity of the training, and how long one should exercise. In terms of form, we are probably more familiar with aerobic exercise. This is a process whereby oxygen provides the required energy to perform and is associated with sustained and elevated activity of both the heart and lungs. The types of exercise that produce this effect include walking, running, and riding bicycles.

An alternative form of exercise is described as anaerobic. This is a term that most will associate with biology lessons in school and nothing more. In fact, it is a form of exercise many of us perform regularly. Examples of this form of exercise include weight training or resistance bands. In other words, activities that require brief but intense bursts of energy. Anaerobic exercise refers to situations where oxygen is not the only energy supplier because the blood is unable to meet the demands of the muscles for this type of activity. Instead, the body reverts to using energy already stored in the body.

A third type focuses on improving agility and is best encapsulated in yoga. Most studies have not shown any difference between aerobic and anaerobic exercise in terms of reducing depression (90, 91). Most research has focused on aerobic exercise and, as a result, has amassed a more extensive evidence base to support its use (90).

Although there has not been much research exploring differences in the effectiveness of the various forms of exercise, there has been research looking at how different intensities of exercise influence efficacy. The upshot of most early studies is that it matters not how intense the exercise is, merely that it takes place in one form or another. However, this is by no means reflected in the findings of all studies on the topic. Dunn and colleagues (92) showed that effectiveness was determined by how many calories were expended.

It sometimes feels that a day does not pass without some reference in the news to how many minutes we should be exercising each day to be healthy. There is unlikely to be a definitive answer. The important thing is to be aware of our activity levels and aim to squeeze into our hectic lives as much as possible.

There have been *post hoc* rationalizations why exercise produces the effects we see. It is undoubtedly the case that exercise improves self-efficacy (90). In this sense, people who adopt a regular exercise regimen demonstrate they are proactive in life by doing what they can to improve their lot, be it physical or mental. Self-worth also improves as a result of supportive feedback provided by others around them (7). Exercising likely provides a necessary distraction from the internal monologue central to depression (96).

There are clear social gains from physical exercise. In many cases, exercise involves contact with other people, be it jogging around a park, attending a gym, or walking to the shop to buy the newspaper (assuming people still do that). Being in the presence of others, even if just fleeting, provides a sense of connection. It also adds an element of competition into the mix. All of this can be harnessed to boost motivation to maintain activity.

Aside from the obvious psychosocial factors, exercise certainly produces biological changes that likely contribute to improvements in psychological functioning (97). Levels of crucial neurotransmitters linked to depression are raised through exercise—increased plasma monoamine—including serotonin, dopamine, and noradrenaline. Exercise also increases free fatty acids. Fatty acids are a great source of energy for the body. Their availability increases dramatically with moderately intense exercise.

Depression is linked to heightened activity of the hypothalamic–pituitary–adrenal (HPA) axis. Such action indicates raised levels of stress (see Chapter 3). Regular exercise helps a person achieve higher levels of resilience when confronted with future incidences of stress.

Endorphin (β-endorphin) is released during exercise. This is an endogenous opioid that has effects comparable to opiates. They are generally associated with prolonged exertion, such as the "high" experienced by runners. As a result, endorphin not only has a soothing effect but also acts as an analgesic, thereby alleviating pain. Therefore, these effects are acute and appear not to play a role in exercise's long-term, sustained impacts.

Neuroplasticity is involved here also. Brain-derived neurotrophic factor (BDNF) is increased through exercise and improves learning and memory formation. Interestingly, from an evolutionary perspective, it makes sense for there to be a close link between physical and mental activities (98). In our distant past, physical effort was often associated with attempts to escape danger. Not only was it necessary to make a quick departure, but it was also essential that appropriate information was learned to better adapt to or avoid such situations at some future point (99).

The main challenge in using exercise as an intervention for depression is compliance. The very nature of depression means that a person lacks drive and energy, which are essential for initiating and then sustaining exercise (100). To help, professionals often tap into techniques associated with motivational interviewing, a procedure shown to be highly effective at producing changes in behaviour (101). Offering exercise programmes catering to the needs of older adults is one way to act to reduce levels of depression among this age group (1).

Regular exercise has been shown to reduce inflammation (102). This inflammation issue is something I shall come back to in Chapter 9. It appears to be implicated in a range of conditions, including depression. This links to the notion that a healthy body is essential for a healthy mind.

Light therapy

As we saw in Chapter 2, there is a form of depression where episodes are determined by the season. This is referred to seasonal affective disorder (SAD) (103), or what is now referred to as recurring major depression with a seasonal pattern (104). It is generally associated with winter. The characterizing symptom here is a significant reduction in activity, increased time spent sleeping, and increased weight gain.

A known treatment for this condition is light therapy. The assumption here is that lowered mood, when related to winter-onset, is due to a reduction in light levels during this season. One method requires individuals to sit in front of a lightbox for around 30 minutes each morning (105). Therefore, increasing a person's exposure to light will offset this deficit. When light enters the eye, one of its effects is to reduce levels of melatonin, the hormone associated with regulating our sleep–wake cycle. There is evidence from some studies of its effectiveness (106). However, little has been written about possible treatment for this condition outside of the winter months. Because this involves exposure to bright light, it might not be suitable for some individuals, especially those taking St John's Wort, as one of the side effects of this remedy is increased photosensitivity. In some cases, people also report headaches, especially those who have experienced migraine (13).

Having looked at a range of possible treatment options, the following section examines how each individual's levels of care are decided. I am referring here to the current stepped-care model. Some of the interventions described earlier are best aimed at mild-to-moderate depression. In contrast, some interventions are specifically designed with more severe cases in mind. In Chapter 8, we will look in detail at some biological treatment options, many of which are aimed at treating more severe symptoms.

Stepped-care model

The premise behind the stepped-care model is that the most effective treatment is offered with the least level of restriction on the individual (107). If a benefit is not derived from the entry-level of care, the next step in the care process is offered. This is the model of care embedded within the current IAPT programme (108). However, the success with which this approach is implemented in real life mostly depends on resources. As we know, resources are particularly scarce in mental healthcare services (7). There is also a leaning towards collaborative care (109). This is where there is a care manager in the form of a health professional who takes responsibility for the individual's well-being (110). This, more often than not, occurs within primary care. Treatment is the focus here, with little consideration of additional follow-up other than that recommended for a particular intervention.

The stepped-care model is an effective way of determining the appropriate level of intervention. The ethos of this approach is that a person is first offered a level of care that is both maximally effective and minimally intrusive. If the situation worsens, a care programme at the next step is provided (26).

Step 1 in this model is appropriate for all suspected cases of depression. It involves assessing needs, active support and monitoring, and referral for additional assessment and treatment. It is common for people at this stage to feel agitated and experience thoughts about taking their own life. Because of that, it is essential that they know how to elicit help should they feel the need.

Step 2 is aimed at mild-to-moderate depression and includes low-intensity psychological therapies, medication, and additional referral if required. There is a need to closely monitor the individual to ensure all appointments are kept. Some of the interventions offered at this step include guided self-help rooted in CBT, computerized CBT (CCBT), or a physical activity programme. Group CBT might also be offered.

Step 3 is appropriate where there has been a minimal response to previous interventions and the level of care demanded by those with moderate-to-severe depression. At this step, medication is offered alongside more intensive psychological therapies. It is usual for SSRIs to be the drug of choice. The therapy packages at this level are more intensive. They may take many forms, including CBT, IPT, behavioural activation, and behavioural couples therapy.

Step 4 is for severe depression with a substantial risk of harm to self or others. This level is characterized by high-intensity interventions, electroconvulsive therapy, crisis service, and possible inpatient care. Such cases generally require input from a multi-professional team to meet their complex and changing needs. When assessing someone for Step 4 care, particular attention should be paid to the possible use of alcohol or other substances, as well as to the presence of a personality disorder. Crisis management is a critical component of the care package. The aim here is to identify potential triggers for specific harmful behaviours, and in so doing, develop strategies to reduce or eliminate them.

In many cases, at this stage, inpatient care is required. During a person's stay in hospital, medication is provided under the strict guidance of the consultant psychiatrist (26). Inpatient care is necessary when there is evidence that the person poses a severe suicide risk or is likely to cause either harm to themselves or others and show signs of extreme self-neglect.

In many cases, there is little evidence to support the worthiness of one model of care over another. However, there does seem to be a growing body of evidence to suggest collaborative care might be an exciting alternative. The main issue here is that this evidence is mainly from the United States, so adoption into a UK system might be complicated (111).

Collaborative care, then, begins with patients and clinicians identifying what the problems are (112). Specific issues are then jointly decided as being the focus of particular interventions. This leads to the identification and training in a range of self-management programmes. This all occurs with access to an appropriate support structure. Follow-ups occur at regular intervals so that the patient can bring to the healthcare professional any specific problem they might still be experiencing. These follow-up sessions also act to reinforce any progress made. This model of care is increasingly evident with the provision of low-intensity interventions of IAPT, as mentioned earlier (113).

One of the main underlying concerns when deciding upon an appropriate level of care is the risk of suicide. When considering long-term goals, there is a solid drive to try to identify strategies that will potentially reduce the risk of suicide, and it is to this that we now turn our attention.

Suicide prevention

In 2013, the World Health Organization (WHO) implemented the first Mental Health Action Plan. Suicide prevention was high on the agenda, with an explicit aim to reduce by 10 per cent the rate of suicide by the end of the decade (114).

Globally, there are over 800,000 suicides each year (figure reported for 2012) (115). For the UK and Ireland, the number is around 6,000 (116). However, this figure is likely to underestimate the actual rate of suicide. This is because the death might be misconstrued as an accident or the fact that it is illegal in some countries impacts reporting accuracy. The actual process of registering death by suicide is complicated. So, for many, the exact cause of death is never known.

We know there is a complex picture when looking at the male-to-female ratio of suicide, with rates depending mainly on the country's wealth. In affluent countries, more men die from suicide than women. However, this ratio falls when one looks at rates in more impoverished areas. Suicides occur more frequently in older adults. However, depending on the country, there are significantly high rates of suicides among 15- to 29-year-olds.

Underpinning many suicides is a sense that the person is alone, with all avenues of support closed to them because of perceived stigma around their condition. This means that, in many cases, deaths because of suicide could have been prevented.

Regarding what we know about major risk factors for suicide, probably the most predictive is a previous suicide attempt (117). Self-harming behaviour is linked to a higher risk of attempted and completed suicide (117, 118). Also, a mental health condition contributes in many cases, especially depression (119), as does alcohol or drug misuse, feeling isolated, medical complaints, unemployment, and financial pressure (116). From a global societal perspective, there are several hugely influential factors at play, including discrimination, violence, abuse, and wars and natural disasters (115).

When exploring what can be done to help prevent suicides from occurring, aside from trying to continue the battle against the stigma surrounding mental health conditions, we know that gaining access to means of achieving the end goal is pivotal. However, when you look at the issue worldwide, there are clear preferences for different groups of people, be it access to guns, chemicals, or footbridges. Except for obvious cases, it is unclear how access to various items could be regulated. It would require a concerted effort to ensure appropriate restrictions are in place.

Access to support is critical in all this. This is especially important for men as evidence indicates men are less likely to talk about feelings that might lead to suicide (120). Nearly three-quarters of the deaths linked to suicide occurred without the appropriate health professional being aware that the person had been experiencing difficulties (121). Restricting the number of tablets prescribed at any one time can reduce the risk of suicide by overdose. There need to be stricter measures in accident and emergency departments to ensure those suspected of being at risk of suicide receive the necessary intervention immediately. It is vital that younger generations are encouraged to explore and talk about their feelings, so schemes at the school level will be helpful and are indeed showing positive outcomes (122).

Approaches to suicide prevention can take three forms. Policies, such as improved access to healthcare services, are aimed at the whole population and are referred to as a universal prevention strategy. Alternatively, specific groups could be targeted, forming selective prevention strategies, such as those who have experienced trauma. The most micro-level of support indicated prevention strategies, focusing on the individual most at risk, such as providing the appropriate level of community support and training in coping strategies (115).

One of the things we have just seen is that in all too many cases, a person's general practitioner is not aware of the severity of someone's depression. In these cases, they do not suspect suicide might be a risk. In previous chapters, we have also seen that depression can be a challenging thing to diagnose, at least early on. We know, too, that making an accurate diagnosis is particularly problematic with older adults. The following section will look at the role of effective communication between patients and doctors.

Effective communication

We saw in Chapter 2 that some GPs are relatively poor at accurately detecting depression. One explanation for this centres around the effectiveness of their communication skills. In particular, GPs who demonstrate excellent communication skills instil an environment in which the patient feels more comfortable talking about their problems, providing the GP with more evidence of distress. In so doing, there is more on which the GP can base their preliminary diagnosis (8). Studies have provided evidence to suggest that, among other things, recognition among GPs that there is a problem and that there is something that can be done about it contributes to better patient outcomes (123). Strangely enough, although skills training for GPs does improve outcomes, it does little to improve how often depression is recognized (124). The effect was partly due to a better experience throughout the care process.

With the growing expectation that we can help direct our treatment, patients and clients no longer expect to be kept in the dark. Reinforcing such an active role can only improve compliance. This will also feed into improving the therapist–client or doctor–patient relationship. However, this largely depends on the personality of the patient and the doctor to a large extent. When looking at the types of complaints patients make, a large proportion is around poor communication. A clinician who is in tune with how the patient is feeling will be better able to take accurate notes that will inform a more precise diagnosis (125). I am, of course, talking about emotional intelligence (see Chapter 4). High emotional intelligence in the clinician improves the service they offer to patients and provides them with greater job satisfaction and lower levels of job stress (125).

Availability of services

Although there has been an increase in the availability of various therapies, it is still the case that many do not receive the level of support they need. One of the main drivers behind increasing the availability of services is public demand, often in the form of user groups, for the commissioning of a particular service. However, there is a financial cost associated with interventions for depression. One-to-one therapies are costly. Given the restrictive budget allocated, there is an ever-present desire to find alternatives to existing interventions that show a comparable level of effectiveness and are less expensive.

As we saw at the beginning of this chapter, IAPT works at the level of primary care to help individuals diagnosed with depression or anxiety return to full functioning as soon as possible. The ethos here is to improve accessibility through an enhanced budget and increase the number of trained staff to deliver the various interventions. There is a broadening out of therapies on offer within this programme, ranging from the high-cost high-intensity therapies, such as CBT, to the low-intensity approaches where therapists are less involved, such as guided self-help.

Summary

In this first chapter on treatment and management strategies for depression, we have looked at psychological approaches. We began by looking at strategies that can be adopted by the individual who is experiencing less severe symptoms of depression. These approaches include using a range of self-help resources with or without the involvement of a therapist. We then looked at various talking therapies covering the entire spectrum and including counselling approaches and more behavioural interventions. We then turned our attention to more cognitively informed CBT and attention training approaches. We also explored how various treatment and management strategies are allocated by referring to the stepped-care model. Finally, the issue of effective communication between patient and doctor, or client and therapist, was highlighted as a way of better improving diagnosis and monitoring and outcome of care programmes. One of the things that we cannot avoid is that demand still outstrips the availability of services. There is no clear resolution to this. In fact, one might only see the disparity between demand and availability worsening year on year as people become more cognizant of their own feelings and know what services are out there. Unless more money is allocated to mental healthcare services, the future is bleak.

References

1   World Health Organization. Depression: Fact sheet 2017. Available from: www.who. int/mediacentre/factsheets/fs369/en/.
2   Great Britain. Department of Health. Fast-forwarding primary care mental health: "Gateway" workers. London: Department of Health; 2002.
3   Department of Health. Improving access to psychological therapies: Implementation plan: National guidelines for regional delivery. London: Department of Health; 2008.   https://www.scie-socialcareonline.org.uk/improving-access-to-psychologi-cal-therapies-implementation-plan-national-guidelines-for-regional-delivery/r/a11 G00000017sXQIAY#:~:text=Improving%20access%20to%20psychological%20 therapies%3A%20implementation%20plan%3A%20national,needed%20to%20 deliver%20the%20implementation%20of%20IAPT.%20
4   NHS England. Adult improving access to psychological therapies programme. NHS England; 2019. Available from: www.england.nhs.uk/mental-health/adults/iapt/.
5   Madhukar H. Trivedi, A. John Rush, Stephen R. Wisniewski, Andrew A. Nierenberg, Diane Warden, Louise Ritz, et al. Evaluation of outcomes with citalopram for depression

using measurement-based care in STAR*D: Implications for clinical practice. Am J Psychiatry. 2006;163(1):28–40.

6 Zimmerman M, Chelminski I, McGlinchey JB, Young D. Diagnosing major depressive disorder X: Can the utility of the DSM-IV symptom criteria be improved? J Nerv Ment Dis. 2006;194(12):893–897.

7 Anderson I, Pilling S, Barnes A, Bayliss L, Bird V. The NICE guideline on the treatment and management of depression in adults. National Collaborating Centre for Mental Health, National Institute for Health and Clinical Excellence. London: The British Psychological Society & The Royal College of Psychiatrists; 2010.

8 Hollon SD, Stewart MO, Strunk D. Enduring effects for cognitive behavior therapy in the treatment of depression and anxiety. Annu Rev Psychol. 2006;57:285–315.

9 Kazdin AE. Evidence-based treatment and practice: New opportunities to bridge clinical research and practice, enhance the knowledge base, and improve patient care. Am Psychol. 2008;63(3):146.

10 Umscheid CA, Margolis DJ, Grossman CE. Key concepts of clinical trials: A narrative review. Postgrad Med. 2011;123(5):194–204.

11 Pagoto SL, McDermott MM, Reed G, Greenland P, Mazor KM, Ockene JK, et al. Can attention control conditions have detrimental effects on behavioral medicine randomized trials? Psychosom Med. 2013;75(2):137–143.

12 Lindseth G, Helland B, Caspers J. The effects of dietary tryptophan on affective disorders. Arch Psychiatr Nurs. 2015;29(2):102–107.

13 Wasserman D. Depression. 2nd ed. Oxford: Oxford University Press; 2011.

14 Schwarzer C, Buchwald P. Social support. In: Spielberger CD, editor. Encyclopedia of applied psychology. Amsterdam; Oxford: Academic; 2004.

15 Harris T, Brown GW, Robinson R. Befriending as an intervention for chronic depression among women in an inner city. 1: Randomised controlled trial. Br J Psychiat. 1999;174(3):219–224.

16 Papakostas GI, Petersen T, Mahal Y, Mischoulon D, Nierenberg AA, Fava M. Quality of life assessments in major depressive disorder: A review of the literature. Gen Hosp Psychiatry. 2004;26(1):13–17.

17 Miller IW, Keitner GI, Schatzberg AF, Klein DN, Thase ME, Rush AJ, et al. The treatment of chronic depression, part 3: Psychosocial functioning before and after treatment with sertraline or imipramine. J Clin Psychiatry. 1998;59(11):608–619.

18 Vittengl JR, Clark LA, Jarrett RB. Improvement in social-interpersonal functioning after cognitive therapy for recurrent depression. Psychol Med. 2004;34(4):643–658.

19 Rogers CR. The necessary and sufficient conditions of therapeutic personality change. J Consult Psychol. 1957;21(2):95.

20 Cain DJ, Seeman J. Humanistic psychotherapies: Handbook of research and practice. Washington, DC; London: American Psychological Association; 2002.

21 Egan G. The skilled helper: A systematic approach to effective helping. Belmont, CA Brookes Cole Publishing; 1990.

22 Egan G. The skilled helper: A systematic approach to effective helping. 4th ed. Pacific Grove, CA: Brooks/Cole; London: Chapman & Hall [distributor]; 1990.

23 Bower P, Rowland N, Hardy R. The clinical effectiveness of counselling in primary care: A systematic review and meta-analysis. Psychol Med. 2003;33(2):203–215.

24 Freud S. On murder, mourning, and melancholia. London: Penguin Books; 2005.

25 American Psychological Association. Psychoanalysis vs. psychodynamic therapy. American Psychological Association; 2017 [December 2017, 48(11)]. Available from: www.apa.org/monitor/2017/12/psychoanalysis-psychodynamic.

26 National Institute for Health and Care Excellence. Depression in adults: Recognition and management. NICE guidelines [CG90]. 2009.

27 Ellis A. Reason and emotion in psychotherapy. 1962. Available from: https://pubmed.ncbi.nlm.nih.gov/31990491/

28 Beck AT. Cognitive therapy of depression. Chichester: Wiley; 1980.

29 Beck AT. The past and future of cognitive therapy. J Psychother Pract Res. 1997;6(4):276.

30 Segal ZV, Gemar M, Williams S. Differential cognitive response to a mood challenge following successful cognitive therapy or pharmacotherapy for unipolar depression. J Abnorm Psychol. 1999;108(1):3–10.

31 Garratt G, Ingram RE, Rand KL, Sawalani G. Cognitive processes in cognitive therapy: Evaluation of the mechanisms of change in the treatment of depression. Clin Psychol Sci Pract. 2007;14(3):224–239.

32 Segal Z, Williams J, Teasdale J. Mindfulness-based cognitive therapy for depression. New York: Guilford Press; 2002.

33 Kabat-Zinn J. Full catastrophe living: Using the wisdom of your body and mind in everyday life. New York: Delacorte; 1990.

34 Williams J, Russell I, Russell D. Mindfulness-based cognitive therapy: Further issues in current evidence and future research. J Consult Clin Psychol. 2008;76(3):524–529.

35 Hunot V, Moore TH, Caldwell DM, Furukawa TA, Davies P, Jones H, et al. 'Third wave' cognitive and behavioural therapies versus other psychological therapies for depression. Cochrane Database Syst Rev. 2013;10:1–46.

36 Miller MC. Therapy for troubled relationships. In: Harvard Health Publications, editor. Harvard Medical School commentaries on health. Boston, MA: Harvard Health Publications; 2019.

37 Lewinsohn PM. The behavioral study and treatment of depression. In: Hersen M, Eisler RM, Miller PM, editors. Progress in behavior modification. Vol. 1. New York; London: Academic Press; 1975, pp. 19–64.

38 Jacobson NS, Martell CR, Dimidjian S. Behavioral activation treatment for depression: Returning to contextual roots. Clin Psychol Sci Pract. 2001;8(3):255–270.

39 Hopko DR, Lejuez C, Ruggiero KJ, Eifert GH. Contemporary behavioral activation treatments for depression: Procedures, principles, and progress. Clin Psychol Rev. 2003;23(5):699–717.

40 Jacobson NS, Dobson KS, Truax PA, Addis ME, Koerner K, Gollan JK, et al. A component analysis of cognitive-behavioral treatment for depression. J Consult Clin Psychol. 1996;64(2):295–304.

41 Ekers D, Richards D, Gilbody S. A meta-analysis of randomized trials of behavioural treatment of depression. Psychol Med. 2008;38(5):611–623.

42 Longmore RJ, Worrell M. Do we need to challenge thoughts in cognitive behavior therapy? Clin Psychol Rev. 2007;27(2):173–187.

43 Hofmann SG, Asmundson GJ. Acceptance and mindfulness-based therapy: New wave or old hat? Clin Psychol Rev. 2008;28(1):1–16.

44 Harris R. Embracing your demons: An overview of acceptance and commitment therapy. Psychother Aust. 2006;12(4):70.

45 Hooper NA, Larsson AA. The research journey of acceptance and commitment therapy (ACT). Basingstoke, Hampshire: Palgrave Macmillan; 2015.

46 Wilson K, Hayes S, Strosahl K. Acceptance and commitment therapy: An experiential approach to behavior change. New York: Guilford Press; 2003.

47 Gilbert PJ. The compassionate mind: A new approach to life's challenges. London: Constable; 2010.

48 Kohlenberg RJ, Tsai M. Functional analytic psychotherapy: A radical behavioral approach to treatment and integration. J Psychother Int. 1994;4(3):175.

49 Wells A. Metacognitive therapy for anxiety and depression. New York; London: Guilford; 2011.

50 Lynch TR, Morse JQ, Mendelson T, Robins CJ. Dialectical behavior therapy for depressed older adults: A randomized pilot study. Am J Geriatr Psychiatry. 2003; 11(1):33–45.

51 Hooley JM, Teasdale JD. Predictors of relapse in unipolar depressives: Expressed emotion, marital distress, and perceived criticism. J Abnorm Psychol. 1989;98(3):229.

52 Christian JL, O'Leary KD, Vivian D. Depressive symptomatology in maritally discordant women and men: The role of individual and relationship variables. J Fam Psychol. 1994;8(1):32.

53 Jones E, Asen E. Systemic couple therapy and depression. Karnac Books; 2000.

54 Fan J, McCandliss BD, Sommer T, Raz A, Posner MI. Testing the efficiency and independence of attentional networks. J Cogn Neurosci. 2002;14(3):340–347.

55 Jha AP, Baime MJ, Sreenivasan K. Attention. In: Ingram RE, editor. The international encyclopedia of depression. New York; London: Springer; 2009.

56 Lutz A, Slagter HA, Dunne JD, Davidson RJ. Attention regulation and monitoring in meditation. Trends Cogn Sci. 2008;12(4):163–169.

57 Eriksen CW, St James JD. Visual attention within and around the field of focal attention: A zoom lens model. Percept Psychophys. 1986;40(4):225–240.

58 Jha AP, Krompinger J, Baime MJ. Mindfulness training modifies subsystems of attention. Cogn Affect Behav Neurosci. 2007;7(2):109–119.

59 Nolen-Hoeksema S. The role of rumination in depressive disorders and mixed anxiety/depressive symptoms. J Abnorm Psychol. 2000;109(3):504–511.

60 Ramel W, Goldin PR, Carmona PE, McQuaid JR. The effects of mindfulness meditation on cognitive processes and affect in patients with past depression. Cognit Ther Res. 2004;28(4):433–455.

61 D'Zurilla TJ, Nezu AM. Problem-solving therapy: A positive approach to clinical intervention. 3rd ed. New York: Springer; 2006.

62 Nezu AM, Nezu CM, Clark MA. Social problem solving as a risk factor for depression. In: Dobson KS, Dozois DJA, editors. Risk factors in depression. London: Academic; 2008, pp. 263–286.

63 Nezu CM, Nezu AM. Problem-solving therapy. In: Ingram RE, editor. The international encyclopedia of depression. New York; London: Springer; 2009.

64 Cuijpers P, van Straten A, Warmerdam L. Problem solving therapies for depression: A meta-analysis. Eur Psychiatry. 2007;22(1):9–15.

65 Nezu AM, Perri MG. Social problem-solving therapy for unipolar depression: An initial dismantling investigation. J Consult Clin Psychol. 1989;57(3):408–413.

66 Christopher G. The psychology of ageing: From mind to society. Basingstoke, Hampshire: Palgrave Macmillan; 2014.

67 Christopher G, MacDonald J. The impact of clinical depression on working memory. Cogn Neuropsychiatry. 2005;10(5):379–399.

68 Lockwood KA, Alexopoulos GS, Kakuma T, Van Gorp WG. Subtypes of cognitive impairment in depressed older adults. Am J Geriatr Psychiatry. 2000;8(3):201–208.

69 Nadler JD, Richardson ED, Malloy PF, Marran ME, Brinson MEH. The ability of the Dementia Rating Scale to predict everyday functioning. Arch Clin Neuropsychol. 1993;8(5):449–460.

70 Kiosses DN, Klimstra S, Murphy C, Alexopoulos GS. Executive dysfunction and disability in elderly patients with major depression. Am J Geriat Psychiatry. 2001; 9(3):269–274.

71 Alexopoulos GS, Kiosses DN, Klimstra S, Kalayam B, Bruce ML. Clinical presentation of the "depression—executive dysfunction syndrome" of late life. Am J Geriatr Psychiatry. 2002;10(1):98–106.

72 Alexopoulos GS, Kiosses DN, Heo M, Murphy CF, Shanmugham B, Gunning-Dixon F. Executive dysfunction and the course of geriatric depression. Biol Psychiatry. 2005;58(3):204–210.

73 Alexopoulos GS, Meyers BS, Young RC, Kalayam B, Kakuma T, Gabrielle M, et al. Executive dysfunction and long-term outcomes of geriatric depression. Arch Gen Psychiatry. 2000;57(3):285–290.

74 Alexopoulos GS, Raue PJ, Kanellopoulos D, Mackin S, Arean PA. Problem solving therapy for the depression-executive dysfunction syndrome of late life. Int J Geriatr Psychiatry. 2008;23(8):782–788.

75 Nezu AM, Ronan GF. Social problem solving as a moderator of stress-related depressive symptoms: A prospective analysis. J Couns Psychol. 1988;35(2):134.

76 Nezu AM, Perri MG. Social problem-solving therapy for unipolar depression: An initial dismantling investigation. J Consult Clin Psychol. 1989;57(3):408.

77 Paul Liberman R, Corrigan PW. Designing new psychosocial treatments for schizophrenia. Psychiatry. 1993;56(3):238–249.

78 Arie S. Simon Wessely: "Every time we have a mental health awareness week my spirits sink." BMJ. 2017;358:j4305.

79 Miller MC. Remembering as a form of therapy. In: Harvard Health Publications, editor. Harvard Medical School commentaries on health. Boston, MA: Harvard Health Publications; 2014.

80 Butler RN. The life review: An interpretation of reminiscence in the aged. Psychiatry. 1963;26(1):65–76.

81 Erikson EH. Identity and the life cycle: Selected papers. New York: International Universities Press; 1968.

82 Erikson EH, Erikson JM. The life cycle completed. Extended/with new chapters on the ninth stage of development (ed. Joan M. Erikson). New York; London: W.W. Norton; 1997.

83 Hsieh HF, Wang JJ. Effect of reminiscence therapy on depression in older adults: A systematic review. Int J Nurs Stud. 1 May 2003;40(4):335–345.

84 Elias SM, Neville C, Scott T. The effectiveness of group reminiscence therapy for loneliness, anxiety and depression in older adults in long-term care: A systematic review. Geriatr nur. 2015 Sep 1;36(5):372–380.

85 Bohlmeijer ET, Westerhof GJ, Emmerik-de Jong M. The effects of integrative reminiscence on meaning in life: Results of a quasi-experimental study. Aging Ment Health. 2008 Sep 1;12(5):639–646.

86 Niederehe G. Psychosocial therapies with depressed older adults. In: Schneider LS, editor. Diagnosis and treatment of depression in late life: Results of the NIH Consensus Development Conference. Washington, DC; London: American Psychiatric Press; 1994.

87 Cheston RA, Christopher GA. Confronting the existential threat of dementia: An exploration into emotion regulation. Cham, Switzerland: Palgrave Pivot; 2019.

88 Stephens T. Physical activity and mental health in the United States and Canada: Evidence from four population surveys. Prev Med. 1988;17(1):35–47.

89 Paffenbarger RS, Jr., Lee IM, Leung R. Physical activity and personal characteristics associated with depression and suicide in American college men. Acta Psychiatr Scand Suppl. 1994;377:16–22.

90 Karwoski L, McCurdy D, Mccurdy D. Exercise and depression. In: Ingram RE, editor. The international encyclopedia of depression. New York; London: Springer; 2009.

91 Lawlor DA, Hopker SW. The effectiveness of exercise as an intervention in the management of depression: Systematic review and meta-regression analysis of randomised controlled trials. BMJ. 2001;322(7289):763–767.

92 Dunn AL, Trivedi MH, Kampert JB, Clark CG, Chambliss HO. Exercise treatment for depression: Efficacy and dose response. Am J Prev Med. 2005;28(1):1–8.

93 Blumenthal JA, Babyak MA, Moore KA, Craighead WE, Herman S, Khatri P, et al. Effects of exercise training on older patients with major depression. Arch Intern Med. 1999;159(19):2349–2356.

94 Babyak M, Blumenthal JA, Herman S, Khatri P, Doraiswamy M, Moore K, et al. Exercise treatment for major depression: Maintenance of therapeutic benefit at 10 months. Psychosom Med. 2000;62(5):633–638.

95 Singh NA, Clements KM, Singh MA. The efficacy of exercise as a long-term antidepressant in elderly subjects: A randomized, controlled trial. J Gerontol A Biol Sci. 2001;56(8): M497–M504.

96 Mynors-Wallis LM, Gath DH, Day A, Baker F. Randomised controlled trial of problem solving treatment, antidepressant medication, and combined treatment for major depression in primary care. BMJ. 2000;320(7226):26–30.

97 Brosse AL, Sheets ES, Lett HS, Blumenthal JA. Exercise and the treatment of clinical depression in adults: Recent findings and future directions. Sports Med. 2002; 32(12):741–760.

98 Vaynman S, Ying Z, Gomez-Pinilla F. Hippocampal BDNF mediates the efficacy of exercise on synaptic plasticity and cognition. Eur J Neurosci. 2004;20(10): 2580–2590.

99 Noakes T, Spedding M. Olympics: Run for your life. Nature. 2012;487(7407):295–296.

100 Blumenthal JA, Smith PJ, Hoffman BM. Is exercise a viable treatment for depression? ACSMs Health Fit J. 2012;16(4):14–21.

101 Rollnick S, Miller WR, Butler C. Motivational interviewing in health care: Helping patients change behavior. New York; London: Guilford; 2008.

102 Flynn MG, McFarlin BK, Markofski MM. State of the art reviews: The anti-inflammatory actions of exercise training. Am J Lifestyle Med. 2007;1(3):220–235.

103 Rosenthal NE, Sack DA, Gillin JC, Lewy AJ, Goodwin FK, Davenport Y, et al. Seasonal affective disorder: A description of the syndrome and preliminary findings with light therapy. Arch Gen Psychiatry. 1984;41(1):72–80.

104 American Psychiatric Association. Diagnostic and statistical manual of mental disorders: DSM-5. 5th ed. Arlington, VA.: American Psychiatric Association; 2013.

105 NHS. Seasonal affective disorder 2015. Available from: www.nhs.uk/conditions/seasonal-affective-disorder-sad/treatment/.

106 Golden RN, Gaynes BN, Ekstrom RD, Hamer RM, Jacobsen FM, Suppes T, et al. The efficacy of light therapy in the treatment of mood disorders: A review and meta-analysis of the evidence. Am J Psychiatry. 2005;162(4):656–662.

107 Bower P, Gilbody S. Stepped care in psychological therapies: Access, effectiveness and efficiency. Br J Psychiat. 2005;186(1):11–17.

108   Health Do. Improving access to psychological therapies: Specification for the commissioner-led Pathfinder programme. In: Health Do, editor. London; 2007. Available from: https://webarchive.nationalarchives.gov.uk/ukgwa/20130123192014/http://www.dh.gov.uk/en/Publicationsandstatistics/Publications/PublicationsPolicyAnd Guidance/DH_074555

109   Bower P, Byford S, Sibbald B, Ward E, King M, Lloyd M, et al. Randomised controlled trial of non-directive counselling, cognitive-behaviour therapy, and usual general practitioner care for patients with depression. II: Cost effectiveness. BMJ. 2000;321(7273):1389–1392.

110   Archer J, Bower P, Gilbody S, Lovell K, Richards D, Gask L, et al. Collaborative care for depression and anxiety problems. Cochrane Database Syst Rev. 2012;10: CD006525.

111   Campbell M, Fitzpatrick R, Haines A, Kinmonth AL, Sandercock P, Spiegelhalter D, et al. Framework for design and evaluation of complex interventions to improve health. BMJ. 2000;321(7262):694.

112   Wagner EH. Managed care and chronic illness: Health services research needs. Heal Serv Res. 1997;32(5):702.

113   Peveler R, George C, Kinmonth A-L, Campbell M, Thompson C. Effect of antidepressant drug counselling and information leaflets on adherence to drug treatment in primary care: Randomised controlled trial. BMJ. 1999;319(7210):612–615.

114   World Health Organization. Mental health action plan 2013–2020; 2013. Available from: https://www.who.int/publications/i/item/9789241506021.

115   World Health Organization. Preventing suicide: A global imperative: World Health Organization; 2014. Available from: https://www.who.int/publications/i/item/9789241564779.

116   Mental Health Foundation. Suicide 2017. Available from: www.mentalhealth.org.uk/a-to-z/s/suicide.

117   Klonsky ED, May AM, Glenn CR. The relationship between nonsuicidal self-injury and attempted suicide: Converging evidence from four samples. J Abnorm Psychol. 2013;122(1):231.

118   Bergen H, Hawton K, Waters K, Ness J, Cooper J, Steeg S, et al. How do methods of non-fatal self-harm relate to eventual suicide? J Affect Disord. 2012;136(3):526–533.

119   Hawton K, Houston K, Haw C, Townsend E, Harriss L. Comorbidity of axis I and axis II disorders in patients who attempted suicide. Am J Psychiatry. 2003;160(8):1494–1500.

120   Wylie C, Platt S, Brownie J, Chandler A. Men, suicide and society. London: Samaritans; 2012.

121   Hewlett E, Horner K. Mental health analysis profiles: OECD Working Paper No. 81; 2015. Available from oecd.org/officialdocuments/publicdisplaydocumentpdf.

122   Katz C, Bolton SL, Katz LY, Isaak C, Tilston-Jones T, Sareen J. A systematic review of school-based suicide prevention programs. Depress Anxiety. 2013;30(10):1030–1045.

123   Ormel J, Van Den Brink W, Koeter M, Giel R, Van Der Meer K, Van De Willige G, et al. Recognition, management and outcome of psychological disorders in primary care: A naturalistic follow-up study. Psychol Med. 1990;20(4):909–923.

124   van Os TW, van den Brink RH, Tiemens BG, Jenner JA, van der Meer K, Ormel J. Are effects of depression management training for General Practitioners on patient outcomes mediated by improvements in the process of care? J Affect Disord. 2004;80(2):173–179.

125   Birks YF, Watt IS. Emotional intelligence and patient-centred care. J R Soc Med. 2007;100(8):368–374.

Chapter 8

Treatment and management
Biological

Antidepressants

First introduced in the 1950s, antidepressants have remained central to the success-ful treatment of depression. Since the release of imipramine, a tricyclic antidepres-sant, the first of its type, the field has grown (1). The following section will expand further on the different forms of antidepressants now available. At the time of their development, antidepressants, as well as antipsychotics, were seen as revolution-ary. In conjunction with advancements in psychotherapy, the once untreatable were seen to make miraculous recoveries. There was a change in perspective, with clini-cians no longer being carers but rather curers of long-term mental health problems. As it might be predicted, the initial euphoria that such medication provided a pana-cea for mental illness (as it was termed at the time) was short-lived. Early drugs, especially antipsychotics, were far from targeted in their action and led to an array of alarming side effects. These side effects were more debilitating than the original symptoms in many cases.

Debates are needed to consider the apparent ubiquity of antidepressants, with concerns about over-prescribing and over-reliance on a quick, chemical fix to help deal with the vicissitudes of life. However, for many, drugs provide the much-needed support to deal effectively with depression.

Prescription of antidepressants should be considered if the person has had a past history of depression, or where the current symptoms have been present for around two years.

Antidepressants vary in terms of their pharmacological impact; which neuro-transmitter system is targeted, in other words. Neurotransmitters are chemical mes-sengers that either excite or inhibit other cells. Serotonin and noradrenaline levels are particularly affected. Drugs act to increase levels of these chemicals, although the exact mechanism behind the improvements in mood is not yet fully understood.

As with all forms of care, the individual is involved at all stages of the pro-cess. This includes the selection of antidepressants. At this stage, the clinician will discuss the various drug options and highlight adverse events associated with each particular drug, the specification of potential side effects, and what might happen once the drug is stopped. There will also be a discussion around possible

DOI:10.4324/9781315688879-8

drug interactions resulting from existing medication and/or known physical health issues. In cases where the person has previously been prescribed an antidepressant, the clinician will explore their experiences of the medication, focusing specifically on its perceived effectiveness and identifying any issues they may have faced when taking it, especially concerning tolerance.

Before a person begins taking the antidepressant, they should be aware of what will happen once they start. For example, the prescriber should stress that there will be no immediate antidepressant effect. Instead, this will take time to manifest. It should also be emphasized that it is essential to continue with the medication for the prescribed period once started. It should be stressed that medicine should be continued even after remission.

Although there have been initiatives to help reduce the prevalence of depression, much work still needs to be done to combat the condition. An epidemiological study conducted in 1995 showed only a third received some form of medication, and it was not always an antidepressant (2). However, this figure is rising.

Offsetting the increased prescribing of antidepressants is a fall in costs. This is because there is an increase in antidepressants available as generic drugs. Generic drugs refer to preparations exactly the same as an existing brand name.

Tricyclic antidepressants (TCAs)

As already stated earlier, a tricyclic, imipramine, was the first antidepressant. We also saw that these early drugs brought with them unexpected and untoward side effects, vastly diminishing their acceptability as a treatment for depression. Another big problem with these first drugs was the genuine risk of overdose and subsequent death. Given that these drugs were heralded as a cure for those with profound depression and its concomitant risk of suicide, the very real fact that there was a high risk of toxicity if taken in excess made the situation far from perfect. This profile of drug action led to the development of a safe form of antidepressant, the selective serotonin reuptake inhibitors (SSRIs), a class of drugs that will be examined shortly.

TCAs block the reuptake of monoamines. Monoamines include noradrenaline (NA), 5-hydroxytryptymine (5-HT), and dopamine (DA), although DA is less affected by this class of drug (3).

Selective serotonin reuptake inhibitors

The selective serotonin reuptake inhibitors (SSRIs) developed out of a response to improving the acceptability of the TCAs available at the time. These drugs were particular in targeting serotonin. First launched in 1987, SSRIs have become the most widely prescribed class of antidepressants. They also addressed the need to reduce the risk of overdose.

Serotonin (5-hydroxytryptamine; 5-HT) is primarily focused around the midline of the brain stem, although there are receptors throughout the central nervous system. The neurotransmitters targeted are the same as those affected by the TCAs.

SSRIs, then, operate by increasing levels of monoamines such as NA and 5-HT. Serotonin is implicated in several processes, mainly regarding mood regulation. However, it is also involved in pain sensitivity, sleep, and arousal, among other things. Low levels of this neurotransmitter are linked to depression, aggression, and suicide (4).

Serotonin transporter (5-HTT)—a protein found in the presynaptic membranes—reprocesses unwanted serotonin. The SSRI class of drugs blocks the work of this transporter protein, thereby preventing the removal of serotonin from sites where it is needed.

SSRIs are the first choice for treating depression. This is because they are effective and are less risky than some other medications. However, constant monitoring is needed when prescribed to older adults as they have been known to interfere with blood clotting and damage the gastrointestinal mucosa. One option is to also prescribe gastroprotective drugs in those at higher risk, such as those currently taking non-steroidal anti-inflammatory drugs (NSAIDs) or aspirin, both of which are known to irritate the stomach lining (5).

One of the main issues with SSRIs is that it can take several weeks before the person can discern a noticeable effect on their overall mood and ability to function. It is not clear why this is the case. However, it does mean that an additional level of support is required during this transition phase.

It is also important to note that SSRIs are efficacious in treating conditions other than depression. These include obsessive–compulsive disorder, panic disorder, and premenstrual dysphoric disorder.

Serotonin and noradrenaline reuptake inhibitors

The class of drugs known as serotonin and noradrenaline reuptake inhibitors (SNRIs) may be used for those who have failed to respond to the more common SSRI treatment. They block the reabsorption of both serotonin and noradrenaline, ensuring that appropriate levels of both are maintained.

Monoamine oxidase inhibitors and reversible inhibitors of MAO-A

Monoamine oxidase inhibitors (MAOIs) act by inhibiting the enzyme monoamine oxidase. These enzymes target monoamines, such as noradrenaline and serotonin, breaking down or metabolizing them. Reversible inhibitors of MAO-A (RIMAs) are a specific subtype of MAOI drugs. They are generally safer than older MAOIs when taken in overdoses.

Melatonergic antidepressants

Melatonergic antidepressants are used to treat recurring major depression with a seasonal pattern. This class of drug is beneficial in restoring better sleep patterns at night without daytime sedation.

Anticonvulsants and mood stabilizers

Anticonvulsants, such as carbamazepine which is generally used to treat epilepsy, and other drugs such as lithium can be used for depression as a mood stabilizer. They help to regulate mood, preventing it from fluctuating wildly.

Third-generation antidepressants

Looking back at the development of antidepressant medication, there are three main waves of development. The first-generation drugs were the tricyclics and monoamine oxidase inhibitors which had a non-specific effect of increasing levels of monoamines either by reducing the metabolism of these neurotransmitters or by inhibiting reabsorption or reuptake. They were far removed from being targeted in their action. The second-generation antidepressants were more specific about what they targeted and were safer. This wave included selective serotonin reuptake inhibitors. There were still issues with the delay between first taking the medication and subsequent symptom improvement. Third-generation antidepressants are not concerned only with the neurotransmitter serotonin. They are described as having a variable mode of action. They are heralded as quicker acting than the previous generation of drugs (6).

Antidepressants for different age groups

There are age-related factors to consider when prescribing antidepressants. In the case of those in their teens, SSRIs have been linked to increased suicidal ideation. As a result, there are strict limits on which medications to prescribe, with fluoxetine (Prozac) being the only SSRI licensed for this age group. Unlike most antidepressants, primarily prescribed by GPs, it is crucial that a psychiatrist prescribe medications with weekly check-ups for the initial month or so for young people. In terms of older adults, prescribers must be cognizant of the increased risk from concurrent medical conditions, such as cerebrovascular disease (7). In addition, there are fears that SSRIs are linked to increased risk of falls in older adults, leading to heightened demand for alternative drugs. However, there is a lack of concrete evidence about causation at the moment (8). Therefore, again, careful monitoring for adverse effects is needed for this age group. More information about age-specific issues relating to the use of antidepressants is presented in Chapter 6.

Sex differences

There is a lack of consistency in the findings of studies that have been designed to see if there were any differences in terms of how men and women respond to the diverse forms of antidepressants. The general assumption is no apparent sex differences (9). However, the clear exception is when considering treating women for depression who are of childbearing age (10).

Combining and augmenting

When another non-antidepressant drug is prescribed in combination with an anti-depressant, it is called augmentation. In some instances, where two antidepressant drugs are jointly prescribed, it is called combination. Such actions should take place only after consultation with a psychiatrist in either case. Only medications that are known to work well in tandem should be selected. However, there may be an increase in the number of side effects experienced by the individual. In which case, benefits should be weighed against the noticeable costs. During such treatment, careful monitoring should occur to ensure no adverse events.

Examples of drugs used in combination or augmentation include lithium, antipsychotics, and other antidepressants. Each type of drug brings specific contraindications relating to health and well-being. In the case of lithium—used in the treatment of bipolar disorder—kidney and thyroid function should be closely monitored. For those at risk of cardiovascular disease, careful monitoring of heart function should also occur. When using antipsychotics, some individuals may experience movement disorders, such as tremor and involuntary, repetitive movements of the body, referred to as tardive dyskinesia. Grouped together, these are described as extrapyramidal symptoms. A person's weight and lipid and glucose levels need to be regularly checked.

Sometimes it is felt necessary to augment an antidepressant with a benzodiazepine. Although justifiable to eliminate extreme agitation or anxiety, there is a risk of dependence for periods exceeding two weeks.

Issues with antidepressants

As with most medications, antidepressants are associated with several side effects, although these are relatively mild and short-lived in most cases. The severity of the side effects is dependent on the dose prescribed (9). Earlier forms of antidepressants tend to be associated with a condition known as dry mouth. The drug causes salivary gland hypofunction (11). In addition, constipation is common here also, as is agitation, dizziness, among others. However, these depend on the class of drug prescribed (12).

TCAs are characterized by a range of symptoms linked to the drug's action on the cholinergic neurotransmitter system, specifically the blocking of acetylcholine. These symptoms include sedation and forgetfulness (13). There are also links between TCAs and increased hypotension and tachycardia. When first taking SSRIs, many report feeling nauseous and more anxious. Headaches are reported too. SSRIs also interfere with sexual functioning in some cases.

One of the more worrying side effects of taking antidepressants is that it might increase suicidal ideation and increase the risk of suicide for some. This appears to be especially the case in adolescents and young adults (9). Because of this, individuals should be warned of this eventuality when they first begin to take the medication. However, the potential for such a risk needs to be weighed alongside the risk of not treating depression.

One option for those who experience side effects on starting a course of antidepressants is to prescribe benzodiazepine if the anxiety and sleep problems are an issue (5). Clearly, this should only be a temporary measure as this class of drug can be highly addictive. Of course, an alternative would be to try another antidepressant. It is entirely dependent on the person's well-being at the time of assessment.

People should not suddenly stop taking antidepressants as several unpleasant side effects have been reported. Symptoms reported include heightened anxiety, diarrhoea, and also disturbing dreams. Because of this, the dose of the drug should be slowly reduced over a few weeks or months. In some cases, liquid forms of the medication can replace pills so that an appropriately small titrated dose can be administered to facilitate this process. This is because it is next to impossible to cut pills accurately to the necessary dose.

One of the controversies surrounding antidepressants and their effect centres on the delay between commencing the drug and any noticeable effect for the patient. The pharmacological effect is immediate; the subjective effect can take weeks.

Compliance

A big problem for healthcare professionals is ensuring a prescribed course of medication is adhered to. The issue of compliance transcends all areas of mental health. The success of any medication rests on the assumption that the drug being prescribed is given at an adequate dose and that the recipient will comply with the instructions provided (14). However, this does not always happen.

Patients should comply with the regimen suggested by the clinician. This is because a particular intervention, or a combination of interventions, are thought to best fit the requirements of the individual, taking all relevant factors into consideration. However, some circumstances prevent patients from complying with these dictates.

High up on the list is the presence of side effects. We have seen that a range of rather unpleasant side effects is associated with antidepressants. One of the main problems is that no two individuals will respond in precisely the same way to a specific drug. This is due mainly to individual differences in how the drug is processed by the body and idiosyncrasies in terms of comorbid conditions and their attendant medications. Strict protocols are published, such as those recommended by NICE, to guide clinicians in treating specific conditions. For many, the first course of action will prove successful. However, there will need to be much trial and error for a large number to attain a successful combination of treatments. During this process, the patient may experience side effects with little to show in terms of alleviation of symptoms.

It is during this time that compliance becomes a real issue. Quite understandably, the individual may challenge the rationale for following the instructions given to them. Doses may be skipped or stopped altogether without the clinicians being immediately aware. Although this may seem a reasonable course of action, it is far from ideal for producing the desired effect. What is needed in such instances is a review of either the dose or class of drug prescribed.

Evidence of efficacy

The primary evidence for a particular drug's effectiveness comes from placebo-controlled randomized controlled clinical trials (RCTs). A placebo—an inert substance—controls the active medication under scrutiny. Although taken as the gold standard for evidence-based therapy, there are unmistakable flaws associated with this methodology.

It would be incorrect to assume that a person receiving a non-active placebo is equivalent to someone not receiving any form of treatment. Even though they are not being given an active medication, they still meet regularly with the research team and clinicians involved in the trial. In this sense, they are receiving various forms of support and input throughout the life of the trial. Besides, spontaneous remission may occur during the trial, depending on the severity of the condition. This would clearly not be due to any form of intervention provided as it would have happened anyway.

There is also the issue of ecological validity to consider here in terms of the people recruited into the trial. In short, those who are actively recruited and participate in clinical trials tend to be less severe in terms of symptomatology. In some cases, people may be excluded if they have a comorbid condition. Because of such factors, there is an increased likelihood that they will recover spontaneously during the trial itself (15).

There are clear ethical reasons for not recruiting those with more severe symptoms onto a trial. This is because there is likely to be a higher risk of suicide on top of the more severe depressive symptoms. So, for this reason, it would be unethical to randomly allocate that person to one arm of the RCT where there is a possibility they will fall into the control condition (9).

Someone who has undergone remission during the active arm of a trial will contribute to the apparent success of the intervention, even though, clearly, they would have experienced symptom reduction regardless. On the other hand, if these spontaneous remissions occur within the control arm of the trial, it will weaken the effect of the treatment under study. It may give the impression that the intervention is not significantly different from the control (9).

It might not be surprising to know that there is a reasonably high dropout rate in clinical trials. Figures vary, but some studies have indicated around 35 per cent do not complete the entire study. This may be due to self-withdrawal, or it might be the fact that a member of the clinical team decides to withdraw individual participants (16). There are various implications of this when looking at the reported outcomes. For many trials, published data reflects only those who completed the whole study. However, there is a growing awareness that an intention-to-treat ethos should be adopted, where findings report data from the entire sample regardless of whether they completed or not.

There are several issues relating to assessing the individual once the trial has started. Even though the majority of RCTs are double-blind—in other words, neither the participant nor the researcher/clinician is aware of to which arm of the trial the person has been allocated—there is nothing that can be done to blind either participant or researcher to the stage at which the assessment is taking place. Because of this, one cannot really control for the expectation of improving the further into a trial someone is assessed (9).

Inevitably drugs come pre-packaged with a range of side effects. The manifestation of side effects will clearly un-blind both participant and researcher. However, to overcome this issue, it is possible to include a placebo control where active drug elements mimic the drug's side effects under trial, but nothing that will actually impact the condition being studied.

For most physical and mental conditions, symptoms tend to fluctuate in severity either across days or, in some cases, within the same day. This is a factor to consider when looking at baseline data collected at the start of a trial. In the case of someone who presents with high levels of symptom severity at baseline, it is only the nature of the condition that symptoms would be rated as less severe at the subsequent assessments. It is merely the nature of the condition. This reflects the ebb and flow of the person's felt experience. This is referred to in the literature as regression to the mean. In other words, a person who rates a symptom as severe on one occasion is likely to rate it closer to the overall mean when next assessed.

However, now is not the place to go into a full critique of RCTs. There are issues not discussed here that make one question some trials' findings. These include the impact of industry funding on how successful a trial appears to be (17), as well as the perennial issue of journals favouring positive outcomes in their published outputs (18). As a final point, although there are clearly problems with RCTs, there is no real alternative at the moment. RCT data still informs decisions about which treatment to recommend for specific conditions. Because of this, we must be mindful of the potential confounds that exist.

Before we move on to look at other things, given we have just spent a reasonable length of time talking about prescribed antidepressants, it is worth considering a readily available alternative treatment.

Alternative treatments

St John's Wort is an herbal remedy. It contains an extract from the *Hypericum perforatum* plant. It has long been associated with the treatment of depression. However, it is still classed as alternative medicine, not licensed in the UK. Just what the active ingredients are that contribute to its antidepressant effect is unclear. However, not knowing the exact pharmacological mechanism for drug action is not unheard of even among licensed medications. You only have to consider SSRIs to see examples of that.

Data on the efficacy of St John's Wort as a treatment for depression is still unclear. There is evidence that it might be helpful in those with mild to moderate depression. However, the validity of such claims needs to be questioned, given the apparent publication bias in the reported findings (19). Less evidence is available that looks at the effectiveness of this remedy for more severe forms of the condition.

There are concerns also around the strength of the various available preparations of St John's Wort. Different products have different strengths and so are not comparable. The composition of over-the-counter remedies is not determined through the same process as licensed products. In other words, the expected evidence base around efficacy or tolerance is not available for such preparations (9). There are also particular concerns over St John's Wort interacting with other drugs (20, 21).

An important caveat when considering over-the-counter remedies is that these should be included in any medication review. There will likely be implications in terms of the effectiveness of the prescribed medication.

Before considering other biological approaches to treating depression, we should consider psychosis. Many diagnosed with depression will experience such symptoms. In instances where a person experiences psychotic symptoms with depression, there is a need to augment treatment with an antipsychotic.

So far, we have focused on treatments and interventions that mainly involve the individual leading a reasonably independent life. In other words, we have been looking at treatment within a person's own home environment, with monitoring occurring through outpatient appointments. In more severe cases, where the levels of risk are high, some form of organized care, often involving hospital stays, is required.

Day hospital

The increasing use of day care as an alternative to inpatient care is a way to reduce some of the costs usually associated with hospital stays. These units provide treatment for those who require an additional element of supervision during their care. However, there is little evidence to show that day hospitals reduce the likelihood of inpatient care further down the line (9).

Inpatient care

Inpatient care is generally offered to individuals who are unresponsive to treatments provided through outpatient appointments. The symptoms are more severe and persistent for those with depression referred to such care. However, again, there seems to be a lack of an overall consensus as to the efficacy of such care compared to that received in outpatient clinics (9) when looking at the reduction of subsequent admissions and overall acceptability among other things.

We now turn our attention to more extreme forms of treatment, ones that require a medical procedure and even surgery. We will examine electroconvulsive therapy, transcranial magnetic stimulation, vagus nerve stimulation, and deep brain stimulation.

Electroconvulsive therapy

Electroconvulsive therapy (ECT) is considered appropriate when a person's life is threatened by their current state. It might be the case, for example, that someone no longer responds to their own internal needs for food and drink, or it may be that they are experiencing severe guilt-fuelled delusions and hallucinations. Often ECT is used to provide a quick response to an escalating situation. In many cases, a person who has been referred for a course of ECT has failed to respond adequately to the current treatment regimen. A systematic review of the literature showed that ECT is an effective short-term treatment for depression, with better outcomes than existing drug therapies (22).

For ECT to go ahead, the person must consent to it after being made aware of the potential risks this treatment might bring. They have the right to withdraw from the procedure at any point. However, it is not always possible to obtain consent from the individual. This is because their condition is so severe that they are unresponsive and experience extreme impairment of function. They may be in a state of life-threatening dehydration and malnutrition. To protect the individual's rights in this situation, the person's carer or supporter will be approached to ensure appropriate treatment. At this stage, the clinical team must ensure the proposed intervention does not go against any existing advance decision provided by the individual.

Because it is a medical procedure, and anaesthesia is used, there are the usual associated risks. During ECT, a person's heart rate and blood pressure increase, which is especially risky if the person has pre-existing heart problems (23). The principal, noticeable side effect of ECT is cognitive impairment following each session. The individual's age being considered is a significant risk factor, with older adults being particularly prone to such difficulties following ECT.

However, one should note that, although there are physical and psychological risks from the administration of ECT, these have to be weighed against the risks associated with the person not receiving the treatment. It is, after all, an issue of quality of life.

Some level of cognitive impairment is inevitable from this procedure. This is why the clinical team needs to consider where best to position the electrodes during the treatment, determine the seizure threshold, and the minimum required electrical dose to induce a seizure (24). Bilateral ECT is the most efficacious in comparison to unilateral ECT. The cost here is the higher likelihood of more pronounced cognitive impairment following treatment. Where unilateral ECT is adopted, a higher stimulus dose is needed to produce the desired effect. However, this again comes at the risk of causing more significant subsequent impairment.

The outcome following each ECT session should be logged using standard clinical assessments. Measures should include examining general orientation and memory both before and after the treatment to quantify retrograde and antero-grade amnesia—loss of memory for events leading up to the treatment and im-mediately after it—resulting from the procedure. This battery of measures needs to also include an indication of the subjective memory complaints experienced by the individual. Once these measures signal remission from depression, ECT should be stopped. If the clinical team assess the severity of the side effects outweigh the benefits, ECT should also be discontinued (5). Such measures will also ensure that, if the level of cognitive impairment is too high, alternative strategies can be considered, such as reducing the dose or changing to unilateral ECT if a bilateral procedure had been previously used.

Following a successful course of ECT, to prevent or reduce the likelihood of relapse, antidepressants should be prescribed. In some cases, antidepressants are augmented with lithium to maximize effectiveness.

The use of ECT has always been enshrouded in a storm of controversy. Initially seen as a revolutionary way to treat previously untreatable conditions, it fell out of favour amidst fears concerning the morality of the technique. Even though debates have raged in the background, the use of ECT continues to this day. There is evidence of a resurgence of belief in the method (25).

In terms of how it works, the mechanisms are still unclear. However, it does appear to influence levels of key neurotransmitters—serotonin and dopamine—like drug treatments (26). Evidence shows that ECT stimulates the release of brain-derived neurotrophic factor, a protein involved in neuroplasticity. Having seen that high immunological function is also linked to depression, more recent research indicates that ECT dampens the immune response (25).

Transcranial magnetic stimulation

Transcranial magnetic stimulation, or TMS for short, is a technique for modulating cortical activity and lends itself to treating mental health conditions such as depression. Repetitive administration of the method—rTMS—produces effects that extend beyond the treatment session.

Depression is associated with changed functioning within the prefrontal cortex, notably decreased left hemisphere activation. There are options for unilateral stimulation of either the right or left dorsolateral prefrontal cortex or bilateral stimulation. rTMS is generally administered on a daily basis for up to six weeks. Each session lasts around 30 minutes. By combining high-frequency rTMS to the left hemisphere and low-frequency rTMS to the right, the argument is that balance is re-established in terms of how the two hemispheres operate (27).

Because it is non-invasive, there is no need for an anaesthetic. It also lends itself to being offered on an outpatient basis. TMS might be considered an option in cases where a person has not responded to a course of antidepressant medication. It might also be an option in instances where antidepressants should not be prescribed, such as for people who cannot tolerate the drug (28).

According to NICE's recommendations (29), there is reasonable evidence that it effectively treats depression in the short term. However, there is a great deal of variation in how people respond. There have been no identifiable concerns with safety.

So far, we have considered non-invasive techniques to treat depression. We will now look at surgical procedures that have proved effective at combatting depression at the more severe end, in cases deemed treatment resistant.

Vagus nerve stimulation

Vagus nerve stimulation (VNS) is a procedure that was initially used to treat epilepsy by reducing the rate of seizures a person experiences. The mechanism of action involves a range of key brain regions, including the amygdala and hypothalamus, resulting from projections of the VNS with nerve fibres terminating in these specific locations (30).

VNS is an option for treatment-resistant depression. The use of VNS in depression stemmed from observations that mood improved among those who were treated with VMS for epilepsy. Indeed, the link with epilepsy is not a new one. The idea that controlled epileptic convulsions could be harnessed medically arose in part from anecdotal reports indicating that, for those with epilepsy, mood following a seizure was often improved. In some cases, depression can be reduced by anti-seizure medication. However, there is a long way to go to build an evidence base for this.

The person receiving this VNS is first given a general or local anaesthetic. This enables the implanting of the electrode that stimulates the left vagus nerve, with leads being inserted subcutaneously that lead to a pulse generator located in the left chest wall. Stimulation of the nerve is not continuous but instead is delivered in short bursts followed by a period of rest. For most, it is a 30-second burst every 5 minutes.

When looking at trial data, up to a half of the sample improved to some extent, with around a third showing full recovery (31), and what's more, this improvement persisted over time. However, participants in some of these early studies were aware of their treatment. These are referred to as open trials. In other words, participants are not randomly allocated to a condition as is the preferred option. However, it is difficult to concoct an RCT that can be used in this case, given the invasive nature of VNS. Where comparison treatments have been incorporated into the study design, the effects have been more negligible but nonetheless significant in some cases. As with many treatments, it is challenging, if not impossible, to predict who might benefit from this procedure; a considerable concern given this is a surgical intervention, with a host of possible complications associated with this type of approach (31), including residual pain and infection. Also, there can be side effects from the stimulation itself. These include discomfort in the neck and surrounding area, headaches, and problems swallowing, among other things. It is also a costly procedure.

Because of all this and the fact that there needs to be more evidence of wholesale effectiveness, VNS should only be considered an option for people who have not responded to a host of other interventions. Evidence to date has not shown an effect in the short term, with improvement only occurring after several months. So, as a treatment, the patient needs to show resolve to see the course of therapy through (31).

Deep brain stimulation

There has been a long and reasonably fruitful history in using deep brain stimulation to treat a variety of conditions. These have included Parkinson's disease and obsessive–compulsive disorder. There is a growing interest in using this technique to alleviate depression.

Deep brain stimulation is where an electrode is inserted into a specific brain area, and electrical stimulation is delivered to this location. As with VNS, a pulse generator is embedded in the chest.

Several smallish studies have been conducted to see if this technique effectively treats depression, particularly depression that has been resistant to previous forms of intervention. The preliminary findings appear encouraging (32, 33). However, more research data from more extensive trials have shown no effect on this technique for this patient group (34). However, the trials were not without limitations; the most important was their relatively short duration (35).

As with many a good idea, there is a concern that its effectiveness will lead to all manner of claims being made for its usefulness to treat myriad complaints. There is a danger of taking a step too far (35). As has been seen with drugs initially designed to improve cognitive functioning in those with mental health conditions, there is an ever-growing market among healthy individuals to take drugs to improve their lot, something that I discuss in Chapter 14 in my book, *The Psychology of Ageing: From Mind to Society* (36). The same will likely be true for more invasive techniques like deep brain stimulation, albeit at some future point in time. People no longer fear surgery if they feel they will be an improved version of themselves at the end of it. Look no further than cosmetic surgery. There is also concern that we are still uncertain how it works in many cases. The effect is relatively clear for something like Parkinson's disease, although not entirely so. Some worrying side effects of the treatment are reported in some instances, mainly linked to impulsivity (37).

However, in the case of something like depression, which is a mood disorder with a whole host of biological, psychological, and social factors thrown into the mix, explanations are lacking. In fact, in some cases, when it was trialled for use with depression, some participants reported feeling more depressed and suicidal (38). A significant difference between a condition like depression and Parkinson's disease is that the nature of the symptoms in Parkinson's disease warrants constant, long-term use of deep brain stimulation. This is because the symptoms are permanent. With something like depression, symptom severity wavers and disappears at varying times. That being the case, it is unfitting to consider a device that continually provides electrical impulses to the brain. Research is ongoing to develop a tool that picks up on specific brain activity. The deep brain stimulation starts only when the requisite profile is detected (39). It is early days yet, and research focuses on post-traumatic stress disorder rather than depression. However, it is an exciting avenue to investigate in the future.

Having explored the various biological treatments for depression in some depth, we need to consider something referred to previously in the chapter, namely treatment-resistant depression. What exactly is it?

Treatment-resistant depression

If it is the case that a person is appearing not to be responding as expected to the chosen package of interventions, then there are several essential points to consider. These are set out in the NICE guidelines, *Depression in Adults: Recognition and Management* (5). Indeed, this section will summarize the main points outlined in this document.

Regarding medication, if there appears to be an inadequate response, the clinician should first check that the prescribed dose is being adhered to. There are many reasons why a person might not take the required amount, including the fear of becoming dependent. Such concerns should be explored at the initial consultation phase. However, it is worth checking that the person is clear about what to expect. A lack of effect may also be due to the presence of side effects that confound the antidepressant nature of the medication.

It is good to monitor changes using an appropriate outcome measure in such cases. It might be the case that, if the medication is being adhered to, and there are no noticeable side effects, there is a need to increase the dose being prescribed. Alternatively, an option might be to switch to another antidepressant. Although there is little evidence to suggest there is, in fact, an advantage to such a move (5), one option might be to consider a newer-generation drug or even a different class of drug. However, there are likely to be tolerance issues with tricyclics and MAOIs.

In previous sections, we have talked about approaches that can be adopted to help prevent a person from experiencing another episode of depression once they have recovered. Relapse is common in depression. Therefore, it is vital to be clear what the implications are of not adhering to a medication regimen. This next section examines this further.

Preventing relapse

Patients should know the importance of continuing their medication following remission. The suggested minimum period is six months (40). There is a significantly reduced likelihood of relapse if this is adhered to. One of the main barriers for those on such medication is the fear that antidepressants are addictive and that the longer they take them, the worse it will be. Although generally argued not to be the case, people report withdrawal symptoms when stopping their medication (41). It has been suggested that an increase in symptom severity following a reduction in drug dose or discontinuation is, in many cases, a side effect of the drug's influence on the body. Rather than a relapse, such changes are signs of drug withdrawal symptoms. Because the depression seems to be returning, drugs are reintroduced, or doses increased. For some, this may be the wrong response (42).

The need for the continuation of antidepressant medication is especially pressing in individuals with residual symptoms of depression being experienced, where there are additional health conditions, or where they face issues within their social environment (5). Again, this is important for individuals who have had several previous episodes of depression.

For those at high risk of relapse, an option is to continue with the prescribed course of medication for at least two years. It is usual for the same dose to be prescribed during this continuation phase (9). This is most important for individuals who have experienced repeated episodes of depression over the years and where there is a significant risk of severe impairment to daily living and/or risk of suicide.

In addition to continuing medication, those considered at particular risk of subsequent relapse should be offered either individual CBT or MBCT. CBT aimed at relapse prevention is delivered to individuals and typically last for about six months, with roughly one session per month, although more may occur in the first couple of weeks. MBCT is usually delivered in groups, with weekly meetings for around two months, followed by four sessions throughout the subsequent 12-month period to monitor progress.

Before ending this chapter, we will look at the power of the placebo. An odd thing to include in a chapter on biological treatments, you might think. Still, there is strong evidence that the placebo effect operates at several levels. We should consider its impact as it is a significant confound for most studies assessing interventions.

Placebo effect

Some have argued that there is an overinflated response among those receiving placebo in clinical trials that aim to explore the effectiveness of antidepressant medication. For one, participants are paid to take part. There is also the amount of attention participants receive from researchers and clinicians during trials. When looking at symptom change in the active arm of the trial, there is a concern that the subjective measures used fail to do justice for the overall effects of the antidepressant. In other words, they do not capture the overall change in well-being (43).

There is much research examining the placebo effect. A placebo was initially defined as a chemical that had no effect on the body. It was pharmacologically inert. Yet, it physically resembled the drug being tested. This enabled researchers to test the pharmacological effects of a proposed new drug in isolation. The term placebo has also been used to describe the prescribing of medication to someone with no disease, but where there is an expectation that they will receive treatment (44). However, the use of the term has expanded considerably. It is no longer tied to the effects of medicine but can refer to situations where there is some form of interaction between patient and doctor, client and therapist. The placebo effect, then, refers to a situation where symptoms are modified by a person's beliefs about what is happening. Indeed, there is a growing interest in embracing the power of the placebo effect and channelling it effectively into mainstream care. However, as one might expect, this is not without opposition (45, 46).

It is certainly not within the remit of this book to come to any conclusion about the efficacy of the placebo effect for healthcare. However, I shall look at how people respond to being placed on a waiting list for treatment. Studies have shown that, among those waiting to receive treatment for depression, a fifth showed a level of improvement over a few weeks when placed on a waiting list. Clearly, many potential confounds here might plausibly explain the improvement, none of which link back to being on a waiting list. Studies have compared the response to a known treatment against either a waiting list control group or a treatment-as-usual (TAU) group. For both types of control, the degree of professional intervention is minimal.

As indicated, there are several possible explanations for the supposed placebo effect. That is why it is such a challenge to researchers. It is impossible to devise a water-tight design when the focus is on treating severe conditions in the real world. So, most methods are flawed to a varying extent in terms of how much interaction people in the control group receive from researchers and clinicians during the trial. Any form of engagement might be sufficient to produce a positive outcome, thereby invalidating any conclusions drawn by the team regarding a placebo effect.

However, it is not all negative. Studies comparing placebo against an antidepressant show potent effects for the non-active intervention, so strong, in fact, that it is difficult in some cases to identify a sufficiently strong indication of a pharmacologically significant impact (9).

Another big problem with this type of research is, somewhat inevitably, publication bias. This issue has been linked chiefly to trials funded by pharmaceutical companies (17). There is certainly evidence to show that, for milder forms of depression, antidepressants offer no advantage, as the condition remits after a finite time, and people generally respond positively to even the most minimal input. The power of the placebo is less supported for the more severe or more persistent form of depression.

Summary

News items about antidepressants pepper the newspapers and news websites. Although there is widespread adoption, their continued use is still and probably will remain controversial. Similarly, with medical procedures. When repeating the phrase, electroconvulsive therapy, it will immediately bring to mind, for a lot of people, scenes from the film *One Flew Over the Cuckoo's Nest*. Indeed, many believe that it is no longer used. The majority are unaware of the more invasive techniques discussed here. It is clear, however, that aside from the psychological approaches set out in Chapter 8, various biological methods can be used to treat often the more severe cases of depression, although antidepressants are commonly prescribed alongside a course of CBT. We have also seen that continuing treatment with antidepressants is an essential strategy to prevent or reduce the severity or frequency of relapse following recovery. Several ethical issues have been raised here and, although it is not really the place to go into many details, implications need to be considered.

References

1   Kuhn R. The treatment of depressive states with G 22355 (imipramine hydrochloride). Am J Psychiatry. 1958;115(5):459–464.
2   Lépine J-P, Gastpar M, Mendlewicz J, Tylee A. Depression in the community: The first pan-European study DEPRES (Depression Research in European Society). Int Clin Psychopharmacol. 1997;12(1):19–30.

3 Mindham R. Tricyclic antidepressants. In: Tyrer P, editor. Drugs in psychiatric practice. London: Butterworth Scientific; 1982, pp. 177–218.

4 Wilhelm K. Serotonin. In: Ingram RE, editor. The international encyclopedia of depression. New York; London: Springer; 2009.

5 National Institute for Health and Care Excellence. Depression in adults: Recognition and management. NICE guidelines [CG90]. 2009. Available from: https://www.nice. org.uk/guidance/cg90.

6 Olver JS, Norman T, Burrows G. Third-generation antidepressants: Do they offer advantages over the SSRIs?-editorial. Curr Ther. 2002;43(7):7.

7 Hickie IB. Antidepressants in elderly people. BMJ. 2011;343:d4660.

8 Gebara MA, Lipsey KL, Karp JF, Nash MC, Iaboni A, Lenze EJ. Cause or effect? Selective serotonin reuptake inhibitors and falls in older adults: A systematic review. Am J Geriatr Psychiatry. 2015;23(10):1016–1028.

9 Anderson I, Pilling S, Barnes A, Bayliss L, Bird V. The NICE guideline on the treatment and management of depression in adults. National Collaborating Centre for Mental Health, National Institute for Health and Clinical Excellence. London: The British Psychological Society & The Royal College of Psychiatrists; 2010.

10 National Institute for Health and Care Excellence. Antenatal and postnatal mental health: Clinical management and service guidance. National Institute for Health and Clinical Excellence; 2007. Available from: https://www.nice.org.uk/Guidance/CG45.

11 Daly C. Oral and dental effects of antidepressants. Aust Prescr. 2016;39(3):84.

12 NHS. Side effects: NHS; 2018. Available from: www.nhs.uk/conditions/antidepressants/side-effects/.

13 Riedel WJ, van Praag HM. Avoiding and managing anticholinergic effects of antidepressants. CNS Drugs. 1995;3(4):245–259.

14 Dunn RL, Donoghue JM, Ozminkowski RJ, Stephenson D, Hylan TR. Longitudinal patterns of antidepressant prescribing in primary care in the UK: Comparison with treatment guidelines. J Psychopharmacol. 1999;13(2):136–143.

15 Khan A, Leventhal RM, Khan SR, Brown WA. Severity of depression and response to antidepressants and placebo: An analysis of the Food and Drug Administration database. J Clin Psychopharmacol. 2002;22(1):40–45.

16 Stassen HH, Delini-Stula A, Angst J. Time course of improvement under antidepressant treatment: A survival-analytical approach. Eur Neuropsychophar. 1993;3(2):127–135.

17 Lexchin J, Bero LA, Djulbegovic B, Clark O. Pharmaceutical industry sponsorship and research outcome and quality: Systematic review. BMJ. 2003;326(7400):1167–1170.

18 Melander H, Ahlqvist-Rastad J, Meijer G, Beermann B. Evidence b (i) ased medicine—selective reporting from studies sponsored by pharmaceutical industry: Review of studies in new drug applications. BMJ. 2003;326(7400):1171–1173.

19 Linde K, Berner MM, Kriston L. St John's wort for major depression. Cochrane Database Syst Rev. 2008;4:CD000448. DOI: 10.1002/14651858.CD000448.pub3

20 Whiskey E, Werneke U, Taylor D. A systematic review and meta-analysis of Hypericum perforatum in depression: A comprehensive clinical review. Int Clin Psychopharmacol. 2001;16(5):239–252.

21 Henderson L, Yue Q, Bergquist C, Gerden B, Arlett P. St John's wort (Hypericum perforatum): Drug interactions and clinical outcomes. Br J Clin Pharmacol. 2002;54(4):349–356.

22 The UKECTRG. Efficacy and safety of electroconvulsive therapy in depressive disorders: A systematic review and meta-analysis. Lancet. 2003;361(9360):799–808.

23   Clinic M. Electroconvulsive therapy (ECT): Mayo Clinic; 2019. Available from: www.mayoclinic.org/tests-procedures/electroconvulsive-therapy/about/pac-20393894.

24   Chung KF. Relationships between seizure duration and seizure threshold and stimulus dosage at electroconvulsive therapy: Implications for electroconvulsive therapy practice. Psychiatry Clin Neurosci. 2002;56(5):521–526.

25   Hamzelou J. Can tainted treatment make a shock return? New Sci. 2016;231(3087):16–17.

26   Yatham LN, Liddle PF, Lam RW, Zis AP, Stoessl AJ, Sossi V, et al. Effect of electroconvulsive therapy on brain 5-HT^2 receptors in major depression. Br J Psychiat. 2010;196(6):474–479.

27   Demirtas-Tatlidede A, Pascual-Leone A. Transcranial magnetic stimulation. In: Ingram RE, editor. The international encyclopedia of depression. New York; London: Springer Publishing Company; 2009.

28   John Hopkins Medicine. Frequently asked questions about TMS. John Hopkins Medicine; 2019. Available from: www.hopkinsmedicine.org/psychiatry/specialty_areas/brain_stimulation/tms/faq_tms.html.

29   National Institute for Health and Clinical Excellence. Repetitive transcranial magnetic stimulation for depression (Interventional procedures guidance [IPG542]). National Institute for Health and Clinical Excellence; 2015. Available from: www.nice.org.uk/guidance/ipg542.

30   Vagus nerve stimulation. In: Tatum WOIV, Kaplan PW, Jallon P, editors. Epilepsy A to Z: A concise encyclopedia. 2nd ed. New York: Demos Medical; 2009. Available from: https://explore.bl.uk/primo_library/libweb/action/display.do?tabs=moreTab&ct=display&fn=search&doc=BLL01015692659&indx=1&recIds=BLL010 15692659&recIdxs=0&elementId=0&renderMode=poppedOut&displayMode=full&frbrVersion=&frbg=&&dscnt=0&scp.scps=scope%3A%28BLCONTENT%29 &tb=t&vid=BLVU1&mode=Basic&vl(297891280UI0)=any&srt=rank&tab=local_tab&dum=true&vl(freeText0)=Tatum%20Epilepsy%20A%20to%20Z%3A%20a%20 A%20concise%20encyclopedia&dstmp=1675062811247.

31   Miller MC. Vagus nerve stimulation: Does it help depression. In: Harvard Health Publications, editor. Harvard Medical School commentaries on health. Boston, MA: Harvard Health Publications; 2014.

32   Bewernick BH, Hurlemann R, Matusch A, Kayser S, Grubert C, Hadrysiewicz B, et al. Nucleus accumbens deep brain stimulation decreases ratings of depression and anxiety in treatment-resistant depression. Biol Psychiatry. 2010;67(2):110–116.

33   Morishita T, Fayad SM, Higuchi M-A, Nestor KA, Foote KD. Deep brain stimulation for treatment-resistant depression: Systematic review of clinical outcomes. Neurotherapeutics. 2014;11(3):475–484.

34   Dougherty DD, Rezai AR, Carpenter LL, Howland RH, Bhati MT, O'Reardon JP, et al. A randomized sham-controlled trial of deep brain stimulation of the ventral capsule/ventral striatum for chronic treatment-resistant depression. Biol Psychiatry. 2015;78(4):240–248.

35   Ridgway A. Short circuit. New Sci. 2015;228(3044):38–41.

36   Christopher G. The psychology of ageing: From mind to society. Basingstoke, Hampshire: Palgrave Macmillan; 2014.

37   Demetriades P, Rickards H, Cavanna AE. Impulse control disorders following deep brain stimulation of the subthalamic nucleus in Parkinson's disease: Clinical aspects. Parkinson's Dis. 2011;2011.

38 Ridgway A. Deep brain stimulation: A wonder treatment pushed too far? New Sci. 21 October 2015. Available from: https://www.newscientist.com/article/mg22830440-500-deep-brain-stimulation-a-wonder-treatment-pushed-too-far/.

39 Dougherty DD, Rezai AR, Carpenter LL, Howland RH, Bhati MT, O'Reardon JP, et al. A randomized sham-controlled trial of deep brain stimulation of the ventral capsule/ventral striatum for chronic treatment-resistant depression. Biol Psychiatry. 2015; 78(4):240–248.

40 NICE. Depression in adults: Recognition and management; 2016. Available from: www.nice.org.uk/guidance/cg90.

41 Wilson C. Nobody can agree about antidepressants. Here's what you need to know. New Sci. 02 October 2018. Available from: https://www.newscientist.com/article/mg23931980-100-nobody-can-agree-about-antidepressants-heres-what-you-need-to-know/.

42 Gotzsche PC. Antidepressants are addictive and increase the risk of relapse. BMJ. 2016;352:i574.

43 Kramer PD. Ordinarily well: The case for antidepressants. Basingstoke, Hampshire; Macmillan; 2016.

44 Youngson RM. Placebo effect. In: Youngson RM, editor. The Royal Society of Medicine health encyclopedia: The complete medical reference library in one A-Z volume. [Fully rev. and updated ed.]. London: Bloomsbury, 2000/2001.

45 Howick J, Bishop FL, Heneghan C, Wolstenholme J, Stevens S, Hobbs FDR, et al. Placebo use in the United Kingdom: Results from a National Survey of Primary Care Practitioners. PLoS One. 2013;8(3):e58247.

46 Schafer SM, Colloca L, Wager TD. Conditioned placebo analgesia persists when subjects know they are receiving a placebo. J Pain. 2015;16(5):412–420.

Chapter 9

Clinical implications and future directions

Future medication

Availability and demand

There is a worrying trend worldwide in the number of prescriptions written for antidepressant medication. In the United Kingdom alone, the number has doubled in the last ten years, with figures of around 30 million rising to 61 million (1). There are many possible reasons for this increase, not all negative. It could very well reflect a greater overall awareness of mental health issues. These figures demonstrate that people can better identify, either in themselves or others, when help is needed. It might also be the case that people are now much more willing to seek advice or support for the problems they face. One would hope both of these operate at some level. Both are positive in driving down the stigma associated with mental health conditions. The problem is one of resources, as usual. Assuming those prescribed antidepressants actually require antidepressants, and this is by no means always the case, one has to consider if antidepressants on their own are the most appropriate intervention. Demand inevitably outweighs availability. Dishing out drugs is the more convenient and the less resource-heavy option. The reality of long waiting lists for psychological interventions is the other, less palatable option for those in need of immediate support (2).

What of serotonin?

The use of antidepressants is now a worldwide phenomenon. There will inevitably be pros and cons to their use. We have also seen that there are issues with taking this class of drug. One is that we do not really know why they work. One of the main problems, as already seen, is that there is a substantial delay after taking SSRIs before any noticeable effect is detected for many. Why this happens is unclear. Some have argued that it is due to a protein in the brain that effectively blocks the distribution of serotonin (3). As with much of this early-stage research, the test subjects were rats. So, while possible explanations might feed into the development of future treatments until human clinical trials are conducted, we are still in the dark about the mechanisms at play here.

DOI:10.4324/9781315688879-9

Increased resistance?

The use of the term treatment-resistant depression has been on the increase, primarily to describe a subgroup of patients who fail to respond to existing antidepressant medications. Indeed, it may be the case that there is a group of patients who do not respond in the expected way. Our growing awareness is due to year-on-year increases in those diagnosed with the condition. However, an alternative explanation for this observation is that it is not the patients themselves who are treatment resistant. Rather, the current gamut of drugs is ineffective, or at least not as effective as once thought. We have already seen a change in perspective with the findings from more recent clinical trials of current medications. The withdrawal of major drug companies from developing new psychiatric drugs is just one symptom of this (4).

Long-term costs

There is growing concern about the implications of long-term use of antidepressants, more specifically, an over-reliance on drugs as a long-term treatment strategy, in terms of public health (5). Clearly, in many cases, antidepressants do work. However, people often struggle coming off the medication. The symptoms associated with withdrawal from antidepressants worryingly mirror the type and severity of symptoms the drug was meant to handle. People complain of increased anxiety, problems with sleep, and difficulties thinking. These side effects can remain for weeks. The severity of the symptoms can be lessened if a person is weaned off the drug slowly over an extended period using increasingly smaller titrated doses. The reality is that it can take months for this to happen successfully without causing the person more distress. The dilemma is whether these effects are merely due to washout from the extended use of the medication or whether they are symptomatic of a return of the depression.

Many of the current drugs operate by raising levels of serotonin. Research has shown that the body compensates for this by reducing its production of this neurotransmitter. This would explain why people might experience the side effects reported when they stop taking their medication (5, 6).

Increasing the risk?

Drugs that work by targeting serotonin come under much criticism. Aside from issues concerning just how effective they really are as an antidepressant, there is the fact that they appear to "work" for several conditions other than depression. The selective serotonin reuptake inhibitors (SSRIs) are ubiquitous in psychiatry. No one really knows why they appear helpful for such a broad spectrum of disorders. There is another thorn in the side of this reign of serotonin drugs. Research shows it might not be just low levels of serotonin implicated in depression but also raised levels (7). This has led to the discovery that different forms of serotonin neurons exist. The theory is that high serotonin in some areas will improve overall mood, but such levels are likely to have a deleterious effect in other regions of the brain (8). It is suggested that this might be why people sometimes report feeling anxious when first taking SSRIs (9).

On top of this, there is growing concern that taking antidepressants might increase the likelihood of future episodes of depression if a person does not receive a psychological intervention (10). In other words, medication alone does not seem to protect the person from future relapse.

It is clear, then, that aside from the various issues surrounding prescribing this class of drug, the current batch of antidepressant medication is not without its problems regarding long-term efficacy. The following section looks to the future to see what is currently being developed to improve the options available to treat this condition.

Unreliable trial data

We are all aware of the rise and rise of antidepressants. Since their inception in the 1950s, antidepressants have been heralded as an enormous triumph, one that led to the successful treatment of those with an often debilitating condition. As seen in Chapter 8, the variety of drugs available to treat depression has proliferated, with almost any age group or combination of symptoms catered for.

A major stumbling block of current treatments is depression that fails to improve with either psychological therapies or drug treatments (11). The theory that depression is caused by a lack of serotonin fed research and development into the SSRIs we are all familiar with. Early trials were complimentary about the apparent efficacy of these drugs. However, to some extent, this particular bubble has been burst, with more up-to-date tests showing a significantly attenuated success rate for these drugs.

One of the main reasons for the discrepancy in findings between recent studies and those carried out beforehand was the profile of the participants who took part in the various trials. When designing trials to test new drugs, great lengths are taken to draw up a set of inclusion and exclusion criteria that might be best seen to serve the purpose of the pharmaceutical industry in the potential future marketing of the drug. As such, the findings may appear to show dramatic improvements in the measures taken, but in terms of generalizability, they are strangely lacking. The screening criteria used are often so strict that the people who participate in the trial bear no resemblance to the proposed future recipients of the drug. For example, people are screened out if they have comorbid conditions, and we know that comorbidity is increasingly a problem for the general population.

Also, doses used are generally below the clinical standard, and the duration of treatment is vastly retracted (12). There are high levels of people withdrawing from the studies in many cases. Such high dropout rates will impact the overall findings, with artificially low remission rates being reported in many instances.

Trivedi and colleagues (12) conducted a large-scale study of citalopram, an SSRI, relevant to real-world patients. In fact, less than a quarter of those included in their study would have met the strict criteria usually set for efficacy trials (13). When comparing the outcomes from the trial separately for those who would have made the grade for standard efficacy trials with those who would not—in other words, the real-world sample—the more homogeneous sample showed better outcomes. Those who would not be eligible for such studies showed poorer response and remission rates, and it took longer for response and remission to occur. The implication here is that the magnitude of effect typically seen in phase III efficacy trials is inflated compared to what would be seen in the real world (13). Indeed, Zimmerman and colleagues (14) reported that less than 10 per cent of patients seen in practice would be deemed appropriate for inclusion in efficacy trials, a figure less than half that reported in the study by Wisniewski and colleagues (13). Another finding from the same team (13) is that the recommended length of treatment might be too short for an effect to be seen in real-world patients. There is also the issue of adverse effects. The level of side effects tends to be lower in the more homogenized samples recruited to clinical trials. The implication is that a less sanitized sample would be at risk of experiencing more drug side effects (13).

Another factor that plays a role in ramping up the apparent effect is that studies concluding a particular compound had no effect, or indeed a negative impact, may be glossed over and "forgotten," with only findings from positive trials making the light of day. This biasing in studies undermines the validity of the approval process carried out by the various regulating bodies. One way to draw a halt to such underhand practices is to ensure that all new trials are registered. That way, it will be possible to audit how many studies were recorded, how many were completed, if the findings were disseminated at conferences, and whether they were later published in peer-reviewed journals. Much is being done to ensure this is standard practice.

Are drug companies losing interest?

The previously prodigious outpourings from the pharmaceutical industry in relation to antidepressants appears to be teetering on the edge of a precipice. With global industries, the likes of GlaxoSmithKline (GSK) and Astra Zeneca, pulling the plug on research into drugs to treat major psychiatric disorders, specifically antidepressants and antipsychotics, the future looks bleak. One representative even went so far as to cite the subjective nature of improvement in mental health as a significant problem when trying to demonstrate the success of a particular drug (15). Medications today still retain their roots in the 1970s. Little has moved on. The focus has remained on modifying levels of critical neurotransmitters. More recent research increasingly presents us with a more complex picture regarding mental health issues. These are complex disorders that require interventions that mirror these intricacies. More research is needed to elucidate how nerve cells are lost, how they can be regenerated, how the immunological response is implicated, and many other factors that complicate the picture (15).

Ketamine

This worrying decision resulted in an endeavour to find plausible alternative treatments. Ketamine has been in the news a lot of late concerning its potential use to treat depression. Probably most commonly known as a tranquillizer used on animals, or indeed as a street drug (special K), it has been shown to produce effects that might be used clinically in humans (15). Ketamine hydrochloride is an *N*-methyl-D-aspartate (NMDA) receptor antagonist. Depression has been linked to over-stimulated NMDA receptors due to high levels of glutamate. The premise here is that ketamine can directly target and block the NMDA receptors. Early studies produced encouraging findings, with evidence that symptom relief occurred within a short space of time compared to the slow burn of current antidepressants (16). One such study showed that low doses of ketamine produced a reduction in symptoms after only three days (17). Ketamine also creates a sense of euphoria and hallucinogenic effect, which, even at the low doses used in such studies, is still detectable by participants, albeit for a short duration, thereby un-blinding them from the randomization in the process. Other studies show an effect with 24 hours (18) even in treatment-resistant depression. The result was observed for about a week.

The neurotransmitter mechanism underlying this effect appears to be glutamate. Glutamate is an excitatory neurotransmitter involved in learning and memory because of its role in synaptic plasticity, the remoulding, in other words, of connections between nerve cells. The essential difference with glutamate is that it is implicated in neuronal repair processes (19). This is key, as studies have shown depression to be associated with neural atrophy (20). It is also the case that once a person experiences depression, they are more likely to experience episodes in the future (21). Taking all this together, it is expected that ketamine initially blocks glutamate receptors. Because of this, levels of brain-derived neurotrophic factor increase. Animal studies show this leads to the growth of new synapses (22). In this sense, it acts to restore communication between neurons more quickly.

There is now growing interest within the pharmaceutical industry to explore the effects of ketamine. There is evidence also that a new compound, GLYX-13, has similar NMDA-mediated effects without the hallucinogenic properties of ketamine (23). This is good news for treating depression, or at least, specific subtypes of depression, including potentially that of treatment-resistant (refractory) depression.

The assumption that the different forms of depression reflect similar underlying mechanisms may not be correct. In this sense, some types might be better suited to drugs that increase serotonin levels, whereas for others targeting glutamate may provide the necessary remedy (11). Therefore, there is a need to develop effective screening tools that will allow clinicians to decide which drug to prescribe.

Lanicemine

Other research has looked at the effect of lanicemine, a drug initially developed to treat epilepsy (24). There was the expected drop in ratings of depression, and the effect appeared to be sustained over time, up to two weeks post-treatment. Using this drug eliminated the hallucinogenic effects of ketamine. The compromise was that the results were not as speedy as with ketamine. There was a lag of two or more weeks. This is comparable to the delay usually seen in standard drug treatments for depression. However, participants in this study were allowed to continue taking their prescribed medication. Of interest, when looking at a sub-sample who did not take any other medication during the trial, there was less of a delay before the effects of lanicemine were noticeable.

Potential biomarkers

Given the current recommendation for first-line treatment is either medication or psychotherapy, it is worrying that less than 40 per cent experience remission—in other words, get better—following their prescribed course of treatment (25, 26). The costs to self and society for opting for the wrong choice can be considerable. The likelihood is that the person will continue to experience high levels of distress and may, in fact, present as a higher suicide risk as a result. It is also highly likely more time will be lost from employment (27, 28).

One way to improve this is to identify biomarkers that could guide the clinician into selecting the most appropriate form of treatment for the individual. Biomarkers have been used with much success in other domains of medical care, such as in the treatment of cancer (29). One recent study has indicated that higher or lower relative averages in metabolism occurring in the anterior insula might be used to predict those who would respond better to CBT than to medication—in this case, escitalopram, an SSRI—and vice versa (30).

If supported by future studies, this finding would seem to make a great deal of sense. The anterior insula is, after all, central to the conversion of bodily sensation into feelings and emotions (31). This region has many connections with other key brain areas, such as the frontal, limbic, and brainstem regions (32). Activity levels in this region also change when a person receives a range of treatments, including medication and mindfulness (33, 34).

There are important implications if such research proves fruitful. Currently, treatment is assigned based on the experience of the clinician. In many cases, this is accurate, although, as we have seen, there is room for improvement. As it stands, if someone is prescribed an antidepressant and then fails to respond to it, in most cases, the person is switched to another antidepressant. The evidence so far from potential biomarkers indicates that some people may respond better to psychotherapy rather than to medication. Therefore, the process of trial-and-error, the only real option available at the moment, will be redundant, and quality of life will improve much more quickly for many patients who experience this troubling condition. There is a caveat, as always, and that is there will still be people who will not respond to either medication or psychotherapy, or indeed a combination of the two (35). The current potential batch of biomarkers will not improve the situation for this group (36).

Using imaging technology

There is hope that, at some point in the future, evidence from imaging studies and other forms of neurobiological assessment can be employed to direct clinicians in making the appropriate choice in terms of intervention (37). We have seen that some symptom clustering are more or less responsive to biological treatments. For example, those who show a disruption in the HPS axis are likely to respond better to medical interventions (38). One potential growth area is better detecting those who are at high risk of suicide (39).

Taking bloods

The next step in ensuring people receive the most appropriate intervention for their problems may be blood testing. As we will explore soon, some depression may be associated with an overactive immunological response, making them more sensitive to potential environmental triggers. They are also less responsive to traditional antidepressants.

A recent study showed that gene expression was different in these patients. They are more sensitive to interferon-α (IFN-α) (40). Interferon is a protein involved in activating the body's immune response. If it is possible to detect this early via a blood sample, it would be possible to respond with the appropriate treatment sooner with a higher likelihood of either preventing or minimizing the depression (41). There is research ongoing exploring the effect of low doses of aspirin in reducing the risk of a person developing several conditions now associated with increased inflammation, including certain cancers and Alzheimer's disease.

Should we screen for depression?

When looking at clinical practice, screening plays a central part in the activities carried out in clinics. The improvement of screening is also seen as being a major focus of research, with its unceasing quest to find the Holy Grail, an accurate way to identify those at risk from specific conditions early on so that either the problem does not develop or, at the very least, treatments can be administered to reduce the impact. This is all good. However, sometimes, things can go awry. Sometimes people become overzealous in their desire to do good. This is particularly problematic in the field of mental health. One area where this is becoming increasingly problematic is in relation to dementia. This is not the place to talk about this here, so I shall refer you to my book, *The Psychology of Ageing: From Mind to Society* (42). What is relevant here is the worry over screening to identify depression early on (43).

As with dementia and other conditions, the concern here is that screening for depression will become standard, just one more thing to be added to the clinical arsenal (43, 44). On the surface, this might seem a reasonable thing to suggest. Why should we not screen as a matter of course for depression? The concern is that it might lead in some cases to false positives, with people being started on treatment for depression when, in fact, they have no real need. That is already happening, so do we wish to compound this? It might be the case that the person is experiencing a transient negative emotion as par for the course of daily life. Over-medicating, especially concerning antidepressants, is already a significant issue (45). Such tactics would only act to accentuate the problem.

On the other hand, screening is far from 100 per cent accurate, so some might still fall through the net. We are already living in an age where we turn to the wonders of pharmaceutical companies to make us feel a little better. Drugs of this nature are increasingly being used as enhancements in the healthy rather than treatments for the sick. As a society, we are certainly not equipped to deal with the current level of individuals with mental health problems, let alone contribute to this by creating more (43).

Earlier in this section, I mentioned inflammation and that some depression could be linked to an overactive immune response. It is to this we now turn. This is not only interesting from the point of view of possibly understanding better the aetiology of some cases of depression, but it also promises new forms of treatment that might contribute to boosting the overall success rate in improving the lives of people with the condition.

Inflammation and immunization

Before we can begin to look at this new and exciting research, we must first appreciate the mechanics of the immune system and its role in causing inflammation. The historical development in our understanding of the immune system is fascinating, especially the burgeoning appreciation of the role of psychology in influencing its operation. For a good overview of this, I would refer interested readers to *Why Zebras Don't Get Ulcers* (46) and *The Balance Within: The Science Connecting Health and Emotions* (47).

The immune system

There is a surfeit of research evidencing clear links between depression and a range of medical conditions. The most prominent ones include heart disease, diabetes, cancer, and Alzheimer's disease. Research has also shown depression as a significant risk factor for such conditions. Depression among those with these and other conditions is higher (48). It is also associated with poorer prognosis and, in some cases, higher mortality.

One explanation for how depression is linked to such a range of conditions is that of immune system dysregulation (49). The immune system is a complex, interconnected system that protects us from invading viruses, bacteria, and other pathogens, including our own cells in the case of tumours. The immune system incorporates the lymphatic system. Lymph nodes are a vital component in the body's defence against invasion. They produce immune cells, called lymphocytes, that protect the body. Lymph nodes are distributed throughout the body. These lympho-cytes are specialized white blood cells. They create immunity so that the body is resistant to future attacks of the same microorganism.

The immune system is intimately connected to other systems within the body, most importantly, from the point of view of this chapter, the central nervous sys-tem. Mental states then can exert an independent influence on immune system functioning. Of interest also is the belief that this communication channel operates in both directions (50).

Cytokines provide one mode by which communication occurs, acting as inter-mediaries between the immune system and the central nervous system. They also help regulate the overall immune response within the body. There are two basic forms of immune response, namely non-specific and specific. The non-specific immune response, as the name suggests, reflects the way the body responds to all foreign entities that invade. Localized inflammation is a typical response to infec-tion or damage to tissue. This response is controlled by proinflammatory cytokines, such as interleukins (IL) 1β and 6, released by macrophages—cells that ingest de-bris, a process called phagocytosis—at the target site. Their presence draws im-mune cells to the location of the damage. On arrival, the lymphocytes engulf and eliminate pathogens, with the remaining wreckage being handled by macrophages.

It is possible to assess the extent of inflammation in a body by determining levels of proinflammatory cytokines. C-reactive protein, released by the liver, is also in higher amounts during an immune response.

Dysregulation of immune response is associated with several conditions, as de-tailed previously. In such cases, the immune response is overzealous or remains in operation longer than is needed. When this happens, the body's own healthy tissue becomes the target for the immune system.

In addition to the non-specific immune response, another form of protection is the specific immune response. Again, as the name suggests, the type of response initiated is determined by the pathogen encountered. A specific immune response can occur simultaneously as a non-specific one. These can be cell-mediated and antibody-mediated immune responses.

Looking first at the cell-mediated immune response, this involves T lympho-cytes, more generally referred to as T cells. They are called T cells because they originate in the thymus gland. The T cell multiplies on recognizing the antigen—the substance that has caused your body to produce antibodies. Different types of T cells are made. Helper T cells activate B cells, which are part of the antibody-mediated response, which is something I will come back to shortly. They also activate macrophages that we know engage in phagocytosis, thereby ridding our bodies of microbes and cell debris. There are also killer T cells. They are called killer cells because they are cytotoxic. In other words, they are lethal to other cells. These attack invading microorganisms by making use of powerful proteins called lymphokines.

I have already mentioned antibody-mediated immunity. In the previous section, I described T cells directly attacking microorganisms. In an antibody-mediated response, lymphocytes, called B cells, work in a manner one-step removed. They produce antibodies. Each antibody works against specific microorganisms by attaching to antigens on its surface. In other words, antibodies adhere to antigen sites and form antibody–antigen complexes.

Before moving on, I need to talk briefly about another mechanism, the complement system. Part of this system is over 20 proteins circulating in the blood. These complement proteins are activated by antibodies. This system helps to destroy microbes, boost white cell activity, widen blood vessels, and remove antigen–antibody complexes.

Evidence of such dysregulation appears in depression, with studies showing up to 50 per cent higher than normal levels of proinflammatory cytokines and C-reactive protein (51), evidence of a heightened non-specific immune response. In contrast, there are also more white blood cells, namely neutrophils and monocytes (52). This indicates that the specific immune response is weaker during depression because internal defence mechanisms are focused on a non-specific response.

Illness behaviour

On releasing proinflammatory cytokines, macrophages set in motion a host of activities aimed at removing harmful invaders and repairing the damage. This activity is not just relegated to the area of bodily injury, but the brain is also affected. Microglia are activated in the brain and secrete additional cytokines. Stress can also induce the same response through elevated adrenaline and cortisol levels, hormones associated with the stress response (53). The resultant effect here is the incitement of an evolved behaviour pattern to support the ongoing immunological response elsewhere in the body. This pattern of responding is referred to as sickness behaviour.

Sickness behaviour refers to responses that aid the survival of the individual and consist of all the behaviour we associate with someone who is sick. This includes lowered mood, stupor, tiredness, lack of appetite, increased sensitivity to pain, and a loss of interest in one's appearance. When we are sick, we conserve energy by reducing our movement. Energy is diverted to fighting the cause of the illness.

When we consider these behaviours, it all makes sense. Being more sensitive to pain allows the person or animal injured to protect the affected part of their body. Reduced grooming in animals means a reduction in the loss of liquids. Loss of interest in eating and drinking reduces and finally ceases the need for defecation, limiting the further loss of fluid and maintaining a clean environment. Together, such behaviour communicates to everyone else what is going on.

When a person feels like this, the upshot is that they tend to withdraw physically and emotionally. They do not feel able to socialize and be active in any way. From an evolutionary perspective, this is ideal behaviour for many reasons. If the person was suffering from a virus, for example, withdrawing from others would curb the spread of the infection. They would also protect themselves from contracting anything else while in their current weakened state. Widespread death resulting from a rapidly spreading virus within an isolated community was all too common in our prehistory, and two decades into the twenty-first century, we find it is still not entirely eradicated.

Unfortunately, as with some of these evolved mechanisms, what was once adaptive in our dim-and-distant past is no longer so. Many chronic conditions we associate with modern life result in sustained inflammation over extended periods. This then means that our brains feel the need to endorse illness-related behaviour. Recent studies have shown that children who present high levels of inflammation are more likely to develop depression or schizophrenia in their teens (54–56).

Notably, there are significant similarities between illness behaviour and depression (57). The behaviours described earlier map directly onto what we see in someone with depression. The argument is the depression shares the same immune-inflammatory pathways. Indeed, sickness behaviour is acute and adaptive, protecting us as we have seen. Depression, on the other hand, is chronic and negative. Chronic inflammation is associated with an autoimmune response. It might be the case that depression could be conceived as some prolonged and maladaptive form of sickness behaviour (58). However, it is more likely to result from an underlying degenerative process.

Treatment and prevention

The fact that inflammation might be implicated in many serious, and in some cases, progressive illnesses too, has the potential of being a major breakthrough, not only in terms of treatment but also in terms of prevention. In this sense, it might be possible in the future to prevent at-risk individuals from developing conditions such as depression and dementia in the first place. The use of anti-inflammatories might be the answer or at least part of the solution for controlling and preventing these conditions (59).

Findings such as this suggest that it might be possible to use anti-inflammatory medication to treat or prevent depression. A study examined the effects of one such anti-inflammatory, infliximab (60). Findings from this trial were encouraging such that symptoms of depression were improved in those who started the trial with high levels of inflammation. This was a small study, so more research is needed to further elucidate the potential mechanisms at play and assess the likely efficacy of such treatments. This is particularly important as the positive effects were only seen for those who had high levels of inflammation at the start, especially when one considers that everyone else fared worse after the course of anti-inflammatory.

In this sense, such treatments might only be efficacious for use among those who have generally elevated levels of inflammation. It is not entirely clear why some individuals have high baseline levels of inflammation throughout their life, although some link it to stress or trauma endured during childhood (61, 62).

There are essential provisos to consider with many drugs, especially when looking at treating conditions in the long term. In this instance, one of the concerns rests on the fact that the implication is to treat people over long periods of time with anti-inflammatory drugs. By their very nature, they exert an immunosuppressant effect. The consequences of this speak for themselves.

Default mode network

An alternative explanation is related to levels of inflammation present in women who give birth. In cases where inflammation levels were high in mothers, the child born had weaker connections in the brain. The default mode network was an area particularly affected here. The default mode network refers to interacting brain regions—the anterior medial prefrontal cortex, posterior cingulate cortex, and angular gyrus (63)—that are active when we daydream when our attention is inward-facing and not on the outside world. This network is, in turn, associated with depression, among other things.

It has been suggested that this network, particularly the anterior cingulate cortex, is overactive and experiences hyperconnectivity in depression and explains why rumination is so prominent (64). In contrast, hypoconnectivity in the posterior medial cortex may explain why depression is associated with the recall of overgeneralized autobiographical memory (65).

Knowledge about the operation within the default mode network might help improve treatment outcomes by assisting clinicians to better predict if a person is likely to be responsive to a particular form of treatment. Hypoconnectivity within the default mode network is associated with a kind of depression that is less responsive to medication (66).

In Chapter 7, we discussed the role of exercise in providing an effective treatment alternative for depression. Exercise is also essential when one considers depression within the context of inflammation. Regular exercise—agreement on the type and duration of the exercise changes so keep an open mind—and a well-balanced diet— this frequently changes also, so please refer to whatever is in today's newspaper and insert accordingly—have been shown to reduce inflammation (67).

Having focused thus far on biological aspects in treating depression, we shall turn our attention to other ways of helping with the condition. The following section is about sleep. Sleep and the importance thereof seem to be in the news reasonably regularly. In fact, this last year has seen a spate of papers and books published about sleep, especially about the health benefits of it. While I am typing, I am reminded of the recent book by Matthew Walker on that very topic (68). Certainly, worth a look if you want to obtain an overview of recent findings.

Sleep

There has been a deeply held interest in sleep. It is something we all do. For some, it is restorative; for others, less so. However, we all know the effects of not getting a good night's sleep. Poor sleep affects not only mood but general cognitive functioning. There are also other medical concerns regarding those who have a poor sleep history. From a neurological point of view, the role of sleep is still unclear.

However, there is a great deal of research exploring just that. Depriving someone of sleep impairs a person's ability to lay down new memories. Likely linked to this is the lower levels of brain-derived neurotrophic factor (BDNF) among those who are sleep deprived as this chemical is involved in regulating new synaptic connections (69).

There is even talk as to whether prescriptive sleep deprivation can help someone with depression. Although a great deal more research needs to be carried out, one recent study showed a substantial improvement in mood following one night of sleep deprivation (70). Just how sleep deprivation could be used therapeutically is still not clear.

One way to improve sleep is through mindfulness meditation (71). Mindfulness practice has expanded exponentially over the last couple of decades or so. There are books, videos, apps, and so on that teach you how to train yourself to engage in mindfulness. Apps we shall consider in more detail soon when we look at the increasing adoption and engagement with technology as an effective means of self-help. First, though, we shall examine the literature on mindfulness and see what it offers for those with depression.

Ubiquitous mindfulness

I have already talked about the ubiquitous nature of selective serotonin reuptake inhibitors in treating depression. However, becoming a close contender is mindfulness meditation. Indeed, meditative practices in treating certain conditions have been given the label "Buddha pill" (72). This refers to it being heralded as a panacea. As we have seen in Chapter 7, mindfulness is a valuable technique that is most often combined with cognitive therapy to help people deal with and recover from depression. Some have argued that mindfulness-based cognitive therapy (MBCT) might even be an alternative to medication (73). Mindfulness meditation aims to facilitate changes in how a person perceives themselves and relates to others. The changes are often subtle but life-changing. This is primarily achieved through a combination of enhanced awareness of breathing, body, and mind. As with most things, there may be downsides.

From a historical perspective, this form of meditation aimed to produce somewhat more radical change than merely to counteract feelings of anxiety or depression or make people more empathetic. In fact, the original purpose of these techniques was to challenge a person's sense of self (74).

So, why am I talking about the ancient practice of meditation here in a chapter on future directions? Mindfulness meditation sessions in relation to treatment for depression usually last for up to half an hour. However, if this was extended to, say, several hours every day, as experienced by those who attend retreats focused on meditative practice, there is evidence to indicate that a small proportion can feel depressed or panicked (75). Obviously, this is only in extreme circumstances. We are talking about meditation rather than specifically mindfulness, but perhaps it warrants further debate.

The concern is that it is not clear why mindfulness meditation works. Some argue that such practices should only be used to distract someone away from distressing thoughts (76). Clearly, this is not the intended premise for mindfulness which is concerned with accepting thoughts rather than active distraction, assuming one adheres to this principle. The argument here is that it might be counterproductive to encourage distressed individuals to not challenge the basis of their thought intrusions.

Rather depressingly, as with early research on antidepressants, the initial tranche of research exploring the validity of mindfulness in treating depression might have presented slightly skewed findings. Williams and colleagues (77) conducted a trial where the outcome was not particularly encouraging for MBCT, with no real difference between it and the treatment-as-usual group.

It must be acknowledged that this technique is somewhat cognitively demanding. We have seen already that people who are depressed or anxious experience severe cognitive deficits (78). Learning to alternate focus from what the body is doing to what the mind is doing and back is challenging, especially in the early stages. Trying not to become emotionally overwhelmed also requires a great deal of effort, again among individuals with known problems, this time in terms of emotion regulation. This is particularly pertinent during phases of the meditation, where one is directed to give the mind free reign before re-focusing on the body or breathing. All manner of distressing material is possible at this stage of the process.

The final section of this chapter focuses on the increasing use of technology in treating depression. Before looking later at the use of virtual reality, we will look at something which most of us own and which is usually within finger-twitching reach, pretty much at all times: the smartphone.

Smartphones

The smartphone is a fantastic development of the trusty old mobile. Gone are the days when people used to skulk in a doorway or, in some cases, stand inside a telephone box to take or make a call on their mobile phone. At the time, it seemed rather odd to be talking into a lump of plastic while in a busy shop or in the middle of the high street (remember those?). Not that many owned one. If you did, you tended to stand out. One might also argue that lurking in doorways or other out-of-the-way places was practical as the original mobiles were around 3 feet long with aerials that extended to the sky, so they could quite easily take out someone's eye. Since then, mobile phones have gradually reduced in size, to the extent that, not that long ago, you needed a magnifying glass to find the thing let alone type in a number or write a text. Then came along the smartphone. A device that is many, many times more powerful than the desktop computers we had when the first mobile phones were on sale. Fantastic yet scary at the same time.

With each generation of smartphones, there is a proliferation of potential uses it could be put to. One very natural area of expansion is in helping with mental health issues. There is now a range of apps that people can download for free (or at a small cost) that aim to improve well-being. Many fantastic apps immediately spring into my mind. There are highly polished apps that lead you through the process of mindfulness meditation, catering for all levels, from novice to expert. Other apps focus on depression itself and incorporate artificial intelligence into their design to create a level of discourse between you and the app. The fact that these apps can provide a source of support wherever you are makes them invaluable, be it as stand-alone exercises or as additions to other more formal modes of support.

What makes such apps particularly apposite is that they can be used by people who may not meet the criteria for a formal diagnosis but would benefit, nonetheless, from this form of informal yet structured support. Also, they offer support to those who may have been diagnosed but have yet to access the necessary care due to long waiting lists.

With the range of available apps, there is also an array of interactivity offered to users. Some are relatively passive, requiring users to merely monitor their mood as it fluctuates across the day. Others offer individualized responses from therapists (79). Many hover somewhere in-between the two extremes. In trying to help people help themselves, so to speak, an essential aspect of self-improvement is making use of our tendency to form habits (80). By their very nature, apps are a finger swipe away. Let's face it, for most of us, that is hardly any distance at all given our obsession with being permanently glued to our devices. In this sense, our obsession with gadgets is used to our advantage. These apps encourage daily activity and can even, in some cases, prompt you to interact. Building a routine, one based on self-improvement, is often what is needed to start many off down this path. Smartphones and tablets offer the perfect forum.

Social media

Linked to smartphones and tablets is the current obsession with social media. At face value, social media is a good thing. It offers a means by which people can keep in regular contact with each other, know what our friends are doing, and share our own thoughts with the wider world. I resisted for a long time but am now on Twitter. I find it really useful, especially in terms of my profession. I also use it as a form of mood repair by following key figures in other disciplines such as history and the arts . . . oh, and otters. There are other platforms that I have yet to explore. Each brings advantages, but there are some distinct disadvantages to such sites. The news is rife with stories about the psychological harm incurred. There is not enough space in this book to deliberate on the pros and cons of social media. Indeed, the long-term effects of this cultural obsession are unlikely to manifest for some time. However, there are worrying indicators of where this may eventually lead us.

Having just watched *Ready Player One*—a brilliant film, by the way—and indulged in a bit of retro 1980s culture as a result—always cathartic—now is probably a good time to write the section about virtual reality and how it can be used in therapy. Virtual reality is no longer merely the stuff of sci-fi; it is no longer restricted to the minority; it is in almost all our homes.[1] We can even turn our smartphones into a virtual reality headset for a few pounds. So, what can virtual reality offer, aside from going on quests to slay dragons or inhabiting a virtual world to replace one that is broken?

Virtual therapy

Virtual reality (VR) refers to a computer-generated environment that allows people to interact in unique and often fantastical scenarios. Individuals manifest as avatars, a virtual body that we can customize as we desire. Importantly, our avatar is unlikely to resemble our physical selves, and there lies many an ethical conundrum. Identifying with our avatar, our virtual self, is called embodiment.

Although the remit of gamers for much of the time, VR has been trialled as a mode of therapeutic intervention. One recent study aimed to see if self-compassion could be enhanced through staged VR interactions (81). In this example, participants were encouraged to express compassion to another person within the VR environment. The role was then reversed. By embodying the person's avatar to whom they had just shown compassion, it enabled them to experience the understanding they had generated themselves first-hand. The premise was to help people become less self-critical. Although such studies are in their early stages, and more rigorous methods are needed to gauge efficacy, there is clear potential for VR as a clinical tool (82). This is encouraging as VR promises a cost-effective tool for clinicians (83).

Summary

In this final chapter, I presented a selection of material that I believe holds much promise regarding how we can better manage and treat depression. We began by looking at potential new medications that may, in the future, surpass the current batch of antidepressants. Only time will tell. Inflammation will likely play a role in better understanding how depression develops and is maintained. We also spent some time exploring what technology has to offer us, especially regarding harnessing the potential of the ever-present smartphone.

Regardless of advancements in technology and theoretical understanding, the reality for many is that they lead lives battling not only their own inner demons but also societal ones. Until we remove the inherent stigma around depression and other mental health problems, well-being can only be improved to a certain extent. It is probably somewhat naive to talk about eliminating stigma. Instead, whatever we can collectively do to sizeably reduce stigma can only be for the better, not only for those with depression but for society at large. We should focus on helping people recover from and better manage their depression rather than reviling them. We are social creatures. Negative attitudes, however they manifest, hurt us and those around us. We need to work together to change public attitudes towards depression.

Note

1 I am aware that, although this is the case for many, the issue of a digital divide still exists and there is no indication that it will disappear anytime soon.

References

1 Digital N. Prescriptions dispensed in the community, Statistics for England; 2016 01/06/2018. Available from: http://digital.nhs.uk/catalogue/PUB20664/pres-disp-com-eng-2005-15-rep.pdf.
2 New Scientist Press Association. Antidepressant drug use in England has doubled in a decade; 2016. Available from: www.newscientist.com/article/2096244-antidepressant-drug-use-in-england-has-doubled-in-a-decade/.
3 Erb SJ, Schappi JM, Rasenick MM. Antidepressants accumulate in lipid rafts independent of monoamine transporters to modulate redistribution of the G protein, Gαs. J Biol Chem. 2016;291(38):19725–19733.
4 Scientist N. Depression, a new hope. New Sci. 2013;219(2927):5.
5 Wilson C. High antidepressant use could lead to UK public health disaster. New Sci. 12 May 2016. Available from: https://www.newscientist.com/article/2087949-high-antidepressant-use-could-lead-to-uk-public-health-disaster/.
6 Read J, Cartwright C, Gibson K. Adverse emotional and interpersonal effects reported by 1829 New Zealanders while taking antidepressants. Psychiatry Res. 2014;216(1):67–73.
7 Barton DA, Esler MD, Dawood T, et al. Elevated brain serotonin turnover in patients with depression: Effect of genotype and therapy. Arch Gen Psychiatry. 2008;65(1):38–46.
8 Forster GL, Feng N, Watt MJ, Korzan WJ, Mouw NJ, Summers CH, et al. Corticotropin-releasing factor in the dorsal raphe elicits temporally distinct serotonergic responses in the limbic system in relation to fear behavior. Neuroscience. 2006;141(2):1047–1055.
9 Geddes L. Total rethink over the causes of depression. New Sci. 2010;207(2770):12.
10 Bockting CLH, ten Doesschate MC, Spijker J, Spinhoven P, Koeter MWJ, Schene AH. Continuation and maintenance use of antidepressants in recurrent depression. Psychother Psychosom. 2008;77(1):17–26.
11 Murphy S. Mood swing: Beyond the serotonin hypothesis of depression. New Sci. 2013;219(2927):34–37.
12 Trivedi MH, Rush AJ, Wisniewski SR, Nierenberg AA, Warden D, Ritz L, et al. Evaluation of outcomes with citalopram for depression using measurement-based care in STAR*D: Implications for clinical practice. Am J Psychiatry. 2006;163(1):28–40.
13 Stephen R. Wisniewski PD, A. John Rush MD, Andrew A. Nierenberg MD, Bradley N. Gaynes MD, M.P.H., Diane Warden PD, M.B.A., James F. Luther MA, et al. Can phase III trial results of antidepressant medications be generalized to clinical practice? A STAR*D report. Am J Psychiatry. 2009;166(5):599–607.
14 Zimmerman M, Mattia JI, Posternak MA. Are subjects in pharmacological treatment trials of depression representative of patients in routine clinical practice? Am J Psychiatry. 2002;159(3):469–473.
15 Van Gerven J, Cohen A. Vanishing clinical psychopharmacology. Br J Clin Pharmacol. 2011;72(1):1–5.
16 Khamsi R. Ketamine relieves depression within hours. New Sci. 2006;191(2565).
17 Berman RM, Cappiello A, Anand A, Oren DA, Heninger GR, Charney DS, et al. Antidepressant effects of ketamine in depressed patients. Biol Psychiatry. 2000;47(4):351–354.

18 Mount Sinai Medical Center. Ketamine shows significant therapeutic benefit in people with treatment-resistant depression. ScienceDaily; 2013. Available from: https://www. sciencedaily.com/releases/2013/05/130518153250.htm.

19 Yang JL, Sykora P, Wilson DM, III, Mattson MP, Bohr VA. The excitatory neurotransmitter glutamate stimulates DNA repair to increase neuronal resiliency. Mech Ageing Dev. 2011;132(8–9):405–411.

20 Kang HJ, Voleti B, Hajszan T, Rajkowska G, Stockmeier CA, Licznerski P, et al. Decreased expression of synapse-related genes and loss of synapses in major depressive disorder. Nat Med. 2012;18(9):1413–1417.

21 Solomon DA, Keller MB, Leon AC, Mueller TI, Lavori PW, Shea MT, et al. Multiple Recurrences of major depressive disorder. Am J Psychiatry. 2000;157(2):229–233.

22 Li N, Lee B, Liu RJ, Banasr M, Dwyer JM, Iwata M, et al. mTOR-dependent synapse formation underlies the rapid antidepressant effects of NMDA antagonists. Science. 2010;329(5994):959–964.

23 Burgdorf J, Zhang X-l, Nicholson KL, Balster RL, Leander JD, Stanton PK, et al. GLYX-13, a NMDA receptor glycine-site functional partial agonist, induces antidepressant-like effects without ketamine-like side effects. Neuropsychopharmacology. 2013;38(5):729–742.

24 Sanacora G, Smith MA, Pathak S, Su HL, Boeijinga PH, McCarthy DJ, et al. Lanicemine: A low-trapping NMDA channel blocker produces sustained antidepressant efficacy with minimal psychotomimetic adverse effects. Mol Psychiat. 2014; 19(9):978–985.

25 Patten SB, Kennedy SH, Lam RW, O'Donovan C, Filteau MJ, Parikh SV, et al. Canadian Network for Mood and Anxiety Treatments (CANMAT) clinical guidelines for the management of major depressive disorder in adults. I. Classification, burden and principles of management. J Affect Disord. 2009;117:S5–S14.

26 National Institute for Health and Care Excellence. Depression: The treatment and management of depression in adults (update). Clinical guideline. 2009;90. Available from: https://pubmed.ncbi.nlm.nih.gov/22132433/.

27 Gaynes BN, Warden D, Trivedi MH, Wisniewski SR, Fava M, Rush AJ. What did STAR* D teach us? Results from a large-scale, practical, clinical trial for patients with depression. Psychiatr Serv. 2009;60(11):1439–1445.

28 Holtzheimer PE, Mayberg HS. Stuck in a rut: Rethinking depression and its treatment. Trends Neurosci. 2011;34(1):1–9.

29 Saijo N. Critical comments for roles of biomarkers in the diagnosis and treatment of cancer. Cancer Treat Rev. 2012;38(1):63–67.

30 McGrath CL, Kelley ME, Holtzheimer PE, III, et al. Toward a neuroimaging treatment selection biomarker for major depressive disorder. JAMA Psychiat. 2013;70(8):821–829.

31 Critchley HD, Wiens S, Rotshtein P, Öhman A, Dolan RJ. Neural systems supporting interoceptive awareness. Nat Neurosci. 2004;7(2):189–195.

32 Augustine JR. Circuitry and functional aspects of the insular lobe in primates including humans. Brain Res Rev. 1996;22(3):229–244.

33 Kennedy SH, Evans KR, Krüger S, Mayberg HS, Meyer JH, McCann S, et al. Changes in regional brain glucose metabolism measured with positron emission tomography after paroxetine treatment of major depression. Am J Psychiatry. 2001;158(6):899–905.

34 Farb NA, Segal ZV, Mayberg H, Bean J, McKeon D, Fatima Z, et al. Attending to the present: Mindfulness meditation reveals distinct neural modes of self-reference. Soc Cogn Affect Neurosci. 2007;2(4):313–322.

35 Thase ME, Friedman ES, Biggs MM, Wisniewski SR, Trivedi MH, Luther JF, et al. Cognitive therapy versus medication in augmentation and switch strategies as second-step treatments: A STAR* D report. Am J Psychiatry. 2007;164(5):739–752.

36 Rush AJ, Warden D, Wisniewski SR, Fava M, Trivedi MH, Gaynes BN, et al. STAR* D. CNS Drugs. 2009;23(8):627–647.

37 Cleare AJ, Rane LJ. Biological models of unipolar depression. In: Power M, editor. The Wiley-Blackwell handbook of mood disorders. Chichester: John Wiley & Sons; 2013, pp. 39–68.

38 Thase ME. Hypothalamic-pituitary-adrenocortical activity and response to cognitive behavior therapy in unmedicated, hospitalized depressed patients. Am J Psychiatry. 1996;153(7):886.

39 Marchand WR, Lee JN, Johnson S, Thatcher J, Gale P, Wood N, et al. Striatal and cortical midline circuits in major depression: Implications for suicide and symptom expression. Prog Neuro-Psychopharmacol Biol Psychiatry. 2012;36(2):290–299.

40 Hepgul N, Cattaneo A, Agarwal K, Baraldi S, Borsini A, Bufalino C, et al. Transcriptomics in interferon-[alpha]-treated patients identifies inflammation-, neuroplasticity- and oxidative stress-related signatures as predictors and correlates of depression. Neuropsychopharmacology. 2016;41(10):2502–2511.

41 Hamzelou J. Primed for depression. New Sci. 2016;230(3072):8–9.

42 Christopher G. The psychology of ageing: From mind to society. Basingstoke; Hampshire: Palgrave Macmillan; 2014.

43 Frances A. Depression screen. New Sci. 2016;229(3058):6–7.

44 Siu AL, Bibbins-Domingo K, Grossman DC, Baumann LC, Davidson KW, Ebell M, et al. Screening for depression in adults: US Preventive Services Task Force recommendation statement. JAMA. 2016;315(4):380–387.

45 Pratt LA, Brody DJ, Gu Q. Antidepressant use in persons aged 12 and over: United States, 2005–2008. In: 76 NDBN, editor. Centers for Disease Control and Prevention; 2011. Available from: https://pubmed.ncbi.nlm.nih.gov/22617183/.

46 Sapolsky RM. Why zebras don't get ulcers: An updated guide to stress, stress-related diseases, and coping. New ed. New York: W. H. Freeman; 1998.

47 Sternberg EM. The balance within: The science connecting health and emotions. New York: W.H. Freeman; 2000.

48 Kessler RC, McGonagle KA, Zhao S, Nelson CB, Hughes M, Eshleman S, et al. Lifetime and 12-month prevalence of DSM-III-R psychiatric disorders in the United States. Results from the National Comorbidity Survey. Arch Gen Psychiatry. 1994;51(1):8–19.

49 Stetler C. Immune system. In: Ingram RE, editor. The international encyclopedia of depression. New York; London: Springer; 2009.

50 Maier SF, Watkins LR. Cytokines for psychologists: Implications of bidirectional immune-to-brain communication for understanding behavior, mood, and cognition. Psychol Rev. 1998;105(1):83–107.

51 Miller GE, Stetler CA, Carney RM, Freedland KE, Banks WA. Clinical depression and inflammatory risk markers for coronary heart disease. Am J Cardiol. 2002;90(12):1279–1283.

52 Herbert TB, Cohen S. Depression and immunity: A meta-analytic review. Psychol Bull. 1993;113(3):472–486.

53 Costandi M. The mind minders: Meet our brain's maintenance workers. New Sci. 09 October.2013. Available from: https://www.newscientist.com/article/mg22029381-000-the-mind-minders-meet-our-brains-maintenance-workers/.

54 Delany FM, Byrne ML, Whittle S, Simmons JG, Olsson C, Mundy LK, et al. Depression, immune function, and early adrenarche in children. Psychoneuroendocrinology. 2016;63:228–234.

55 Leza JC, García-Bueno B, Bioque M, Arango C, Parellada M, Do K, et al. Inflammation in schizophrenia: A question of balance. Neurosci Biobehav Rev. 2015;55:612–626.

56 Miklowitz DJ, Portnoff LC, Armstrong CC, Keenan-Miller D, Breen EC, Muscatell KA, et al. Inflammatory cytokines and nuclear factor-kappa B activation in adolescents with bipolar and major depressive disorders. Psychiatry Res. 2016;241:315–322.

57 Maes M, Berk M, Goehler L, Song C, Anderson G, Gałecki P, et al. Depression and sickness behavior are Janus-faced responses to shared inflammatory pathways. BMC Med. 2012;10:66.

58 Huang Y, Henry CJ, Dantzer R, Johnson RW, Godbout JP. Exaggerated sickness behavior and brain proinflammatory cytokine expression in aged mice in response to intracerebroventricular lipopolysaccharide. Neurobiol Aging. 2008;29(11):1744–1753.

59 Mohammadi D. Brain under siege. New Sci. 2015;226(3027):38–41.

60 Raison CL. The promise and limitations of anti-inflammatory agents for the treatment of major depressive disorder. Inflammation-Associated Depression: Evidence, Mechanisms and Implications. 2017:287–302.

61 Baumeister D, Akhtar R, Ciufolini S, Pariante C, Mondelli V. Childhood trauma and adulthood inflammation: A meta-analysis of peripheral C-reactive protein, interleukin-6 and tumour necrosis factor-α. Mol Psychiat. 2016;21(5):642–649.

62 Pariante C. Neuroscience, mental health and the immune system: Overcoming the brain-mind-body trichotomy. Epidemiol Psychiatr Sci. 2016;25(2):101–105.

63 Goldstein-Piekarski AN, Williams LM. A Neural circuit-based model for depression anchored in a synthesis of insights from functional neuroimaging. In: Neurobiology of Depression. London, United Kingdom: Elsevier; 2019, pp. 241–256.

64 Berman MG, Peltier S, Nee DE, Kross E, Deldin PJ, Jonides J. Depression, rumination and the default network. Soc Cogn Affect Neurosci. 2010;6(5):548–555.

65 Williams LM. Precision psychiatry: A neural circuit taxonomy for depression and anxiety. Lancet Psychiat. 2016;3(5):472–480.

66 Dichter GS, Gibbs D, Smoski MJ. A systematic review of relations between resting-state functional-MRI and treatment response in major depressive disorder. J Affect Disord. 2015;172:8–17.

67 Woods JA, Wilund KR, Martin SA, Kistler BM. Exercise, inflammation and aging. Aging Dis. 2012;3(1):130–140.

68 Walker MPA. Why we sleep: The new science of sleep and dreams. London: Penguin Books; 2017.

69 Giese M, Unternährer E, Hüttig H, Beck J, Brand S, Calabrese P, et al. BDNF: An indicator of insomnia? Mol Psychiat. 2014;19(2):151.

70 Wolf E, Kuhn M, Norman C, Mainberger F, Maier JG, Maywald S, et al. Synaptic plasticity model of therapeutic sleep deprivation in major depression. Sleep Med Rev. 2016;30:53–62.

71 Howell AJ, Digdon NL, Buro K, Sheptycki AR. Relations among mindfulness, well-being, and sleep. Pers Individ Differ. 2008;45(8):773–777.

72 Farias M, Wikholm C. Ommm . . . Aargh. New Sci. 2015;226(3021):28–29.

73 Kuyken W, Hayes R, Barrett B, Byng R, Dalgleish T, Kessler D, et al. Effectiveness and cost-effectiveness of mindfulness-based cognitive therapy compared with maintenance antidepressant treatment in the prevention of depressive relapse or recurrence (PREVENT): A randomised controlled trial. Lancet. 2015;386(9988):63–73.

74 Farias M, Wikholm C. Panic, depression and stress: The case against meditation. New Sci. 13 May 2015. Available from: https://www.newscientist.com/article/mg22630210-500-panic-depression-and-stress-the-case-against-meditation/.

75 Shapiro DH, Jr. Adverse effects of meditation: A preliminary investigation of long-term meditators. Int J Psychosom. 1992;39(1–4):62–67.

76 Ellis A. The place of meditation in cognitive behavior therapy and rational-emotive therapy. In: Shapiro DH, Walsh R, editors. Meditation: Classic and contemporary perspectives. New York: Aldine; 1984, pp. 671–673.

77 Williams JMG, Crane C, Barnhofer T, Brennan K, Duggan DS, Fennell MJV, et al. Mindfulness-based cognitive therapy for preventing relapse in recurrent depression: A randomized dismantling trial. J Consult Clin Psychol. 2014;82(2):275–286.

78 Christopher G, MacDonald J. The impact of clinical depression on working memory. Cogn Neuropsychiatry. 2005;10(5):379–399.

79 Rutkin A. Therapist in my pocket. New Sci. 2015;227(3038):20.

80 Calder PC, Carding SR, Christopher G, Kuh D, Langley-Evans SC, McNulty H. A holistic approach to healthy ageing: How can people live longer, healthier lives? J Hum Nutr Diet. 2018;31(4):439–450.

81 Falconer CJ, Rovira A, King JA, Gilbert P, Antley A, Fearon P, et al. Embodying self-compassion within virtual reality and its effects on patients with depression. BJPsych Open. 2016;2(1):74–80.

82 Zeng N, Pope Z, Lee JE, Gao Z. Virtual reality exercise for anxiety and depression: A preliminary review of current research in an emerging field. J Clin Med. 2018;7(3).

83 Fodor LA, Coteţ CD, Cuijpers P, Szamoskozi Ş, David D, Cristea IA. The effectiveness of virtual reality based interventions for symptoms of anxiety and depression: A meta-analysis. Sci Rep. 2018;8(1):10323.

Chapter 10

Postlude

COVID-19

The finishing touches to this book were made during the COVID-19 pandemic. COVID-19—coronavirus disease—is caused by the SARS-CoV-2 virus. The infection leads to respiratory problems that can quickly turn fatal. During this time, nations across the entire planet fought to control and prevent the further spread of the deadly virus. The mortal threat of the coronavirus was clear from the outset. However, following close on its heels was the clear and present danger it posed to mental health.

Inevitably, peoples' mental health was adversely affected by a combination of the existential threat of the virus and the various imposed lockdowns. Instances of depression increased during this period. Multiple studies have been conducted with differing findings. One meta-analysis of data gleaned from the general public indicated that depression was seven times higher during the pandemic (1). It also became apparent, as time progressed, that inequalities in health and mental health worsened. Different sectors of the community experienced COVID in very different ways.[1]

One thing is clear, and that is the rise in the prescription of antidepressants during this time.[2] This is symptomatic of both a rise in depressive thoughts and actions and a response to a lack of access to talking therapies. Mental health services in the UK were stretched, to say the least, before COVID and have been unable to meet the demands of those in need during the lockdown.

Evidence from previous coronavirus outbreaks, such as SARS (severe acute respiratory syndrome) in 2002 and MERS (Middle East respiratory syndrome) in 2012, showed that some people were affected in the longer term by a range of psychopathology, including depression (2). This seems to be due to the virus directly infecting the central nervous system. An alternative explanation is that such damage to the nervous system may be mediated by the immune response (3). Although anti-inflammatory reactions occur to prevent damage to vital systems, sometimes systematic inflammatory response syndrome (SIRS) kicks in following a severe infection like pneumonia resulting from the coronavirus. SIRS has been responsible for fatalities as it can cause multiple organ failures (4). Psychopathology in such cases results from immune cell activation in the brain producing chronic inflammation. This, in turn, can lead to damage of brain tissue (5). The body's immune

DOI:10.4324/9781315688879-10

response to infection can precipitate a cytokine storm—an exaggerated immune response—resulting in neuroinflammation (6). Studies have also shown that coronaviruses can cause damage to neuronal tissue due to their neurotropic potential (7); in other words, their ability to attack the nervous system. However, the link between COVID-19, inflammation, and depression is not as clear-cut (8).

On top of this, of course, are the psychological responses to COVID-19. Fear, insecurity, isolation, and trauma, all common during this time, contribute to depression (9). This was exacerbated in those who experienced mental health problems before the outbreak (10). Depression was higher among those who were hospitalized for more extended periods. There is also evidence indicating that depression is more prevalent among younger age groups (11). Higher engagement with social media, and the increased risk of exposure to the fake news it all too often brings, could in part account for this effect (12). Of course, all ages are affected by scaremongering from the various news outlets. The World Health Organization reflected this, directing people to only seek information about the virus once or twice each day and access only reliable sources.³ The enticement to "doom scroll" likely contributed to this deleterious effect.

As already indicated, those disadvantaged before the pandemic experienced the worst outcomes (1). Depression was higher among the unemployed, low social status groups, those who lacked social support, and people who had experienced financial loss (13). It reflects poorly on governments across the globe that the pandemic has only widened the gap further between the haves and have-nots and heightened discrimination against the discriminated-against.

It is also clear that the physical and psychological effects of COVID-19 do not necessarily disappear once a person has apparently recovered. Many now face the challenges of long COVID. Symptoms are numerous and wide-ranging and include fatigue, cognitive problems, heart palpitations, insomnia, and, most pertinent here, depression.⁴ We will be living in the shadow of this virus for many years to come. Although scientists have warned us for years that a pandemic was highly likely, we will be better prepared for the next one, perhaps, given this current wake-up call. This is inevitable given the connected global societies in which we all live.

Although much has been written about the harmful effects of the COVID outbreak, studies are beginning to emerge suggestive of positive outcomes in some instances. Because of restrictions, people reported being more able to spend time on activities they valued. They were more appreciative of aspects of their lives they had previously taken for granted (14). In many cases, the changes in personal routines led to a reassessment of their life and, with it, a solid disinclination to return to their pre-pandemic existence. Such positive outcomes were higher for females, younger age groups, those cohabiting, people in employment, and individuals in good health.

The pandemic threat has yet to transition to an endemic nuisance, with new variants occurring regularly, and with it, a fear that a new strain will be resistant to the vaccines that are currently making the rounds globally (although, sadly, distribution is by no means equitable). It is still too early to assess the long-term impacts across the various levels of society. Included among these are the emergent mental health concerns of those touched by the virus but who survived.

Notes

1 www.health.org.uk/news-and-comment/blogs/emerging-evidence-on-covid-19s-impact-on-mental-health-and-health
2 https://media.nhsbsa.nhs.uk/news/nhsbsa-releases-summary-mental-health-stats
3 www.who.int/publications/i/item/WHO-2019-nCoV-MentalHealth-2020.1
4 www.nhs.uk/conditions/coronavirus-covid-19/long-term-effects-of-coronavirus-long-covid/

References

1 Bueno-Notivol J, Gracia-Garcia P, Olaya B, Lasheras I, Lopez-Anton R, Santabarbara J. Prevalence of depression during the COVID-19 outbreak: A meta-analysis of community-based studies. Int J Clin Health Psychol. 2021;21(1):100196.
2 Rogers JP, Chesney E, Oliver D, Pollak TA, McGuire P, Fusar-Poli P, et al. Psychiatric and neuropsychiatric presentations associated with severe coronavirus infections: A systematic review and meta-analysis with comparison to the COVID-19 pandemic. Lancet Psychiat. 2020;7(7):611–627.
3 Klein RS, Garber C, Howard N. Infectious immunity in the central nervous system and brain function. Nat Immunol. 2017;18(2):132–141.
4 Chen C, Zhang X, Ju Z, He W. Advances in the research of cytokine storm mechanism induced by Corona Virus Disease 2019 and the corresponding immunotherapies. Chin J Burns. 2020;E005.
5 Wu Y, Xu X, Chen Z, Duan J, Hashimoto K, Yang L, et al. Nervous system involvement after infection with COVID-19 and other coronaviruses. Brain Behav Immun. 2020;87:18–22.
6 Dantzer R. Neuroimmune interactions: From the brain to the immune system and vice versa. Physiol Rev. 2018;98(1):477–504.
7 Desforges M, Le Coupanec A, Dubeau P, Bourgouin A, Lajoie L, Dube M, et al. Human coronaviruses and other respiratory viruses: Underestimated opportunistic pathogens of the central nervous system? Viruses. 2019;12(1).
8 Mazza MG, De Lorenzo R, Conte C, Poletti S, Vai B, Bollettini I, et al. Anxiety and depression in COVID-19 survivors: Role of inflammatory and clinical predictors. Brain Behav Immun. 2020;89:594–600.
9 Carvalho PMM, Moreira MM, de Oliveira MNA, Landim JMM, Neto MLR. The psychiatric impact of the novel coronavirus outbreak. Psychiatry Res. 2020;286:112902.
10 Vindegaard N, Benros ME. COVID-19 pandemic and mental health consequences: Systematic review of the current evidence. Brain Behav Immun. 2020;89:531–542.
11 Wang C, Pan R, Wan X, Tan Y, Xu L, McIntyre RS, et al. A longitudinal study on the mental health of general population during the COVID-19 epidemic in China. Brain Behav Immun. 2020;87:40–48.
12 Ustun G. Determining depression and related factors in a society affected by COVID-19 pandemic. Int J Soc Psychiatry. 2021;67(1):54–63.
13 Nguyen HC, Nguyen MH, Do BN, Tran CQ, Nguyen TT, Pham KM, et al. People with suspected COVID-19 symptoms were more likely depressed and had lower health-related quality of life: The potential benefit of health literacy. J Clin Med. 2020;9(4):965.
14 Williams L, Rollins L, Young D, Fleming L, Grealy M, Janssen X, et al. What have we learned about positive changes experienced during COVID-19 lockdown? Evidence of the social patterning of change. PLoS One. 2021;16(1):e0244873.

Index

acetylcholine 39–41, 115, 157
adverse effects 107, 112, 114–16, 138, 153, 156–7, 175
aetiology 11, 44, 179
alcohol 2–3, 23, 25, 93, 97–9, 106, 110, 143–4
alexithymia 80, 92
alternative treatments 160
amygdala 21, 41–2, 81–3, 164
anhedonia 1, 5, 16, 50
antidepressants *see* biological treatment; compliance 113, 141, 145, 158–9; costs 173; efficacy 107, 114, 155, 159–60, 174–5; issues with 157–8; future 172–7; risk 173–4; side-effects 158
anti-inflammatory medication 42, 182–3
antipsychotics 107, 157, 161
anxiety 2, 6–7, 13, 19, 21, 23, 26, 48, 62–4, 83, 105, 108–9, 120, 138, 146, 157–8, 173–7, 184–5
apathy 41, 69, 135
assessment 5, 11, 18, 25–6, 31–2, 38, 67
attachment 45–6, 52–3, 106
attention 2, 25, 50, 60–9, 71–2, 83, 131–2
attention training 72, 131–2
automatic processing 61–2, 64

Beck, A.T. 26, 45, 49–50, 61, 126
bereavement 6–8, 106, 112
bipolar disorders 17–8, 26, 157
biological model 37–39
biological treatment: anticonvulsants 156; antidepressants 13–4, 27, 37–42, 69, 91, 96, 99–101, 107, 112–7, 135, 153–8, 160, 163, 166–8, 172–9, 185, 187, 193; deep brain stimulation 161, 165; combining treatment 157; electroconvulsive therapy (ECT) 6, 143,

162, 168; ketamine 176–7; lanicemine 176–7; melatonergic antidepressants 155; monoamine oxidase inhibitors (MAOIs) 114–5, 155, 166; reversible inhibitors of MAO-A 155; selective serotonin reuptake inhibitors (SSRIs) 101, 114–5, 143, 154–7, 172–4, 177; serotonin and noradrenaline reuptake inhibitors 155; third-generation antidepressants 156; transcranial magnetic stimulation 163; tricyclic antidepressants 105, 114–5, 153–4, 166; vagus nerve stimulation 164
biomarkers 42, 177
blanking 66
blood samples 178
brain-derived neurotrophic factor (BDNF) 141, 176, 184
broaden-and-build theory 50–1

cancer 12, 42, 91–2, 96, 178
cerebrovascular disease 41, 111, 156
caregivers 100, 112, 137
Child and Adolescent Mental Health Services (CAMHS) 106–7
clinical trials 114, 122, 159, 167, 172–3, 175
cognitive attentional syndrome 71
cognitive deficits 2, 26, 28, 60–84, 111, 115, 135, 162–3, 185
cognitive processes: *see* attention; automatic processing; controlled processing; executive function
cognitive model 49, 126
cognitive reactivity 52, 127
cognitive theory of depression 61; *see also* Beck, A.T.
cognitive vulnerability 51–2
communication 98, 131, 138, 145